S0-BNX-654

# The ICE CREAM CONNECTION

*Helen Hokinson, My Best Girls, E. P. Dutton and Company, New York, 1941*

"*I'm punishing myself for being a naughty girl yesterday in Schrafft's.*"

# The ICE CREAM CONNECTION

## All you'd love to know about ICE CREAM

### RALPH POMEROY

PADDINGTON PRESS LTD
THE TWO CONTINENTS PUBLISHING GROUP

**Library of Congress Cataloging
in Publication Data**

Pomeroy, Ralph, 1926-
The ice cream connection.

1. Ice cream, ices, etc.  I. Title.
TX795.P65  641.3'7'4  75-11170
ISBN 0-8467-0062-X
LC 75-11170

Computer typeset by Input Typesetting Ltd.
4 Valentine Place, London S.E.1. England

Designed by Richard Browner
Assisted by Colin Lewis and Richard Johnson

Drawings by Julian Graddon and Phil Dobson

**IN THE UNITED STATES**
**PADDINGTON PRESS LTD**
**TWO CONTINENTS PUBLISHING GROUP**
30 East 42 Street, New York City, N.Y. 10017

**IN THE UNITED KINGDOM**
**PADDINGTON PRESS LTD**
231 The Vale London W3

**IN CANADA**  distributed by
**RANDOM HOUSE OF CANADA LTD**
5390 Ambler Drive
Mississauga, Ontario L4W 1Y7

# CONTENTS

"My advice to you is not to enquire why or whether, but just to enjoy your ice cream while it is on your plate, that's my philosophy."

**Thornton Wilder,** *The Skin of Our Teeth*

"We dare not trust our wit for making our house pleasant to our friends, and so we buy ice-creams."

**Ralph Waldo Emerson,**
*Man the Reformer*

There's more to ice cream than melts in the mouth. It's not just a food. It's a luxurious extravaganza, an erotic trip, a visual treat, a luscious, cool, sinus-penetrating, sado-masochistic weight-producer, all-this-and-heaven-too, mother's milk, winter in a spoon, a social ploy, food freaks' turn-on, the poets' flower of milk, a childish throwback, a dinner's apotheosis, many things to many men.

It appears every day in millions and millions of people's lives. One of its containers – the classic cone – is considered one of the great design ideas of the century. You eat it! No waste. The recycling circle *par excellence*. Some days, hot summer ones especially, it seems to be everywhere. In leafy backyards. Hawked in suburbia. Carried along chic avenues. Beside the sunny sea.

Carefree by carfare, by bicycle, by high-heel and bare foot, pilgrimages are made to polka-dotted, jello-like chandeliered, nouveau nostalgic nirvanas where lazy-day, overhead fans cool the dreamy-eyed heads of flavor fetishists out to take-off on the flavor of the day, the week, the month, the year, the epoch! Standing in line at dipping counters, sitting in actually antique booths, dawdling in classy restaurants, yearning in gourmet gallimaufries. Good ice cream, awful ice cream, incredible ice cream, superb ice cream by the bar, the scoop, the soda, the sundae, the cup – by the brick, by the gallon, by the ton – moving from mound to mouth. Presidents serve it. Shahs are given it in costly forms. Celebrities have it flown in from afar. Journalists laud and condemn it. Whole books are devoted to ways of making it, molding it, serving it, cherishing it.

Ice cream has been fought over by fan and foe, denounced by prude and pulpit, flaunted by kings and queens, co-featured in films. Fred and Ginger have stopped dancing long enough to trade witticisms over it. Lana Turner has cooled her fevered prow by it. Stern Measures as to its manufacture have been debated by governments. Poets have mocked with it. Great chefs re-invented it. It has been the symbol of Sybaritic wealth – the rarest, the most exotic, frozen ambrosia. And equally, the suspect, soot-specked treat of slum urchins. Its past goes back thousands of years and its future seems endless.

That's why, when I began this book I felt that there was a real need for something other than one more cook book, or history, or do-it-yourself-er. I recalled a poem I love, a play that haunts me, a charming scene from a Broadway musical, a fragment from Gilbert & Sullivan. I remembered certain contemporary works of art, certain scenes in movies, my own childhood memories of fresh-fruit, ice-cream summers in Illinois.

Ice cream I liked and didn't like, like now and don't like. The ravings of addicted friends. Legendary stories of special perfections and glorious concoctions, some of which turned out to be true. I was curious about mass manufacture. Living for some time in California I had been able to watch improvements in quality wine production, and I learned there are similarities between the people who produce the best ice cream and their grape-growing counterparts. They are very serious and love what they're doing, and the world seems to be paying them more and more attention. The clouds of guilt and accusations of childishness seem to be clearing away. It's fun to be able to talk about ice cream *not* as some forbidden fruit.

Of course there is ice cream and ice cream – "Tell me what you are made of and I will tell you your worth." Noble charge!

Nice to be reminded that for years the only public places where women could be seen without damaging their reputations were dispensaries of delicious goodies. Interesting contrast with the negative nature of men-only bars and pubs – in the former, the good and the beautiful gathered together!

I have neither climbed every mountain nor followed every rainbow. And I certainly have not tasted every ice cream.* I haven't yet been to Moscow or Bombay, but I know people who have. In any event, although I am sometimes critical, the reader will soon discover that this is not what could be called a "critical" text. I leave that to others. My aim has been fo find out as much about ice cream, from as many angles as possible. And as I read and asked and talked and wrote I found that the amount of iceberg showing would be pretty much the same if I worked at it for another ten years. Like a child "picking pebbles on the shore of a boundless ocean" (Sir Isaac Newton), I found myself a kind of curious tourist among the ices, a beach-comber along sundae shores – not to mention a bit of a glutton among the bookshelves.

* Which more and more came to stand also for ices, sherbets, and close relatives of the ice cream family, including euphemisms like "frozen desserts" and "cold sweets."

I found that in the half-century since 1925 everything has gotten faster and faster and bigger and bigger with more and more happening, but it all seems to have more to do with events than with history (yet, anyway). Perhaps personal, I admit. But the evolution of refrigeration, the increase in knowledge brought about by television and travel, the breakdown of many food prejudices (when I was a kid, garlic wasn't allowed in the house even if it *did* ward off vampires), while major in their effect, don't seem to have *quite* the sharp focus of individual achievements.

Of course, as on any journey, some places are by-passed, some closed to foreigners, some lingered over out of sheer interest and love, some negatively experienced. Some end up being missed due to simple exhaustion, while others emerge as too complicated to get to. In the case of this book, one question led to a dozen new ones. To glance through an industry trade magazine is to learn of new retail and wholesale outlets, new products, new inventions, new flavors, more and more names of ice cream manufacturers, large and small.

Right now we seem to be going through a period of nostalgia having to do with the "innocence" and "simplicity" of ice cream. You find people talking about the good-old-days of ice cream. Which, it appears, means the days when a single scoop cone cost only 5¢, when real whipped cream was served at this place or that, when a Wall's container was trimmed with black-and-white checks, and Good Humor had "lucky sticks" that meant a free ice cream bar when you ate your way down to one. It means one's very first soda, one's very first *shared* soda. It means a reward for going to the dentist. It means telling about unexpected ices discovered on trips to foreign countries; the times when you got to lick the dasher.

Not everyone enthuses, as some people do, over roast dog, or fried ants, or wheat germ, or pork, or even beefsteak. But it *has* been suggested that no one exposed to really good ice cream has ever rejected it. All I know is that in the United States alone Americans were eating as much as 786,000,000 gallons of ice cream per year by 1974 and spending as much as $500,000,000 per year on ice cream novelties alone. Somebody out there obviously loves the stuff!

It must be me and you.

# ORIGINS

Contemporary China looking very ancient. Snow and ice have always been plentiful. This photograph was taken in the Kirin province.
– *China Reconstructs, February 1975*

# or "Drinking Out of Ice"

Histories differ. The history of ice cream seems to differ considerably. Legend and fact meet and part in a kind of dance of persuasion: This is true. *This* is true. So the dance goes. According to some authorities the Chinese had enjoyed a form of water ices – snow mixed with lemons, oranges, and pomegranates – for several thousand years by the time the memorable Marco Polo brought back from his Far Eastern journey a recipe for a sherbet-like dessert containing milk. The news spread rapidly from Venice to all of Italy.

On the legend-inaugurating side, King Solomon's reference in the Book of Proverbs to "the cold of snow in the time of harvest" *could* be construed as the refreshment of chilled wine in the heat of hard labor. Legendary too is the report of Richard the Lion-Hearted's return from the Crusades with the knowledge of how to make a form of orange ice given him by Saladin, Sultan of Egypt and Syria.

The Romans liked to remove peach stones and pack the peaches with snow, thereby creating an exquisite dessert frozen from *within*. Alexander the Great, on one of his campaigns, ordered trenches dug and filled with straw-protected snow so that he and his retinue might enjoy cooled fruit and drink. During the same period the Emperor Nero sent slaves in relays up into the Appennines to insure a steady supply of snow which he then had mixed with honey and fruit juices.*

The great Hippocrates had warned many years earlier that "It is dangerous to heat, cool, or make a commotion all of a sudden in the body . . . because everything that is excessive is an enemy to nature." Evidently his admonitions went unheeded. He was fully aware of human nature as well: "People will not take warning and most men would rather run the hazard of their lives or health than be deprived of the pleasure of drinking out of ice." One only has to observe any of today's cigarette smokers luxuriating in the face of official warnings to see the truth of the noble physician's complaint.

Ices were introduced to Sicily by the Saracens in the 9th Century, and it is said that the ruling Arabs sucked out birds' eggs and filled them with blossom-flavored water which they then buried overnight in snow. More recent histories tell of the snows of Etna – plentiful both in winter and summer – having been bequeathed to the Church as a source of revenue for the bishopric of Palermo whose incumbent ceremonially blesses them.

It is not too surprising that it was the Italians who improved cooling methods. They achieved this by placing beverage containers in a dish of ice or snow combined with saltpeter, thereby speeding up the process. The possibility of over-cooling these beverages and discovering "ices" seems more than likely.

Meanwhile, in what is now Mexico, an Aztec general sent to round up fugitive Totonac Indians was overwhelmed by an extraordinary smell permeating the jungle. He discovered that it emanated from pods produced by a yellow orchid. He returned to the court of his King, Montezuma, who imaginatively mingled this new-found treat, called vanilla, with the bean of the cacao tree into a liquid which he then chilled. It was this drink which historians tell us he served the Spaniard Cortez. One doesn't know whether the general was rewarded or punished for returning without the Totonacs he'd been sent to find.

Back in Europe Catherine de Medici, the young bride of the future Henri II of France, brought along her own chefs and thereby introduced ices and sherbets to the French. She and her court may have known the forefather of actual ice cream: there appear about that time written references to milk sweetened with honey and then frozen into a food poetically dubbed "the flower of milk." It's pleasant to imagine that in Elizabeth's England there also could have been a near ice cream. That exotic-sounding drink, "syllabub under the cow," might even have been frozen (the palaces and great houses of the time had ice-houses in which ice cut from rivers and ponds was harvested and stored in straw against the coming summer). This consisted of a girl milking a cow that gave a cream-rich milk into a large bowl

An engraving by Isabey done in 1827. One of a series on manners. In this case somewhat languorous ladies enjoying ice cream.
*Mary Evans Picture Library.*

of sweet white wine, causing it to froth and foam.

There is no doubt about Charles I. His French chef served a frozen dessert which so pleased His Majesty and his guests that he commanded the recipe be kept a secret. There are conflicting accounts as to the fate of this chef. One states he was given £500 per year to keep mum. Another report mentions only £20. A third tells of his beheading for giving the secret away – an event that couldn't have occurred before Charles' son James II – or *his* chef – learned it, as James was extremely fond of this exclusively royal dessert and even ordered a dozen dishes (at the steep price of £1 a dish) while encamped with his army.

The beginning of the dissemination of this Lord of Concoctions took place in Paris where, not surprisingly, a Sicilian *limondier,* Francesco Procopio, opened the first cafe where he served *iced* cream (as it was first known) and sherbets. No longer was ice cream to be reserved for the very rich. Although these were still the beneficiaries of elaborate novelties. Vatel, chef to Louise XIV, at one of the king's banquets "caused to be served before each guest, in silver gilt cups, what was apparently a freshly laid egg, colored like those of Easter, but before the company had time to recover from their surprise at such a novelty at dessert, they discovered that the supposed eggs were delicious sweetmeats, cold,

and compact as marble." Shades of Arabs 700 years before!

The example and success of Signore Procopio – who changed his name to Procope and whose celebrated establishment survives as a restaurant to this day in the rue de l'Ancienne Comedie – was widely imitated. Paris saw the opening of several hundred cafes, many boasting their own ice cream. Some of these refreshment shops were very beautiful. Most were run by Italians with names like Coltelli, Tancredi Latino, Biago Villa, Santorio, and Controso. The Glacerie of a certain Godette was especially beautiful – all glass through which patrons could see to all parts of a large garden.

No one knows exactly when the transition from ice to ice cream actually took place, but in the New World a dinner guest of Governor Bladen of Maryland wrote a letter from the colony stating, " . . . we had a dessert no less Curious; among the Rarities of which it was Compos'd, was some fine Ice Cream which, with Strawberries and Milk, eat Most Deliciously." Communications from Vienna told of ice cream being indulged in year-round. And the French and English were both starting to produce recipe books containing directions for making frozen desserts. A famous one, written by a Mrs. Glasse, directed: "Take two Pewter Basons, one larger than the other. The inward one must have a close Cover, into which you are to

put your Cream, and mix it with Raspberries or whatever you like best, to give it a Flavour and a Colour. Sweeten it to your Palate, then cover it close, and set it into the larger Basin. Fill it with Ice, and a Handful of Salt; then let it stand in this Ice three Quarters of an Hour, then uncover it, and stir the Cream well together; cover it close again, and let it stand Half an Hour longer, after that turn it into your Plate."

In Paris the Duc de Chartres served his guests ice cream decorated with his coat of arms carved in the cream itself. At the same time Brillat-Savarin had traveled to the new United States and reported in his celebrated work, *La Physiologie du Gout,* that nobles who had fled from *his* country's revolution were finding a means of survival through their knowledge of and taste for food.

An interesting footnote to history is that in the very year of the French Revolution, Mrs. Alexander Hamilton is known to have served ice cream to the first man to become President of the United States – George Washington.

---

* A custom even practiced in the 20's. Mrs. Lloyd B. Wescott – then Barbara Harrison, daughter of the last Governor of the Phillipines – was invited to cocktails by the Glaoui, chief of the Berbers in Morocco. The drinks were chilled with snow brought from the 12,000-foot snow line of the Atlas Mountains via a chain of runners. The snow was also used for other cooling and freezing.

Don't be misled — see that it is
# A1 ICE CREAM

A1 Stands for the Best, the Purest Ice Cream.

*There can be No Better*

**6 CARTS OUT DAILY**, all specially constructed, Hygienic and Dust-proof. Motor Vans cater for the Suburbs.

Parties and Dances catered for          Delivered Any Time.

Particulars from:

## "A.I." ICE-CREAM FACTORY,
### 89, Hope Street, Cape Town.

# Eating Winter with a Spoon

In England, a prevalence of hand-drawn, hand-painted carts. Ice cream vendors from the 1890's to the 1930's. A common sight, recognizable by their attractive decorations – like all true folk expression, traditional and individual at the same time. Most have striped overhead awnings redolent of hot Italian skies.

Among those shown here: Young ladies and little boys at Hampstead; a bowlered seller in Richmond Row and Fox Street; before a handsome Art Nouveau window; even in January before St. Clements Dane Church; Saffron Hill in April – "pure ices" and fine wooden tubs.

" ICE-CREAM AND GINGER-BEER."

## The Penny-Ice Man

IN summer when the sun is high,
  And children's lips are parched and dry,
An ice is just the thing to try.
So this young man who comes, 'tis plain,
  From Saffron Hill or Leather Lane,
A store of pence will quickly gain.
"A lemon ice for me," says Fred;
  Cries Sue, "No, have a cream instead."
"A raspberry!" shouts Newsboy Ned.
"What fun! Although we're now in June,
  It feels"—says Ned—"this afternoon,
Like eating winter with a spoon!"

# ICES IN SICILY

The Villa Giulia Gardens in Palermo, with a wide double carriageway and broadwalks on the shore beneath the fortified seawall, were laid out in the second half of the eighteenth century. Here in the days when the Bourbon sovereigns, Ferdinand and Maria Carolina, were using Palermo as a capital while in exile from Naples during the Napoleonic Wars, there used to be sociable assemblies in the evenings, the officers and gentry conversing, strolling or listening to music from bandsmen seated in an eagle-surmounted stone tribune. The fashionable mob would bow as the King and Queen passed, heads lowered in succession like ears of corn and poppies rippled by a zephyr and, the ritual over, retire to chatter anew, eat ices or nibble Sicilian trifles. This was the *ora dei gelati*.

The Marina still has its shady walk below the rampart and its superb view across the bay to the Gibraltar-like mountains of the Conca d'Oro, but it is no longer a smart rendezvous, though two cafes serve ices and sweet cakes at tables under poplars and beneath Erythrina trees that have cockscomb blossoms in the spring. Nowadays, North Italian ices are imported, coming by ice-conditioned railway wagons met at stations by ice-conditioned motor trucks. There has been a struggle by the new and imported against the old and local. The ice war has now come to a deadlock. After an initial success, the invaders from the North are being held back by the Mediterraneans, though with difficulty and only because a core of conservative Sicilians of all classes prefer their old customs, including traditional dishes. So it is by no means at every café in Palermo that Sicilian ices are to be found. Dagnino's in the Piazza Politeams, a firm founded a hundred years ago, is one of the few.

Another is Iliardi's on the Marina below the Trabia and Lampedusa Palaces, also an old establishment. A big change in the use of the Marina, by nannies and children in the morning and by fashionable strollers in the evening, came during the late war, when its extremities, between the Porta Felice and the Villa Giulia Gardens, suffered from Allied bombing; later the use of the roadway by cars and the filling in of the foreshore by bombed debris, that put the sea at a greater distance, further altered the character of the area.

Since nothing can destroy the view and there is a strong liking for freshly made Sicilian specalities by the people, the Marina remains popular at holidays, if not as popular as it once was. It is at the heart of old Palermo though removed from the bustle of narrow streets of the ancient city and there can be savored not only ices, but the atmosphere of the past of a capital where many civilizations have met.

The coffee-shops have their offices and kitchen in the rampart itself, in what were once carriageways, sally-ports and service gates to the Palaces; there the proprietors superintend the cutting of fresh fruit and the mixing of ingredients, but they will come out to linger and discuss their trade with clients at the tables.

It is an accepted fact in their belief that ices, which are not mentioned by Apicius, gastronomic authority of ancient Rome, were first introduced to Sicily by the Saracens. Since the Arabs arrived in 827 A.D. and ruled, from Palermo, until the Norman Conquest in 1072, the history of ices in Europe is well over 1,000 years old. It is a likely tale, for Sicily is one of the few places where ice and snow are close at hand in very hot summers. It was the custom until a few years ago to pack the ice and snow into grottoes half way down the mountains and from there bring loads to the city at night on donkeys and mules. Today electrically driven machines have replaced the hand-turned, wooden ice-making pail, the shape in metal though larger, being much the same. The ices made include flavoring with almonds, orange blossom, honey, nougat, pistachio, lemons, figs, black salsify, cannella or cinnamon, *fichie d'Indie* or prickly pears, *gersi neri* or mulberries and the popular jasmine or *gelsomino. Scorzonero* or salsify ices are favorites with the clergy, possibly because of their subdued coloring, black and white. . . .

Some of the ices are made to resemble slices of red watermelon with seeds of chocolate, others mixed with cake and cream are somewhat like the well-known 'English Soup' served elsewhere in Italy, though firmer, and called Cassata, a word some say is by origin from the Arabic for 'sliced'. There are several kinds of them much favored in Sicily. *Caffè bianco* is made with coffee, though white in color, a secret of the Iliardi family.

Another secret recipe is of ices for invalids, from chicken and meat with strengthening herbs. It is even said that there are aphrodisiac ices, but only made in winter and reserved for the nobility.

These secrets, at least in the Iliardi family, have been handed down in each generation from father to son, and it is a long-lived family, the last two elders being eighty-eight and one hundred and three. According to them, ices were first made in Sicily by Arabs sucking birds' eggs and filling them with water flavored by blossoms which were then buried in the snow for a night until ready to be transported to Palermo, packed in straw. . . .

In Italy . . . each city had, and still has, an annual opening date for ice-making that varies according to the climate, and it is always in a traditional place or cafe that the ices are eaten. If the first gastronomic use of ice in Western Europe was owed to the Arabs and Sicilians, the Russians and Americans extended its usage. The *granita* or sorbay, a crunched or water ice, said to have come to Western Europe via Russia in the eighteenth century, was however not taken alone but between courses as a digestive during long banquets and dinners, a usage the Arabs and present-day Sicilians would feel was beneath the deserts of a true ice, the gelato, or fruit-ice in general, the *semi-freddo* or parfait and the *mantecato* or milky ice. The origin of the word sorbay is from the Arabic *sharbah,* taken into the Turkish and Persian vocabularies as meaning to drink, and sherbet is from the same source. In Sicily, ices must have been found good indeed to be favored by all the successors of the Arabs and to last so long. The Normans in Sicily, in the golden age of Frederick the Second, and later the Angevins and the Spaniards when they in turn ruled, all ate and enjoyed them. Nelson's younger sailors and powder-monkeys, if allowed a shore when his fleet anchored off Cape Gallo, must have liked them as a change from salt beef, ship's biscuits and rum. The Bourbons it is known favored them; eating ices in public was *à la mode* under them in the nineteenth century. In the late war, British and American soldiers, stopping their jeeps to buy them, were enthusiasts.

Sicilian ices still have such moments of success renewed. Recently the mixed caste of the ball scene in *The Leopard* by Lampedusa being filmed in Palermo took them with delight. In the courtyard of the Gangi Palace, demure looking ladies in crinolines and diamonds, fluttering their fans, dangling their dance-cards, side-whiskered and handsome young officers, stripped to the waist in the great heat, swords and white kid gloves beside them, waiting their turn in the ball, gobbled or licked them with evident pleasure, blue or black eyes rolling equally. In the stifling nights of a long midsummer and near the cooler dawns, in and about the lamp- and candle-lit Palace or driving home over the stone-flagged streets of old Palermo, in fast cars or almost as fast Victorias drawn by galloping nags, members of the Company might sometimes be seen enjoying them, as did other invaders, Arabian Emirs and their courts from North Africa a thousand years before.

from *"Ices in Sicily"* by Gerald de Gaury,
*The London Magazine*, October 1963.

A *sorbetto* – an Italian sherbet (or ice) vendor in southern Italy from a lithograph by Muller.

The Bettman Archive

19

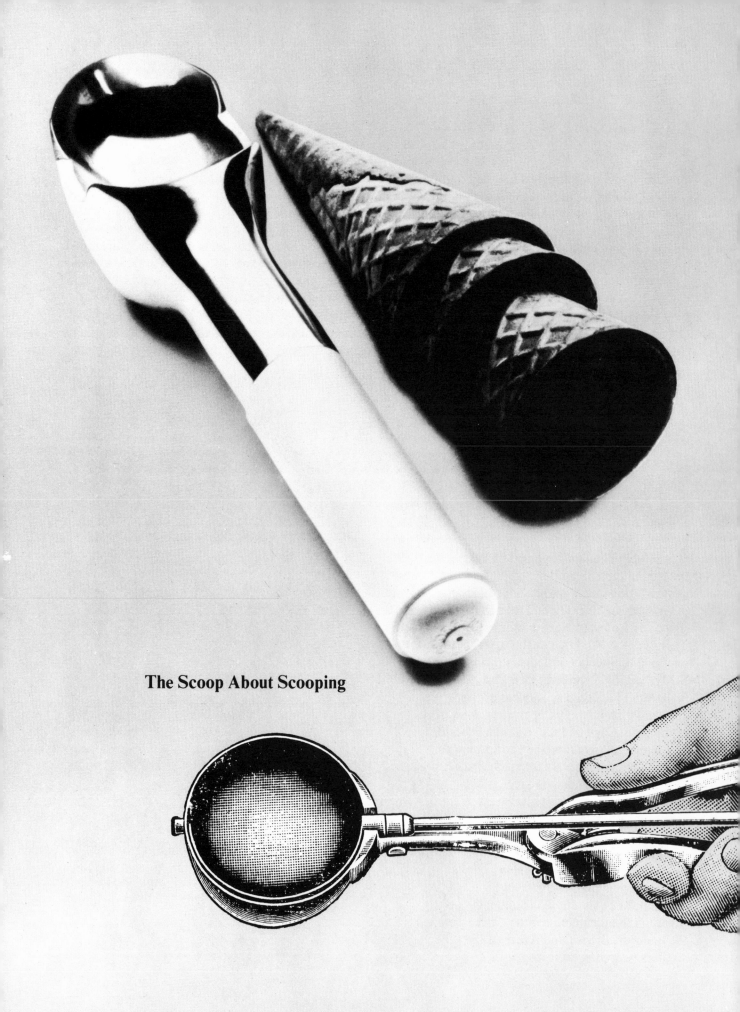

**The Scoop About Scooping**

The newest ice cream scoop is *eutectic*\* and contains an anti-freeze which makes it easier to use than traditional trigger-scoops.

According to Lyons Maid, "To get correct yield, take the scoop and cut into the ice cream to a depth of about half an inch. Draw the scoop in a circular motion around the container until it is full. Work the scoop into the ice cream one layer at a time toward the center of the container. Ensure that the ice cream is kept as level as possible. Deposits and thin layers of ice cream around the sides of bulk containers become sandy and unpleasant. . . ."

Wash and dry the scoop thoroughly after use. A number 24 scoop is two inches in diameter and the standard scoop for cones. Should get 24 level scoops from a quart of ice cream. A number 12 scoop, two and three-quarter inches in diameter, is the standard scoop used for making sundaes.

Ice cream should be served soft enough to reveal its full flavor. The proper temperature will depend on how it is made and what it is made of. Chocolate, for example, melts faster than vanilla so it can be served at a lower temperature than vanilla. If it is too hard, forcing the scoop into it will release air incorporated into it and spoil its texture and appearance.

---

\* *eutectic* – "an alloy or mixture whose melting point is lower than that of any other alloy or mixture of the same ingredients."

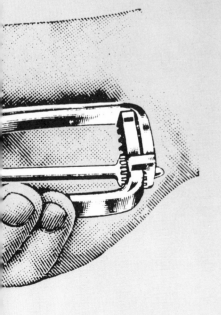

# "DELECTABLE MOUNTAINS"

The title derives from a wonderfully imaginative book by e. e. cummings called *The Enormous Room*. The book has nothing to do with ice cream, but the phrase just seems too good not to use. One of the difficulties in doing a book on ice cream is that, like sex, everyone has his or her favorite kind. And – have you noticed? – it always turns out to be the "best" kind as well. Asking someone at a party or meeting what they know about ice cream is to chance informational over-load. Invariably there seems to be yet another place you've never heard of. This can be delightful of course – as well as endless. However, there *are* examples of consensus and I would like to deal with them here. A warning: some may prove to be more like foothills than mountains in the experiencing.

In California, Southern that is, several names leap to many minds. Wil Wright in Los Angeles is one. Back in 1964 Lucius Beebe wrote that "the supreme hallmark of affluent sophistication is to serve a spectacular ice cream confection by Wil Wright at one's parties, to send Wil Wright's uncommonly costly confectioneries as gifts or, if you are in the teen-age brackets of well-upholstered celebrity, to command soda fountain specialties at one of Wil Wright's several dispensaries of caloric splendor . . . not only a status symbol but a burgeoning cult, at first in Southern

California and then as far afield as Dallas where they enjoy an exclusive franchise at Neiman-Marcus' millionaire trap." Wright began above a garage in Beverly Hills in 1945. He and his partners, Mart Conley and Bill Walsh, opened their first parlor on the Sunset Strip. They emphasized quality and costliness (Bollinger when champagne was called for, 40-year Hennessy for their cognac) and it worked. By 1964 there were ten shops and a couple of franchises and grosses were reported as nearly a million dollars a year. Even then, Nesselrode Bula sold for $2.75 a quart. A dish of ice cream in one of the parlors was listed at 75¢. Wright produced superb molded desserts, combining ice cream and water ices: an ocean liner of chocolate macaroon and black cherry; a fruit bowl of flavors to match the fruit shapes. Stars like Ingrid Bergman (chocolate mocha) had their favorites flown to Europe packed in dry ice. Rita Hayworth was quoted as replying to a question about what she wanted above all for her birthday, "Never mind the cabochon emeralds, just send me a hundred quarts of Wil Wright's Nesselrode Bula."

According to a more recent report (by George Christy in *Los Angeles*) there are now only eight Wil Wright parlors – still decorated in red and white with bent-wire chairs and marble-topped tables, still making a superior

Nesselrode Bula (fruit, chestnuts, rum and brandy), but with the vanilla and many other flavors rating a "blah." Evidently the so-called European Fruit Ices are still "frozen to perfection" however. Christy's verdict on them: "out of this world."

Aided and abetted by Judy Baldwin, Christy worked out a guide to L.A. based on ice creams, ices and sherbets, sodas, and particularly hot fudge sundaes. And it seems C.C. Brown's still exists. Clarence Clifton Brown claims to have invented the first hot fudge sundae in 1906. His place is in other hands now and the team found the sauces too sweet and too rich for the most part, but they serve "one of the best ice cream sodas" in town and the sundaes sport real whipped cream.

Highest praise is given to Clancy Muldoon's (there are two of them): "pure and sweet, velvety-smooth and refreshing to the last lick." Flavors are chosen from about 150. Things like mandarin orange, apple strudel, canteloupe, butter brickle, with around "14 per cent butterfat and 85 per cent overrun (as little air as possible)." Muldoon works with a single batch freezer. He also serves a Honeymaid ice cream – pure honey, raw unprocessed sugar, fresh eggs and cream, no artificial flavoring. The places themselves are what can be called "ice cream counters" rather than parlors (the same as Bud's and Polly Ann's and the original Swensen's in San Francisco). Sherberts are "outstanding," the lime and grapefruit deserving of "international fame."

Another counter place, Bennett's Ice Cream Shoppe in the Farmer's Market, dispenses ice cream a bit "too rich" though undeniably delicious. Fresh peach (in season) and banana marshmallow rate "four stars" (out of a possible five). Sherbets are also described as very good.

After praising the neo-nostalgia decor of Swensen's Ice Cream Factory (L. A. wing) – ceiling fans, real marble tables, etched mirrors, etc. – C & B award their ice cream four stars. The same for their sundaes (more on Swensen's later).

The guide ends with mention of Gills' Old Fashioned Ice Cream in the Farmers Market; Altadena Ice Cream, one of those places springing up which use all natural ingredients and nary a chemical stabilizer; and Brockmeyer Ice Cream – another

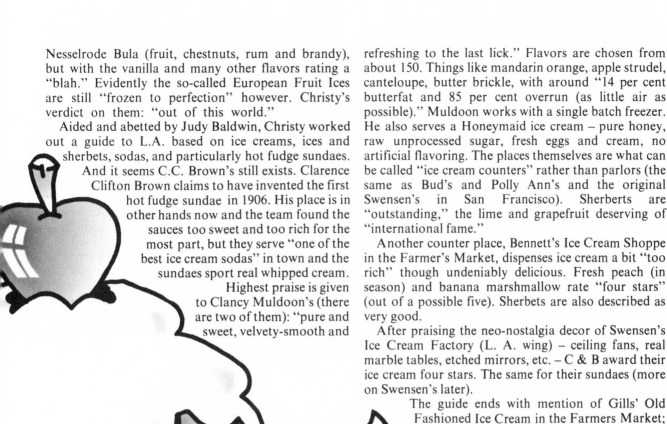

"naturally made goodie" available in most supermarkets in the area and branching out into other states. They list ingredients on their packages – something of a rarity in the industry.

In 1971 Gael Greene, one of the half-handful of top writers on ice cream, did a similar guide to New York City in *New York*. (Most mysteriously, there is no mention of ice cream or ice cream parlors in Kate Simons' famed *New York: Places and Pleasures*). Greene discusses several of the Big or Big-ish companies I'd like to write about elsewhere, and then goes on to say she finds Carvel's soft ice cream "like sweetened shaving foam" but *has* enjoyed their rum raisin. 101 Varieties of Yum Yum on Amsterdam Avenue announces some enticing flavors like canteloupe a la mode, Burgundy punch, bubblegum, but the taste is "thin" and worse than Carvel at its non-best. A place called Camel's Hump on West Third Street often serves Arabic ice cream, "apricot and pistachio – almost solid fruit or solid nuts, glued together by clotted-cream and perfume-scented gum arabic. Rich, chewy, unusual and sublime." Alwan's Oriental Confectionary in Brooklyn carries it too. The Ice Cream Connection (I did not know about it until researching this book) on St. Marks Place is "into" goat's milk and organic honey – inevitable in these days of trying to have your health-cake and eating it too. They also dip out cow-derived ice cream: fudge ripple, peach brandy with actual bits of peach, apple (also with bits of fruit). Ms. Greene: "How does goat's milk ice cream taste? I tried peach. The first taste is peach. The second taste is goat." Another West Third Street place, Health E. Snack, a couple of doors from the Camel's Hump, does a strawberry shake with organic strawberries and sells goat's milk ice cream by the scoop. The cone is made with wheat germ, natch (pun *int*ended).

Interestingly, Ms. Greene has something to say about Wil Wright's way out west. She quotes something called "top executives" at Wright's as saying, "There isn't anyone that [sic] approaches our butterfat." 20 per cent in their vanilla, 16-20 in other flavors. As though *that* were the sole criteria for the best ice cream! It's not. It's the right percentage of butterfat in relation to the other ingredients. People, like a movie theater executive she mentions, still have it flown to them. Mention of a nationally franchised "fun food and ice cream" to be called "Wil Wright's America" is made, but unknown to me so far and none of my efforts to get answers to letters of enquiry has produced any results. Parlor-wise the *New York* list includes The Flick on

Second Avenue – so underlit it's "almost like eating ice cream in a closet" though admittedly amid "handsome mahogany" (no rating of the ice cream); Hicks, a somewhat plastically "old fashioned" fruiterers on East 49th Street much beloved by women shoppers, whose "fruit-laced flaming and hot fudge extravaganzas are a special joy" along with a thirst-quenching "Lemonsher, with raspberry sherbet and floating berries." Old-Fashioned Mr. Jennings – who was once the "manic prankster soda chef" at Hicks – is reported to be running a red-white-and-blue place on East 70th Street which a writer acquaintance described to me as thought to be "safe" for the offspring of the neighborhood's better-heeled. I couldn't locate it. In *Town & Country* it was reported in 1973 that Mr. Jennings was "doing his thing" on the ninth floor of Bonwit Teller.

The Trattoria's (Pan Am Building) *tartufo* was found to be an "honorable, unashamed steal from Tre Scalini in Rome's Piazza Navona" [note that for your next Italian trip] but served far too frozen. Lorenzo Dolcino is responsible for the outstanding ice cream. Blended in small amounts several times a week from nothing but the finest ingredients obtainable. Next to no overrun (that business about air again) and high butterfat content. Lovely lemon ice, *granita di caffe,* but the pistachio is rated "bland."

Rumplemayer's on Central Park South conjures up a whole world of gentility and family excursions for tea and cakes and elegant confections. It continues to offer the "undiluted best" down (or up) to classic French fan biscuits. (Christy in a 1975 article recommends their caramel nut, chocolate mint, hot fudge pecan sundae).

Ferraro's on Grand Street, happily characterized by Ms. Greene as the "Deux Maggots of Little Italy," blends its *gelato* on the premises: 8 per cent butterfat and low overruns which makes it heavy (in the sense of being filled with good things). A world of spumone, tortoni, ices and gelati.

And what of Schrafft's with its dropped-f sign of gilt letters? Phasing, if not phased entirely out. High quality, lady-like (small to some) portions elegantly served in the "right" way – in glass dishes upon lacey paper doilies. Blum's (of San Francisco origin) is reported "listless" and apparently suffering from "transplant shock," but with good ice cream – "burnt-almond especially." Well, it's nothing like its former Polk Street self in San Francisco *its* self. The decline there was sealed by the disappearance of real whipped cream. Still pink in color, if not in condition, it goes on its plastic way at Macy's in Union Square and a small place on Union Street. Thomforde's, in Harlem, since 1903, boasts a carved mahogany soda counter and frosted glass ("everything a bit too sweet"); Jahn's in the Bronx, since 1897: Seventeen "Ice Cream Emporiums" today. ("Nothing wrong" with the ice cream, but they use Whipt-Rite all over the place where real cream should rule) and, like so many fine parlors, the once grand Richmond Hill Jahn's is now a place of "scarred, dark stained paneling . . . half hidden behind rosewood formica, and the magnificent gaslights, chandeliers, and . . . advertising memorabilia are flanked with hanging baskets of artificial flowers and American flags." Serendipity on East 60th Street is a camp confectionery-boutique which is delightful to sit in (check the airy upstairs). Things like Apricot Smush – somewhere between ice cream and sherbet, and frothy – and Hot Chocolate served cold and slushy with cream on top flecked with chocolate, are customer favorites. Huge sundaes. Mr. Waffles on West Eighth Street and the Acropolis on First Avenue are also mentioned in Ms. Greene's report.

Friends have told me of a tiny place – more awning than anything else – on West 4th Street, Ma Somebody's, which has only Home Made Ice Cream as its designation;* the Agora up on Third Avenue with a turn-of-the-century interior transplanted from a once-thriving parlor in Haverstraw, New York – a melody of cabinetry and frosted mirror, stained-glass and beaded chandeliers with an onyx soda fountain (angostura pineapple, cherry or coffee rum, daiquiri have been singled out); Kron's on an upper floor along Madison Avenue, supposed to sell incredible chocolate ice cream – *only* chocolate. Recently (too late for review as they say in the newspapers), the Liberty Cafe Ice Cream Convention opened on West 64th Street near Lincoln Center. I know nothing about its frozen confections, but the building was once a warehouse (The *Liberty* Warehouse maybe?) with a wonderful "Pop" replica of The Statue of Liberty on its facade.

Sari Staver Sheldon, writing in the March, 1975 issue of *Chicago,* offers a very helpful guide to ice cream eating in the Chicago area. Evidently more Chicagoans eat ice cream than either New Yorkers or Los Angelinos. Ms. Sheldon enlisted six other people to first test a number of locally available ice creams. As usual, there were some surprises. They found Walgreen's (a big drugstore chain) vanilla cheap, flavorful and like good homemade. While Vala's, the most expensive, proved "awful." The highest-rated chocolate only came up to the 7th-rated vanilla. Goldenrod was graded best with a "nice, okay flavor." Considering both vanilla and chocolate, the testers ranked Homer's first, Baskin-Robbins second, Walgreen's third, Mitchell's fourth, Marshall Field's fifth, Peacock's sixth, and Goldenrod's seventh. The top three averaged 12 per cent butterfat while the following three contained a higher 17 per cent. Goldenrod was two-thirds less expensive than Vala's – which it owns – and scored higher.

The article went on to list ice cream stores and parlors. Baskin-Robbins (a number of Chicago stores) has its local ice cream made by Dean's – very successfully duplicating B-R flavors, according to the writer. " 'Very berry' is full of real berries – raspberries, blueberries, boysenberries, olalliberries; fruit tree sherbet contains slices of pears, cherries, mandarin oranges, peaches, pineapples." Bresler's 33 Flavors (22 stores) were found to be "thin and anemic" and to "lack pizazz." Kumquat sherbet was "insipid" and butter brickle lacked "distinctive flavor." But maple nut and maple divinity had "strong, pleasant tastes." Buffalo's on Irving Park Road and West Dempster in Morton Grove insist they make their own ice cream. They don't. Hawthorn Mellody makes it for them (at least in the Irving Park Road store). The decor of the latter is described as unchanged from earlier days – "massive, high-backed wooden booths and buffalo murals" with a "genuine old-fashioned touch." Vanilla, "nothing special." Chocolate, "mild and pleasant." Hand-whipped cream, "delicious." But all in all, a "disappointment." Crystal Palace in the famous old Marshall Field and Company department store on North State Street rates a star and is newly "an elegant 1890s-style ice cream parlor. Stained-glass archways and ribbon-glass chandeliers, potted palms and hanging plants, and Victorian-style mirrors and carved cupids" making it "Chicago's classiest ice cream parlor." "The high-ceilinged room is decorated in pink and green, right down to the neatly folded cloth napkins . . . You can sit in wire-backed chairs at small tables at the soda bar, where you'll be able to watch the young soda jerks in action." It sounds wonderful! As for the ice cream, it is offered in eight standard flavors plus rotating special. Frango mint is rated "delicate", chocolate peanut butter, "scrumptious." Commercial hot fudge sauce was "overly sweet." But there is also a homemade one you should ask for. Take-home ice creams (along with dry ice) available on 7th floor. Dr Jazz Ice Cream Treats on Montrose is "gadget and gizmo-filled." Free silent films are shown in the evenings. Hawthorn Mellody ice cream in a dozen flavors. French vanilla, "rich, tasty." Mint chocolate chip, "delicately flavored." Two specials: peanut butter milk shake, "very rich and very peanutty"; fresh orange cream (juice of two oranges mixed with vanilla ice cream), nice and "creamy." Hot fudge. "slightly grainy but very tasty." Another shop scheduled to open on Chicago Avenue in Evanston. If you ignore the No Smoking signs, "a siren goes off, red lights blink, overhead fans begin to turn." Gasper's on West Washington Street will create and flavor for you if you order at least five quarts. "For the discriminating ice cream eater." Brandied egg nog is "heavily spiked with French brandy." Special order desserts available with several days notice, are "visual and gustatory delights."

---

* Demonstrative of the often incestuous world of ice-creamania is a fact, reported by the columnist Herb Caen in the *San Francisco Chronicle* to the effect that "*New York* magazine [obviously an issue other than the one containing Ms. Greene's guide] picked the ice cream at a place called Mother Buckas' as the best in Manhattan, little knowing that all of Mother's recipes come from the celebrated Bud (Bud's Ice Cream) Edlin of our village, Maureen Pratt and Mark Falk, Mother's owners, came here from N.Y. to learn Bud's secrets, then bought his recipes for $3,000 . . ."

Hemingway's Moveable Feast on North Lincoln Plaza, is the only place in town offering hand-packed Vala's ice cream. From around 15 to 30 flavors depending on the time of year. Some of the "very best" – mocha chip, rum raisin, macadamia nut, Bavarian cream fudge, praline. Fresh peach "needs more flavor." Big black cherry "has a piece of fruit in every bite." Mandarin orange sherbet "makes all the other orange sherbets seem anemic." Margie's on North Western is the kind of place beloved by gourmands. "Largest creations in town." "Foot-long" banana splits. "World's Largest Sundae" made with half gallon of ice cream. Highlander's premium ice creams. Homemade toppings. Hot fudge, "tasty, milk-chocolaty." Fresh fruit sundaes in season. Ting-a-ling on West Division gets a star. Truly homemade ice cream. Tiny shop opened in 1928. Eight wooden booths. Ice cream is quite simply "superb." Chocolate chip, butter pecan, coconut are Ms. Sheldon's favorites. Maple milk shake, "rich and delicious." Hot fudge topping, "marvelous" (though the banana involved was "mushy and overripe"). Hot caramel sauce, "unsurpassed." In-season canteloupe, strawberry, raspberry, blueberry, and peach sundaes.

The guide goes on to list and comment on David's and The Gayety in South Chicago and several places in the suburban north and northwest – among them Homer's in Wilmette. Opened in 1935. Quality unchanged. Twenty-five flavors, all homemade. Praised: banana, chocolate and mint chip, fresh peach (summer only). Hot fudge, "exceptional." Dry ice. Howard Johnson's on Sheridan Road in Wilmette (other places). Twenty-eight flavors. Praised: cinnamon apple, mocha chip, peppermint stick. Peacock's, another star-winner. On Davis Street in Evanston and Skokie Boulevard in Wilmette. Twenty-eight "terrific homemade flavors" – mocha chip, chocolate almond, cinnamon. "Excellent" hot fudge. Coffee soda, "like a hearty cup of fresh-brewed coffee." Very generous servings. Take-home toppings and ice cream. Dry ice. Sweet Shop on Elm Street in Winnetka. Dozen flavors (Homer's) along with homemade toppings. Fresh fruit sundaes in season. Treat Shoppe on Frontage Road in Northfield and on Mill Pond in Long Grove. Both shops filled with antiques. Frontage Road: 9 flavors of Homer's ice cream. Chocolate and mint chip and fresh peach (in season), "superb." Long Grove serves Peterson's ice cream. Happiness Is on Oak Park Avenue, Oak Park. Nine premium flavors. Pistachio, butter pecan, peppermint, "particularly good." Petersen's on Chicago Avenue and Lake Street in Oak Park. Twenty-eight flavors made by people some of whom have worked there since 1919! Cinnamon, banana, lemon custard, run raisin, all "super."

In suburban south and southwest Ms. Sheldon chooses the following: Kaffel's Cone Shoppe (The Grainery, Franfurt, at intersection of Routes 30 and 45). Up to thirty flavors of homemade ice cream. "Top notch" rum raisin, chocolate peanut, banana cream. Huge scoops. Cunis Candy Shop (East 162nd in South Holland). New location for store opened in 1930's. Fourteen flavors. Homemade. English toffee, maple

nut, fresh peach (in season), "very good." A star for Mitchell's Candie and Ice Cream shop (Dixie Highway in Homewood). Another relocated shop dating back to the 30's. A "gem of a shop" with "no gimmicks, no fancy names, just rich, down-home goodness." Fifteen flavors. "Some of the best ice cream around." Chocolate chip, pistachio, chocolate almond, "outstanding." Hot fudge, "all-time favorite." Fresh fruit sundaes (in season). Homemade, take-home toppings. Insulated bags. Plush Horse (86th Place, Palos Park and East Front Street, Wheaton). Dozen flavors of "superb" homemade ice cream. Palos Park favorites: creme de menthe, brandied peach, butter cream, old-fashioned, Hawaiian delight. Fresh fruit sundaes (in season).

The guide ends by noting Carson Pitie Scott's (State Street) Heather House Ice Cream Pie; Food For Life's (North Lincoln) "natural" ice creams and "fantastic granola topping"; Good Humor's (roaming the streets) "super" chocolate éclair and toasted almond flavors; Kennessey's (West Belmont and Elmhurst Road, Mount Prospect) high butterfat homemade ice cream – "great" vanilla, coffee cognac, "deep, dark, rich" chocolate;" Lutz's (Montrose Avenue) beautiful outdoor garden;Lady Borden ice cream; house special of two ice creams, brandy, fruit and whipped cream; Ideal Candies' (North Clark Street) "terrific homemade fudge sauce," Highlander's ice cream; Maxim's de Paris' (North Astor) "unsurpassed elegance," Louis Sherry ice cream, profiterôls and cherries jubilee, strawberries Romanoff highly praised. The Ninety-Fifth's (floor of the John Hancock Center) Vala's ice cream served with a view, Baked Alaska, Cherries jubilee, etc.; Treasure Island Food Mart's (North Broadway, etc.) Highlander's ice cream, hand-dipped cones at 15¢; Truffles' (Hyatt Regency, East Wacker Drive) Häagen-Dazs ice cream – "rich, dense, almost too heavy;" Woolworth's (all over town) Borden's ice cream, double-dip chocolate sodas, "great buy."

But even so thorough an investigation can't win 'em all. No mention is made of The Palmer House Hotel which an old (and trusted) friend wrote me "still really does have the world's best chocolate ice cream."

Other places across the land praised and recommended by Mr. Various and Ms. Sundry are: The Chocolate Shop in Kalamazoo; Millers Dairy Farm in Eaton Rapids (responsible for a combo of pickles and ice cream!); Stroh's Ice Cream Parlor in the On-the-Hill shopping Center in Grosse Point – all three in Michigan; Fitzgerald's in Albuquerque, New Mexico. Bing's in Mexico. Dysart's in Cedar Rapids, Iowa. Snelgroves and the Pink Pantry, both in Salt Lake City, Utah. Deering Ice Cream Shops in Maine. A Peterson's in Marion, Massachusetts.

A postcard from Jane Howard, a former Life-Time editor, dated 21 Jan. 1975, contained the following enthusiasm: "I've discovered another good ice cream, served at the Algonquin Hotel in Pembrine, Wis., made I believe by a Wisconsin firm called Barclay's. It was superb."

And on and on it goes . . . .

TOASTED SUZIE IS MY ICE CREAM
– Gertrude Stein

# SOCIETY & TH

Like any pleasure, the enjoyment of eating such things as ices and ice cream could not be reserved forever for one special class. Charles I attempt to keep ice cream "to himself" was bound to fail. And it wasn't too long before Catherine de Medici's "novelty," which she brought to France, found its way to the burgeoning cafes of Paris. Caesars, Kings, and Presidents were soon to be joined by the likes of merchants, professionals, and the gentry – "persons of great refinement" of course. In the early 19th century the presence of society ladies and their followers in confectioners' "genteel" ice cream saloons was equaled by the enthusiastic customers who could be seen clustered around the carts of street vendors. By mid-century this democratization was perfectly symbolized by the appearance at the Crystal Palace of Queen Victoria and her Consort, who inspected the refreshment rooms. Under the headline "The Great Exhibition," the *Morning*

# SINFUL SODA

*Post* of June 9, 1851, reported that:

"On Saturday, during the Queen's visit to the Exhibition, Her Majesty inspected the refreshment rooms which adjoin the machinery in motion, where the royal party was received by Messrs. Schweppe, Welch and Masters, the contractors for supplying refreshments.* Her Majesty and the royal party partook of some refreshment, and also of some cream ices, produced by the ingenious machinery of Mr. Masters for freezing by artificial means, and which on this occasion was put in action by *steam power*. The singular powers of this machine were explained to the royal party by the inventor in person. The production of ice instantly, by the simple means exhibited, seemed most agreeably to surprise both the Queen and the Prince, who

* J. Schweppe & Co. were entrusted with supplying refreshments at the Great Exhibition. They sub-contracted to Younghusband & Son and Masters & Co.

29

LONGING FOR LICKINGS.

were curious to be clearly informed of the processes employed for the purpose. Mr. Thomas Masters, of the Royal Polytechnic Institution, Regent Street, is the inventor, and he has in operation daily, in the Western Refreshment Room, an apparatus capable of freezing nearly 100 quarts of dessert ices every fifteen minutes. The machines, however, are not limited to making dessert ices; they can be made to produce cylinders of *solid ice,* sufficiently large to hold a decanter of water and several bottles of wine. These cylinders are made in the form of castellated towers, and have a very novel appearance; they not only cool the wine and water placed in the center, but diffuse a most agreeable coolness to the atmosphere.''

A cartoon of the same period points to another aspect of the pleasures provided by frozen confections – the reaction of puritanical types who saw in them a substitute for the evils of alcohol (this was to have interesting results later on). In fact, it may have been one attempt to allay the fears of critics of the Exhibition who grimly warned of "thieves and vagabonds" – not to mention drunks – who would infest the "temple dedicated to industry" and turn it into a hotbed of moral degradation. The cartoon seems to suggest that such a "temperate exhibition" would actually have an uplifting effect on the "ruined working classes."

This judgmental tone appears earlier in the treatment of three Parisians eating ices by Louis Leopold Boilly, in which there are pronounced erotic overtones and a curious exposure of auto-enjoyment like that of children – a kind of

30

sensuous selfishness, a touch of "me-me-me!"

But "suspect" or not, more and more people were "being seen" eating ice cream. New York's fashionable ladies found that they could go unescorted to such places as Taylor's or Thompson's ice cream saloons. That last word bears a closer look. Unescorted women *had* been going to confectioners like Guerin's and Palmo's Cafe des Mille Colonnes – both on Broadway – where, along with such things as chocolate, coffee, ices and sandwiches, *liquor was served.* One could even partake of a touch of the forbidden Mediterranean world by ordering an absinthe or a glass of maraschino. Reportedly, both Taylor's and Thompson's sold no liquor and were the epitome of irreproachable elegance filled with flowers and plants, gilt-framed mirrors, marble and gold leaf, red plush and dark, polished wood; pictures of turn-of-the-century luxury as we think of it today.

These were the great days of Delmonico's and Sherry's and Schrafft's – the latter begun by a prominent Boston candy-making family who sold their New York franchise to a Mr. Frank G. Shattuck. Louis Sherry was from Vermont but he had the French touch and had to move twice from his original location at Sixth Avenue and 38th Street to Fifth Avenue and 44th Street – the very center of social activity in New York. Stanford White, the famed architect, was called in to design the new building and everybody who was anybody found their way to it. J. Pierpont Morgan was a fixture. Delmonico's was already established on the opposite corner and the two firms shared the world of society and celebrities for more than twenty years. John Drew and Ethel

Three Parisians eating ice cream by Louis Leopold Boilly (1761-1845). An oddly sensuous treatment: The opposite-to-innocent picture of ice cream eating.

31

Young women crowded along a soda
fountain. From the *Century
Magazine,* July, 1901.

Barrymore, Richard Harding Davis, Mrs.
Stuyvesant Fish and the leader of New York
society, Mrs. Astor, were among the happy
throng. There is a revealing (no pun intended)
story told about Mrs. Fish and Mrs. Astor. It
seems that Mrs. Fish and her friend Mrs. Burke
Roche scandalized "all New York" when they
copied the new London fashion and appeared in
public on a Sunday in low-cut gowns and without
hats. This so upset everyone that Mrs. Astor felt
compelled to save the situation and break her rule
of never dining in a public place. She dutifully
appeared at Sherry's dressed in what was
discreetly described as a "coquettish" white satin
dress and wearing the "tiniest headress" as to
make no matter. One can imagine the gratitude
felt by Messrs. Sherry and Delmonico.

Parallel with the spread of ice cream was the
popularity of soda water. "Invented" by John
Matthews in the 1830's, it led to the soda
fountain. The combination of the soda fountain
with the drugstore was achieved by Elie Magliore
Durand in Philadelphia (again!), where the
fineness of his store – all mirrors, marble and
mahogany – and of his company (he was even
visited by Lafayette) led to the first connection of
a drugstore with a social scene. Another
Philadelphian, Eugene Roussel, a parfumier from
France, had the idea of flavoring his soda water
with syrups like lemon, sarsaparilla and ginger.
The soda-dispensing machinery was the next
thing to be upgraded. A Massachusetts gentleman
named Gustavus D. Dows began designing
fountains in Italian marble and sparked the
treatment of soda fountains as works of
"sculpture" which culminated in the mad

An advertisement published in
1911. Images of social
propriety and romantic
possibility are associated with
the marble-and-mirror world of
the soda fountain.

A superb example of the rather wonderful limits soda fountains reached in the beginning of this century: the fountain at Hegeman & Co., Druggists, New York in 1907.

PRECEDING PAGE:
The meeting place for *tout* New York, Delmonico's, in the 1880s.
*Courtesy of The New York Historical Society.*

extravaganzas some costing $40,000 or more – at the end of the century.

The syrup, the soda fountains, the drugstore, led eventually to the ice cream soda itself. There are reasons for this related to the persistence of the puritanism I referred to earlier. For some reason the "righteous" were very much against such things as something they called "sucking soda" – especially on the sabbath. Was it the soda itself? Or the people and places in which one encountered it? In any event, it appears that soda water was the friend of the Devil.

Then, around 1874 as far as we know, another Philadelphian, Robert M. Green, happened on the first *ice cream* soda. It was at the Franklin Institute where he had a concession during their semi-centennial celebration. He had been serving a syrup and carbonated water drink which also

Backstage at Sherry's, the famed meeting place of New York society. This is the ice cream department photographed around 1903.

involved cream and he ran out of the latter. He substituted ice cream and the results were sensational. According to Paul Dickson's *The Great American Ice Cream Book,* Green had been "averaging $6 a day with the first drink" and he ended up "taking in over $600 a day" by the time the exhibition closed. Two years later, at the Philadelphia Centennial celebrations honoring the signing of the Declaration of Independence, the exclusive rights to sell ice cream sodas were bought by James W. Tufts, who immediately erected an enormous fountain which gave him just as enormous publicity. By April 8th, 1893, *The Critic* was already able to call the drink "our national beverage the 'ice-cream soda'."

But the Puritans weren't long to follow. Even though there were, by this time, more soda fountains than bars in New York, which would

Like the couple in Charles Dana Gibson's drawing, these  society folks also appear relaxed in evening dress.

This turn-of-the-century cartoon carries the strong suggestion that hooliganism, premature smoking and God knows *what* forbidden games are somehow connected with eating ice cream.

*seem* to suggest the triumph of Temperance, the Puritans attacked the ice cream soda too. Really an impossible bunch! They wasted no time in getting after this newest excuse to sip soda water on Sunday and it too was forbidden (hard as this may seem to believe). But matters took another, inventive turn, and by leaving *out* the carbonated water the sundae was arrived at sometime between 1896 and 1900. The unusual spelling of the word "sundae" is again due to pressures from the usual group who *now* objected to using the name for the Lord's Day for anything so frivolous. I blush to mention that my birthplace, Evanston, Illinois, was among the first to complain against something called the "Sunday Soda Menace." Again, its name merely changed, the latest delicious concoction caught on.

rasp the cone with the right hand firmly but gently between thumb and at least one but not more than three fingers, two-thirds of the way up the cone. Then dart swiftly away to an open area, away from the jostling crowd at the stand. Now take up the classic ice-cream-cone-eating stance: feet from one to two feet apart, body bent forward from the waist at a twenty-five-degree angle, right elbow well up, right forearm horizontal, at same level as your collar-bone and about twelve inches from it. But don't start eating yet! Check first to see just what emergency repairs may be necessary.... Checking the cone for possible trouble can be done in a second or two, if one knows where to look and does it systematically. A trouble spot some people overlook is the bottom tip of the cone. This may have been broken off. Or the flap of the cone material at the bottom, usually wrapped over itself in that funny spiral construction, may be folded in a way that is imperfect and leaves an opening. No need to say that through this opening – in a matter of perhaps thirty, or at most, ninety seconds – will begin to pour hundreds of thousands of sticky molecules of melted ice cream.... It is a grim moment. No one wants to eat a cone under that kind of pressure, but neither does anyone want to end up with the bottom of the cone stuck to a messy napkin. There's one other alternative ... increase the waist-bend angle from twenty-five degrees to thirty-five degrees, and then eat the cone, *allowing* it to drop out of the bottom onto the ground in front of you! ...

So far, we have been concentrating on cone problems, but of course there is the ice cream to worry about, too. ... Frequently the ice cream will be mounted on the cone in a way that is perilously lopsided. This requires immediate corrective action to move it back into balance – a slight pressure downward with the teeth and lips to seat the ice cream more firmly in and on the cone, but not so hard, of course, as to break the cone.... Sometimes, trickles of ice cream will already (already!) be running down the cone toward one's fingers, and one must quickly raise the cone, tilting one's face skyward, and lick with an upward motion that pushes the trickles away from the fingers, and (as much as possible) into one's mouth.... If it isn't possible to decide between any ... of the ... basic emergency problems ... allow yourself to make an arbitrary adjudication; assign a "heads" value to one and a "tails" value to the other, then flip a coin to decide which is to be tended to first. Don't, for heaven's sake, *actually* flip a coin.... Just decide *in your mind* which came up, heads or tails, and then try to remember as fast as you can which of the problems you had assigned to the winning side of the coin ...

In trying to make wise and correct decisions about the ice-cream cone in your hand, you should always keep the objectives in mind. The main objective, of course, is to get the cone under control. Secondarily, one will want to eat the cone calmly and with pleasure. Real pleasure lies, not simply in eating the cone, but in eating it *right* ... proceed with it in an orderly fashion. First, revolve the cone through the full three hundred

*Fox Photos*

Maybe not exactly the lick of love, but a start.

and sixty degrees, snapping at the loose gobs of ice cream; turn the cone by moving the thumb away from you and the forefinger toward you, so the cone moves counter-clockwise. Then, with the cone still "wound," which will require the wrist to be bent at the full right angle toward you, apply pressure with the mouth and tongue to accomplish over-all realignment, straightening and settling the whole mess. Then, unwinding the cone back through the full three hundred and sixty degrees, remove any trickles of ice cream . . . eating the ice cream off the top. At each bite, you must press down cautiously, so that the ice cream settles farther and farther into the cone. Be very careful not to break the cone. Of course, you never take so much ice cream into your mouth at once that it hurts your teeth; for the same reason, you never let unmelted ice cream into the back of your mouth. If all these proceedings are followed correctly, you should shortly arrive at the ideal – the way an ice-cream cone is always pictured. . . . You have taken an unnatural, abhorrent irregular, chaotic form, and from it you have sculpted an ordered, ideal shape. . . .

At last you can begin to take little nibbles of the cone itself, being very careful not to crack it. Revolve the cone so that its rim remains smooth and level as you eat both ice cream and cone in the same ratio. Because of the geometrical nature of things, a constantly reduced inverted cone still remains a perfect inverted cone no matter how small it grows, just as a constantly reduced dome held within a cone retains its shape. Because you are constantly reshaping the dome of ice cream with your tongue and nibbling at the cone, it follows in logic – and in actual practice, if you are skillful and careful – that the cone will continue to look exactly the same, except for its size, as you eat it down, so that at the very end you will hold between your thumb and forefinger a tiny, idealized replica of an ice-cream cone, a thing perhaps one inch high . . . *then* you can hold the miniature cone up for everyone to see, and pop it gently into your mouth.

from "How to Eat an Ice-Cream Cone"
by L. Rust Hills
*THE NEW YORKER*, August 24, 1968

It tastes good the wrong way round too!

45

From 20's vans, loaded with leaky containers of ice cream wrapped and packed in salt and ice, to modern refrigerated monsters delivering bulk packages; from the charming blue and gold Lyons livery vans and Dreyer's Ford trucks, to the transportation and delivery of ice cream over greater and greater distances – distribution has continually improved so that consistent temperatures can be maintained, a crucial element in the distribution of quality ice cream. Until recently, refrigerator trucks had to keep temperatures at –20° to prevent melting. This meant that ice cream producers couldn't manufacture and deliver ice cream products economically within more than a 150-mile radius. But thanks to a technical innovation called "No Drip" which Good Humor has introduced recently that keeps ice cream at 0°, that appears to be changed. The process has to do with a stabilizer that is "100 per cent natural and FDA approved." Tests have shown that this new process can withstand five thaw and freeze cycles without damage to flavor or shape.

COLONIALIZATION

It seems fitting that in America, a country destined to become a Nation of Advertisers, the first proper advertisement for ice cream should appear. *And* in New York. The advertisement was placed in The *New York Gazette-Mercury* by a London caterer named Philip Lenzi and it offered to supply ice cream "to the gentry along with various confections." It didn't take long for others to follow his example and advertisements began to appear with increased regularity.

On the highest social level, George Washington had ice cream made at Mount Vernon using the preferred pewter. And it is known that he spent over £50 on a visit to New York City in the summer of 1790. Easily understandable to anyone familiar with Manhattan heat – then or now. Thomas Jefferson, a man of great inventiveness and superior taste devised a frozen dessert which appears to have been a forerunner of Baked Alaska – an elaborate recipe enclosing the ice cream in a warm pastry.

Ice cream was definitely fashionable, a necessary part of social prestige. In Paris the *bombe glacé* (literally "ice-bomb") had become the rage and it was the thing to be seen eating it in the cafés of the arcaded Palais-Royal. The wife of America's fourth President, Dolly Madison, enchanted her dinner guests by surprising them with her favorite dessert – a strawberry mixture described by one of her guests as "a large shining dome of pink ice cream." This she served on a silver platter on a table "set with French china and English silver, laden with good things to eat." (The great lady is immortalized as the name of a modern ice cream product and a brand of contemporary home freezer.) In W. S. Arbuckle's treatise on ice cream, published in 1966, there is a photograph reproduced of a room in "Ashland," the Kentucky home of Henry Clay, showing a table on which – as the caption reads – the visitor "can see this very beautiful china received by Mrs. Henry Clay in 1827 for serving ice cream." The caption continues, remarking on Mrs. Clay's preference – shared with Mrs. Madison – for strawberry ice cream. Did these good ladies know that their passion for frozen desserts was similarly expressed by none other than Beethoven, who once noted his concern over the mild winter's effect on the coming summer's supply of ice?

But word and opportunity were spreading. As early as 1806 a series of "gardens" opened in New York: Charles Barnard's "United States Garden"; John Contoit's "New York Garden" – where customers could eat and drink beneath the leafy bowers of Broadway; and Mr. Ensley's "Columbian Garden" which announced several new flavors – including raspberry and pineapple – a portent of things to come. Ice cream parlors were appearing elsewhere as well. Usually they were associated with confectioners. At the start of the new century New Orleans could boast a number of such places,

An imaginative reconstruction of one of Dolly Madison's parties at which guests were served ice cream prepared by her black cook Augustus Jackson.

61

California Historical Society, San Francisco

The "Fountain Head" ice cream saloon opened by Alberto Peri in the Californian mining town of Marysville in 1860. The local newspaper reported that "It is already a favorite place of resort. The warmer the weather the more popular it will become. A living fountain in the interior . . . adds much to its refreshing atmosphere"

including one in the celebrated Exchange Coffee-House. In Philadelphia, Mrs. Madison's former cook – a black man named August Jackson – opened his own ice cream shop.

Ten years earlier an anonymous cry was heard in the streets: "I Scream for Ice Cream." The call came from vendors pushing carts and selling something called "hokey-pokey," a dubious dish defined by *The American Thesaurus of Slang* as "cheap ice-cream sold by peddlers." A considerable understatement. It was more ice than cream, and far more than a street-cry away from the fine frozen ices and creams sold by the established confectioners. In 1974 a bookseller in New York told me that when she was a little girl her mother wouldn't allow her to buy hokey-pokey because of the filthy conditions under which it was made and sold (this over a hundred years later)! A New York newspaper also complained about the boisterousness of the vendors. Children, with their characteristic candour, even made up a rhyme which goes:

Hokey Pokey
Penny a glass
All fresh from the donkey's ass.

A famous American company was to run into similar trouble in the 60's.

An event that occurred during the same period was to have considerable impact later on: the manufacture by a young Englishman of the grand-daddy of the soda fountain – an apparatus for creating carbonated water.

Part of the reason for the increasing availability of ice cream was the introduction as far back as the 1780's of a freezer with rotary paddles which is the secret of keeping the mixture smooth during the process of freezing. It was a refinement that increased the feasibility of manufacturing a quality product on a reasonably commercial scale. Even so, it was not until more than half a century later that Jacob Fusell, a Baltimore milk dealer, was to establish the first wholesale manufactury in the world. Before that considerable event, a woman named Nancy Johnson invented the hand-cranked freezer. She failed, however, to patent her discovery and one William G. Young took out a patent two years later. He experienced the usual multiplication of patented improvements by others that all inventors suffer from and held the field only briefly.

Fusell, on the other hand, was busy expanding. From Pennsylvania and Maryland he spread to Washington, D.C. and Boston, and, eight years later, to New York. He was so successful he shared his success with his good friend Perry Brazelta. The march to the West had begun. Actually, the Middle West – places like Chicago and St. Louis. It was not until the later part of the century that wholesale production spread even as far as Arkansas. And in any case the process was still done by hand.

Perhaps it should be noted here that a small company begun by the Basset family in and near Philadelphia, Pennsylvania, and considered by many still to be producing the finest ice cream in the world, was stirring (no pun intended) in the yard of their dairy and produce farm where a horse turned the crank of the freezer.

A charming chapter in this history belongs to an enterprising gentleman named Albert Peri. In the 1850's, he and his wife opened a dancing school in the California mining town of Marysville (named for one of the members of the tragic Donner party) on the trail to the mines running through the Sacramento Valley. Their school was located in the Water Works Hall and lessons were given Tuesday and Friday nights from 7:30 to 10:00. Private lessons could be arranged.

In the 1880's soda water dispensing became an elaborate art. "Fountains" were created by such companies as Matthews, Puffer, Tufts and Lippincott and given grandiose and fanciful names like "Commonwealth", "Minnehaha", and "Transcendent."

L. Haaag del.

In April, only a year before the outbreak of the Civil War,* the Peris opened an "Ice Cream Saloon" which they called the Fountain Head. The *Daily Appeal,* April 27, 1860, reported: "Monsieur and Madame Peri's Ice Cream Saloon in the Water Works Building is a very neat, elegant and genteel place. It is already a favorite place of resort. The warmer the weather the more popular it will become. A living fountain in the interior of the saloon adds much to its refreshing atmosphere." Like the rest of his colleagues, M. Peri served ice cream in connection with the art of catering and the production of candies. The same newspaper carried a story three years later headlined "Artistic Piece of Work," and described Peri's show window in which could be seen "a temple of liberty, done in sugar, of large size and symmetrical proportions. Occupying the center of the lower portion on the first floor of the temple is a statue of Washington. In the hall of the second story is a figure representing Ceres or some other female who has an especial affection for agriculture, which she exhibits by embracing a sheath [sic] of wheat. The dome is surmounted by a genuine American flag . . ." Some years later, after a prolonged absence to visit Paris and London, Peri returned to build a new confectionery this time equipped with the latest thing – a "Soda Fountain" ordered in New York and complete with silver ornaments and five different Italian marbles.

In the same year that M. Peri opened his new "saloon," an Italian named Gatti began the commercial production of ice cream in England. His product was the custard type familiar to the English. It was sold in "cornets" made of dough baked in the shape of sea shells. In London the famous firm of Gunter's in Berkeley Square was the subject of a book entitled *Gunter's Modern Confectioner: A Practical Guide to the Latest and Most Improved Methods for Making the Various Kinds of Confectionary With the Manner of Preparing and Laying Out Desserts Adapted for Private Families or Large Establishments.* The work was compiled by William Jeanes "Chief Confectioner at Messrs. Gunter's, Confectioners to Her Majesty". "Her Majesty" was, of course, Queen Victoria. And, alas, Gunter's is no more.

---

* Typical of the sort of thing that goes on during every war was the practice of molding ice cream with spun sugar into forms depicting forts, cannon, turrets, etc.

Ragamuffins pausing in their work to buy hokey-pokey, an inferior form of ice cream, in the Bowery section of New York City in the last century.

# Hand-made,

A type of hand freezer

New versions of the classic hand-cranked freezer, invented in the middle of the last century by Nancy Johnson, are still widely used. There are also small modern electric home-freezers available in many large department stores. The standard ice tray in refrigerators can also be used to make ice cream at home. It seems to me that the directions – not to mention the prose – given by Maria Parloa in her *New Cook Book*, published in Boston in 1883, are hard to improve on:

*An ice cream freezer is a great luxury in a family, and will soon do away with that unhealthy dish – pie.*

*No matter how small the family, nothing less than a gallon freezer should be bought, because you can make a small quantity of the cream in this size, and when you have friends in, there is no occasion to send to the confectioner's for what can be prepared as well at home. With the freezer should be purchased a mallet and canvas bag for pounding the ice fine, as much time and ice can be saved.*

### Directions for Freezing

*Pour the mixture that is to be frozen into the tin can, put the beater in this, and put on the cover. Place in the tub, being careful to have the point on the bottom fit into*

*the socket in the tub. Put on the cross-piece, and turn the crank to see if everything is in the right place.*

*Next comes the packing. Ice should be broken in large pieces, and put in a canvas bag, and pounded fine with a mallet. Put a thick layer of it in the tub (about five inches deep), and then a thin layer of salt. Continue this until the tub is full, and pack down solid with a paddle or a common piece of wood. After turning the crank a few times add more salt and ice, and again pack down. Continue in this way until the tub is full. For a gallon can, three pints of salt and perhaps ten quarts of fine ice will be required.*

66

# Home-made and ...

by Udico

Electric ice cream freezer

Remember that if the freezer is packed solid at first, no more ice or salt is needed. The water must never be let off, as it is one of the strongest elements to help the freezing. If more salt than the quantity given is used, the cream will freeze sooner, but it will not be so smooth and rich as when less is used.

Turn the crank for twenty minutes – not fast at first, but very rapidly the last ten minutes. It will be hard to turn when the mixture is frozen. Turn back the cross-piece, wipe the salt and ice from the cover, and take off the cover, not displacing the can itself. Remove the beater and scrape the cream from it. Work a large spoon up and down in the cream until it is light and the space left by taking out the beater is filled. Cover the can, cork up the hole from which the handle of the beater was taken, put on the cross-piece, and set the tub in a cool place until serving time. Then dip the can for a few seconds in water that is a trifle warm, wipe it, and turn on the dish. Rest it for a moment, and lift a little.

If the cream is to be served from a mold, remove it when you do the beater. Fill the mould and work the cream up and down with a spoon. This will press the cream into every part and lighten it. Cover the top of the mold with thick white paper, put on the tin cover, and bury in fresh ice and salt.

There are a great many good freezers. The Packer is especially suited to family use. It turns so easily that any lady can make her own creams. For the first twelve minutes a child can work it. It is made of the best stock, and will last many years. The cogs on freezers should be oiled occasionally. When you have made cream, see that every part of the freezer is clean and perfectly dry before putting away.

# Freeze-it-yourself

One of the newest developments in the ice cream explosion is the return of the home freezer – most often electric – which can be used in the usual way or placed either in refigerator freezing compartments or home freezers depending on size. Of course type and practicality differ from country to country. Electric power is not universal in kind and Americans tend to own far larger freezer compartments than their European counterparts. There are not too many makes as yet but those available are not, for the most part, too expensive.

In the United States the most readily available are those such as Salton, Inc. made in the Bronx. Capacity, one quart. An in-freezer machine attractive in design. Plastic in several colors. A fan pulls the cold air around the metal can. The Proctor-Silex model, as advertised by Macy's, is an avocado-colored plastic bucket freezer that "gets up to four quarts of rich homemade ice cream." A friend of mine and a superb cook recommends the Kitchen Aid model which fits onto their mixer. Somewhat expensive. The J. E. Porter Company of Ottawa, Illinois, offers a variety of charmingly designed "Dolly Madison" freezers – electric and hand-cranked. Capacity, two to six quarts. The "Williamsburg" model has a very useful see-through cream can cover. Their biggest seller – "more than 2 million in America" – is the "Husky" (which I have seen at Selfridges in London), a red fiberglass tub. All the above require crushed ice and rock salt.

As does the Cornwall, one of two freezers pictured in Hammacher Schlemmer's catalogue (the other comes from Spain). Made in Canton, Mississippi, the Cornwall comes in a four or six quart capacity. The tub is leak-proof and warp-proof, has a "wood-tone finish," see-through can cover, and chrome handles. The Spanish freezer is by Odag and requires no crushed ice or rock salt. Capacity: one quart.

Strong, high-impact plastic. Two other in-freezer freezers from Europe needing no ice or salt are the French Seb – one-quart capacity (according to the *New York Times*, March 29, 1975, its stirring paddles "automatically retracted above the surface of the mixture, which had barely begun to freeze around the outside" and instructions "called for unplugging the appliance but leaving it in the freezer an additional one and a half hours until completely frozen") – and Gelcrem – metal alloy with two chromium paddles that churn in opposite directions and driven by a belt that "slips" when the mixture has thickened enough to stop them, thus preventing the motor from burning itself out. It too has a one-quart capacity. Siberia is another French freezer.

The in-freezer freezers usually have electric cords capable of passing between the rubber gasket and the door of the freezer so they can be plugged into an electric outlet. According to the *Times* (and from my experience) the European models need a ground (or "earth" in Britain).

The Richmond Cedar Works of Danville, Virginia also produces electric and hand-cranked freezers of four, five and six quart capacities. Like the Cornwall model they have plastic dashers that are easy to wash.

In most cases there are accompanying booklets which explain the function of the freezers, adding bits of history, recipes and other helpful information.

While it can, as they say, be great fun making ice cream it does require quite a bit of time and attention and can be quite expensive – there's no point in using anything but the best ingredients – and there seems to me a bit of a myth going on about the "good old days." I find it impossible to believe that one could produce a finer ice cream than that made by some of the companies dealt with in this book. But of course that is entirely a personal matter.

# TABLEAU AT TWILIGHT

I sit in the dusk. I am all alone.
Enter a child and an ice-cream cone.

A parent is easily beguiled
By sight of this coniferous child.

The friendly embers warmer gleam,
The cone begins to drip ice-cream.

Cones are composed of many a vitamin.
My lap is not the place to bitamin.

Although my raiment is not chinchilla,
I flinch to see it become vanilla.

Coniferous child, when vanilla melts
I'd rather it melted somewhere else.

Exit child with remains of cone.
I sit in the dusk. I am all alone,

Muttering spells like an angry Druid,
Alone, in the dusk, with the cleaning fluid.

OGDEN NASH, FAMILY REUNION
from *Verses from 1929 On*,
Little, Brown & Co.
Copyright 1942 by Ogden Nash.

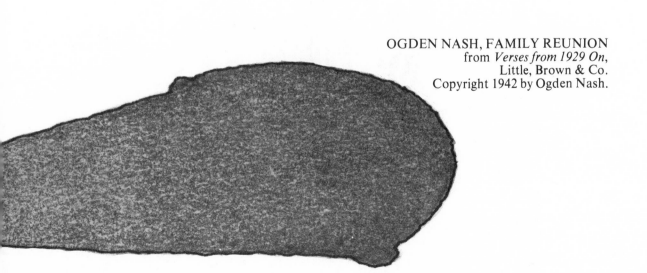

*Collection: Myron Orlofsky. Photo: Rudolph Burckhardt.*

"Ice Cream Soda" by Roy Lichtenstein.

# ICE CREAM AS ICON

## IMAGES OF ICE CREAM IN 20th CENTURY ART

For many people a certain cluster of associations with ice cream – even visual ones – persist: children and childishness, suggestive sensuality, indulgence, dietary insensitivity or foolhardiness. As an image in painting and sculpture ice cream has only come into its own since the advent of "Pop Art" in the 1960's. Although a painter of the quality of Boilly depicted it in the 18th century in France, no Impressionist I know of has painted it. Odd abstinence on the part of painters who dealt lavishly with food and drink, giving us wonderful records of the wreckage of meals on sunlit tables and picnics beside sparkling water. Was it because ice cream melted?

Maybe it was because they were men. Another persistent social attitude has it that sundaes and sodas are for women. If a man wants refreshment he heads for the nearest café or bar. This, of course, is pretty much true. Especially as far as *public* places are concerned. The habit of taking home a quart or so of ice cream for the family is now fairly widespread (at least in the United States) but still relatively new. So, while we can easily connect Degas with absinthe and Bonnard with breakfast, I can't think of a single Monet or Renoir featuring someone well into a chocolate sundae. A shame really. Both could have pictured it unforgettably.

In the American 30's a few artists did deal with the subject. While earlier the great illustrator Charles Dana Gibson chose to show the romance in sharing a soda, William Glackens – a sort of New World Renoir – depicted a somewhat lonely moment in a soda fountain: two women "properly" dressed in hats and white gloves, one with her back to the other. Not friends or acquaintances, but city strangers like the people in many of Edward Hopper's paintings. The young woman on the right has swiveled round on her stool and is wiping her mouth prior to leaving. She stares into space. Later, Isabel Bishop – a master chronicler of shopgirls – shows some caught in a typical New York situation redolent of summer afternoons.

After World War II and the triumph of Abstract Expressionism, the art movement known as "Pop" reintroduced images and found in food the perfect symbol for ironic commentary on affluence and accepted ideas as to what constitutes a proper subject for a work of art – what truly can be said to represent The Beautiful. Andy Warhol elevated the Campbell's Soup can into a series of mock-heroic icons (he later created for Schrafft's a very idiosyncratic TV commercial involving a sundae). James Rosenquist took from the scale and method of painting billboards *his* version of the "grand." All through the 60's Claes Oldenburg produced sculptures of sundaes, pies à la mode, ice cream bars (including a set in imitation fur!), and giant cones. Wayne Thiebaud painted cones and banana splits in creamy oils that echoed the richness of their subject matter. Some of the eroticism associated with ice cream comes through in Richard Lindner's "Ice," in which fetishism is combined with Americana and the suggestiveness of hot-and-cold. In "Ice Cream Soda" (1962) Roy Lichtenstein produced an apotheosis of an ice cream soda – five feet high and as stylized as a Japanese floating-world print.

This disorientation of scale is continued in the 70's by a number of so-called "New Realists," among them Don Nice in his watercolor of an over-lifesized cone. Audrey Flack, another of the "new" or "photo" realists, creates ironic statements about advertising imagery, excess, and the practice of reproducing paintings which are taken from photographs by means of photographs, while at the same time rejoicing in the sheer, beautiful yucky yummy-ness of it all.

Concurrent with these movements but, as always in art, independent of them, other artists have also employed images of ice cream. Harold Bruder caught his wife and son on Fifth Avenue at Central Park indulging in a Good Humor; and his daughter, in a moment of southwestern sunshine, watching her brother lick the wooden spoon of his Dixie Cup. Maryan paints a fierce, erotic "Personnage" with splayed legs and lolling tongue. While 'J. Nutt' of the Chicago group known as "The Hairy Who" – whose images and attitudes are colored by the world of comics – aims at the outrageous by the addition of surrealism and the erotic. Very much off on his own is the surrealist H. C. Westerman, who manages to make something rather nasty out of the overtones of waste and self-gratification implicit in his construction "A New Piece of Land."

Isabel Bishop's portrait of thoughtful shop-girls in the wartime summer of 1942 resting a moment to enjoy cones of their favorite ice cream.

William Glackens' "The Soda Fountain", 1935, which catches perfectly the "properly dressed" (hat and gloves) young woman enjoying a lunchtime treat in the 30's.

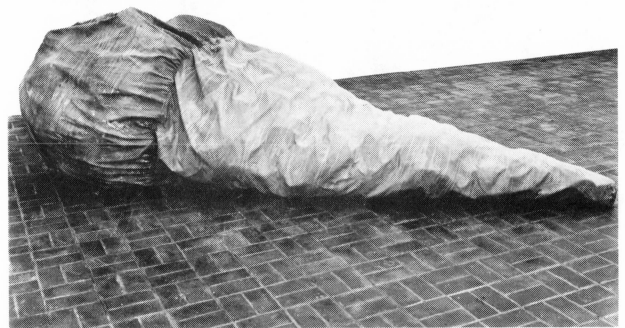

"Floor Cone (Giant Ice-Cream Cone)". Claes Oldenburg's famous ten-foot long construction of canvas filled with pieces of foam rubber, paper cartons and painted with liquitex and latex. Oldenburg has done a whole series of drawings and sculptures involving ice cream which have become synonymous with the "Pop Art" movement.

"Proposed Colossal Monument for Park Avenue, N.Y.: Good Humor Bar" by Claes Oldenburg.

*Collection: Joseph H. Hirshhorn Museum*

"Arizona – Winter Afternoon" by Harold Bruder. Another example of this painter's work in which the world of childhood and sunny pleasure is connected with ice cream.

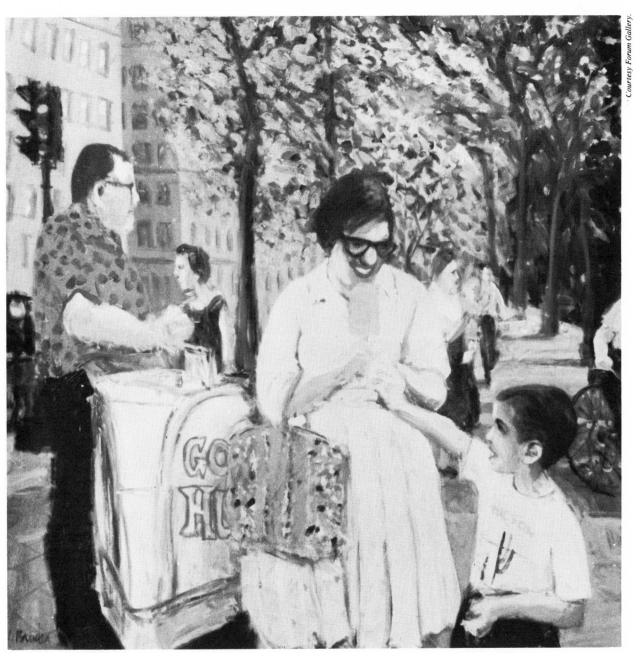

"Sunday and Ice Cream" by Harold Bruder.

"Banana Split" by Wayne Thiebaud.

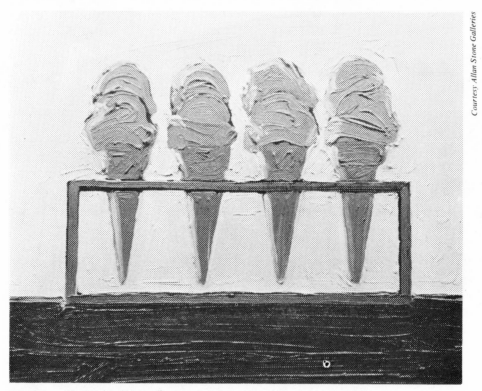

"Pink Cones" by Wayne Thiebaud.

"Banana Split Sundae" by Audrey Flack.

"Pound Cake Sundae" by Audrey Flack.

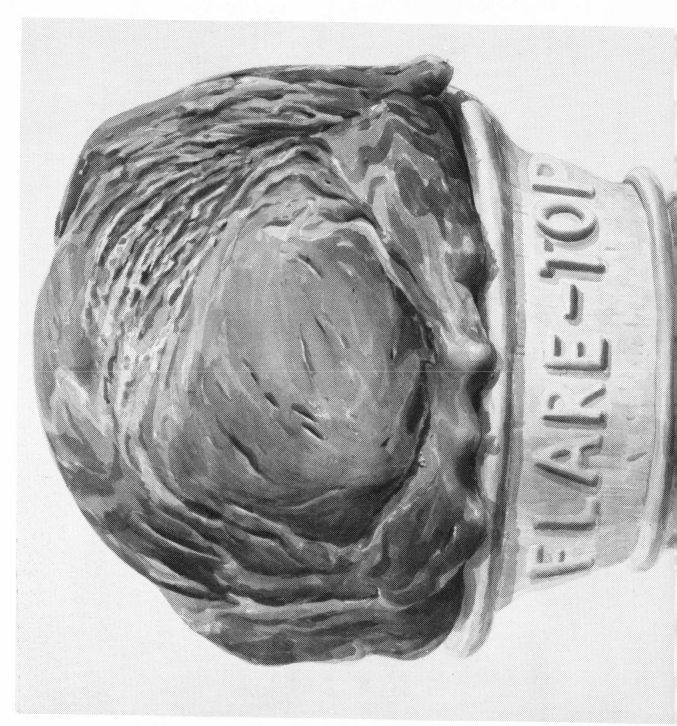

"Chocolate Ice Cream Cone" by Don Nice.

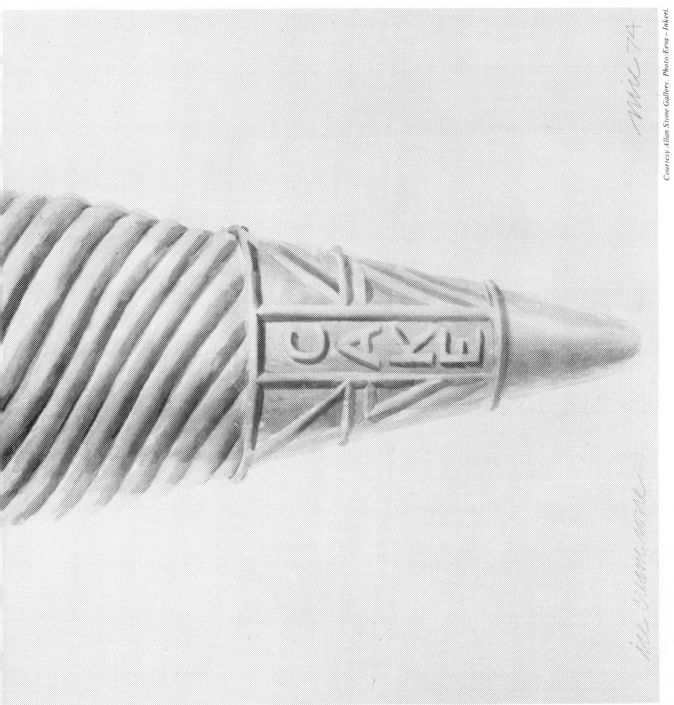

"Ice" by Richard Lindner.

*Courtesy Allan Frumkin Gallery. Photo: Nathan Rabin.*

"Personnage" by Maryan.

*Double Decker*

"Double Decker" by William Snyder.

"Triple Dip" by Ben Shahn.

"A New Piece of Land" by H. C. Westermann.

A page from a booklet put out by the Hairy Who, a group of Chicago painters involved with comics and pop surrealism.

*Courtesy Robert Sumner Photo: Gerald Pates*

Tiny ceramic lapel pins by the California artist Robert Sumner found at "The Artifactrie" on Vine Street in Berkeley, California. Left to right: Good Humor (with a bite out of it); Twin Popsicle (lemon, orange, cherry); postage stamp to show scale; Sundae (strawberry ice cream with chocolate sauce and cherry); Double Dip Cone (chocolate and strawberry).

Handmade toys made of synthetic foam and washable toweling. Created by Marshmallow, two Argentinian girls named Anita and Sylvia.

# Measures for Measure

Most governments have issued directives and passed legislation "controlling" the production of ice cream and related frozen products, but to do any serious justice to them a writer would have to have a team of translators and a couple of years.

For example: the Austrian *Bundeskammer der Gewerblichen Wirtschaft* (Federal Chamber of Industry) puts out a 67 page book-let titled "Speise Eis Fibel" or "Ice Cream Primer" with sections devoted to Microbiology, Ways of Preparation, Heat Treatment, Purification, Test Sampling, Eating Arrangements, Basic Regulations, Raw Materials Index, Nomenclature. And of course measurements are given in litres and grams. *You* read it! At least the Bundeskammer has a sense of humor (see accompanying illustration).

The Swiss work under an Ordinance issued in 1936. Pierrot Ice Cream, one of the largest and best Swiss manufacturers – the "commun des Centrales Laitières de Berne, Genève, Sant-Gall et Zurich," quotes some of the country's regulations in an attractive promotional booklet. Pasteurization and homogenization are mentioned as being important. Sweet cream and sugar as well. "Graisse lactique" (butterfat I expect) must not go lower than 8 per cent. However, if fresh fruit is involved it can go as low as 6 per cent. Authorized designations are "*crème glacée, Eiscreme, Rahmeis*", etc.

In England, controls are set jointly by the Minister of Agriculture, Fisheries and Food and the Minister of Health under the Food & Drug Act of 1955. A sampling follows: *Citation and commencement* 1. These regulations may be cited as the Ice Cream Regulations 1967; and shall come into operation on 4th January 1971 . . ." Eight pages of small print follow. Terms like "artificial sweetener," "composite article of food," "container," "food," "human consumption" are defined. "Ice cream" means "the frozen product intended for sale for human consumption which is obtained by subjecting an emulsion of fat, milk solids and sugar, with or without the addition of other substances, to heat treatment and either to subsequent freezing or to evaporation, addition of water and subsequent freezing, whether or not fruit, fruit pulp, fruit puree, fruit juice, sugar, flavoring or coloring materials, nuts, chocolate or other similar substances have been added before or after freezing, and includes any ice-cream present as an ingredient of any composite article of food, but does not include any sherbet, sorbet, water ice or ice lolly described as 'sherbet', 'sorbet', 'water ice' or 'ice lolly', as the case may be.

" 'Parev ice' includes Kosher ice and means the substance intended for sale for human consumption which resembles ice cream and which (a) is usually known as Parev ice or Kosher ice, and (b) contains no milk or milk derivatives . . . shall contain not less than 5 per cent fat and not less than $7\frac{1}{2}$ per cent milk solids other than fat . . .

"Any ice-cream described as 'dairy ice-cream,' 'dairy cream ice' or 'cream ice' contain no fat other than milk fat or any fat present by reason of the use as an ingredient of such ice cream of any egg, any flavoring substance or any emulsifying or stabilizing agent." And so on in the necessary round-robin legalese of qualifying phrases which usually lead me to think I'm reading the same-thing-only-different like a character in *Alice In Wonderland*.

Next comes packaging. And labeling. No one is allowed to sell, consign or "deliver in a container" anything described as "ice cream" if it contains any other fat than milk fat (allowing for contents as part of any other ingredients). *Unless* the words "contains non-milk fat" appear "in immediate proximity". Knowing how carefully buyers read what they buy you can see how *that* can be handled! And what if you need glasses? And there's an alternative – the words "contains vegetable fat" "may appear" – would *you* use them?

But to give the British credit (and maybe other countries too) you can't use the words "ice cream", or "dairy ice cream", or "dairy cream ice", or "cream ice", or "milk ice", or "Kosher ice" if it doesn't meet the already stated requirements. And (my favorite part) you can't use any pictorial device "which refers to, or is suggestive of, butter, cream or milk or anything connected with the dairy interest . . ." Unless . . . And they go through it all again.

BUT, such are the ways of the language known as "Compromise Quibble" that IF, *if* you comply with all these requirements, then "Nothing in these regulations shall prevent the use in or on any label, ticket, notice or advertisement of . . . the expression 'ice cream' . . ."

Commercial ice cream in the United States must contain a minimum butterfat content of 8 to 14 per cent; a minimum 1.6 pounds of total food solids per gallon figured after an overrun of 80 to 100 per cent; weigh a minimum of 4.5 pounds per gallon. It may be created from *any* of the following: sweet cream, plastic cream (a kind of quite rich dairy cream surprisingly), frozen cream, whole milk, skim milk, buttermilk, butter, butter oil, nonfat dry milk, condensed milk, evaporated milk, powdered whey solids, or malted milk. The law is oddly precise about one kind of ice cream however: "French" ice cream *must* contain eggs.

"Economy" ice cream, i.e. dried products chiefly, mixed with a large percentage of air, as much as 60 to 80 per cent; must contain minimum milk fat (10 to 12 per cent), can contain *maximum* stabilizers and emulsifiers, and (normally does) artificial flavors.

Only in 1949 were ice creams and other frozen products legally defined in France; it is still difficult to find out what they are made of. Jealous manufacturers keep their formulas secret. Legally, *Sorbet* (sherbet) must consist of a minimum 10 to 15 grams of fruit per 100 grams of product. *Crème glacée* (ice cream): proportions of milk, cream, sugar and flavoring are fairly constant. The minimum amount of sugar, fats, water is prescribed in relation to the flavor involved –

vanilla, coffee, chocolate, pistachio, and praline are a little richer than fruit flavors. *La glace aux oeufs* (ice cream made with eggs) should consist of egg yolks and pasteurized milk in a proportion of 7 grams to 100 grams of product, sugar and natural flavoring. *La glace à . . . ou glaces au syrop* (literally, "the ices of . . . or syrup ices"), made partly of water and sugar with milk or cream added, must, if flavored with fruit, contain 10 to 20 grams to 100 grams of product. All artificial flavorings are strictly forbidden. Only natural extracts are allowed to reinforce tastes. The only coloring allowed is that allowed confectioners: caramel for brown; chlorophyll for greens; cochineal for red.

 **BUNDESKAMMER DER GEWERBLICHEN WIRTSCHAFT**

**SPEISE EIS FIBEL**

 Herausgegeben vom Wirtschaftsförderungsinstitut der Bundeskammer und der Bundesinnung der Konditoren

The Emperor of Ice Cream

Call the roller of big cigars,
The muscular one, and bid him whip
In kitchen cups concupiscent curds.
Let the wenches dawdle in such dress
As they are used to wear, and let the boys
Bring flowers in last month's newspapers.
Let be be finale of seem.
The only emperor is the emperor of ice cream.

Take from the dresser of deal,
Lacking the three glass knobs, that sheet
On which she embroidered fantails once
And spread it so as to cover her face.
If her horny feet protrude, they come
To show how cold she is, and dumb.
Let the lamp affix its beam.
The only emperor is the emperor of ice cream.

WALLACE STEVENS
from *The Collected Poems of Wallace Stevens,*
Alfred A. Knopf.

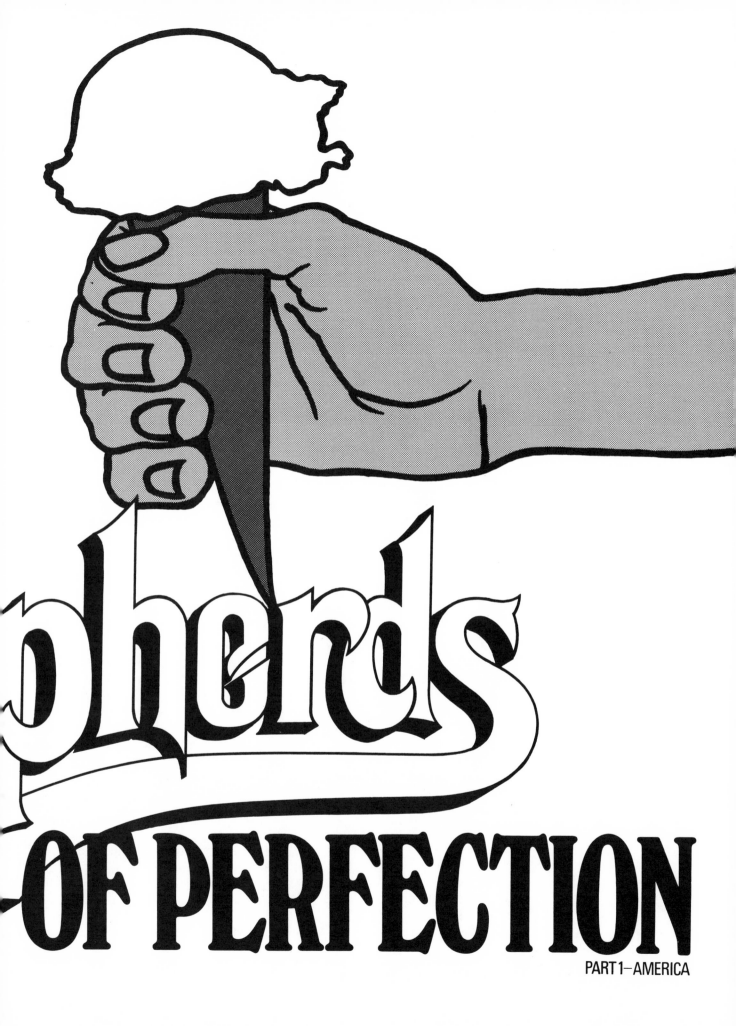

pherds

OF PERFECTION

PART 1—AMERICA

If criteria were all, and one could arrive at the right ones, there'd be small problem in choosing and listing the finest ice creams, ices, etc. But there are overlaps and underlaps (not to mention over*sights*). Large-but-superior production ends up being opposed to small-but-so-what? output. Miniscule and marvelous would probably be the closest thing to a good test: maximum control with least diffusion of effort. But how explain that a tasting of 14 brands of Coffee Ice Cream in New York, from luncheonette home-made to superchain factory-formed, could result in Howard Johnson's ice cream being listed as number one among the top three and described as "brilliant, unsurpassed flavor (must be savored in competition to be fully appreciated) . . ."? I'm afraid the reader will simply have to read back and forth between various sections of this book and come up with his/her own conclusions. And, after all, what it all *tastes* like to the individual is the sensible finale.

Reading along you will come upon the findings of writers such as Dickson, Greene, Christy and Howard. The latter mentions a place called Bott's in California (as does Dickson) as being in Berkeley. Actually it is on College Street near Ashbury which I'm pretty sure is still in Oakland (about which Gertrude Stein once quipped "There's no There There" – no longer truly true as it now boasts a terrific Art Museum and a marvelously restored Art Deco Movie Palace which houses its symphony orchestra) on the *way* to becoming Berkeley.

One purist criterion for the best could be a preference for places not serving any other food (cooked food at least) and *ideally* prohibiting smoking (as in some of the greatest French restaurants). Places where the owner-creators seem as idiosyncratic as shepherds tending their flock of prize flavors. (I can't honestly attest to there *never* being a cigarette lit, but to my mind to try to smoke and enjoy superb ice cream at the same time can only be described as dumb – although the sensuous pleasure of eating ice cream *after* inhaling certain kinds of smoke is not unknown to many.)

In San Francisco – one of the top four I.C. towns, Philadelphia, New York and Boston being the others – "**Bud's**", a place the size of a "submarine wardroom" (to quote Jack Shelton, locally acclaimed for his by-subscription-only restaurant guide) located at Castro and 24th Streets turns out day-to-day supplies of extremely creamy, rich (too rich to some) utterly delicious ice cream. One has to wait in line – come rain or come shine – but there are people to meet and hundreds of advertisements and announcements to read stapled up on the community billboard outside. The classic trio – V., C., & S. (Vanilla, Chocolate, Strawberry) – are wondrous and so is a Red Raspberry full of "rasp" and a Pumpkin ("little tendrils of fresh pumpkin lace this velvety, nutmeg-spiked masterpiece" – Shelton again). Butterfat averages around 16 per cent. Between 20 and 30 flavors are listed above the dipping counter and it can be hell trying to decide which to order. Bud has "perfected" nearly 70. Portions are generous and everything tastes exactly like its name, as in bittersweet bittersweet and peachy peach. There are cones, floats, malts and shakes and sundaes described by many as the best in the world. An interesting criticism was registered by a local journalist a while back. He complained of a change-over from plastic to wooden spoons which, he wrote, have a "woody taste" and interfere with the taste of the ice cream. (He keeps a plastic spoon in his car).

Al Edlin ("Bud") has been making his own ice cream for 25 years. He has no interest in opening any franchises and has only expanded to the extent of moving his new freezer next door. He does supply another Bud's in Tiburon across the bay, which he doesn't own, along with a parlor named Raskin Flakkers, a coffee house called Munchins, a place called The Konery and several Bay Area restaurants (it was his ice cream at Des Alps which elicited Mr. Shelton's superlatives). As in several similar places (if comparisons can be made) the word "decor" would be excessive. Pink and green wallpaper stripes the walls. Crepe paper cones descend from the ceiling. Amusing cartoons enliven the windows and a nifty "pop art" sign outside shows a hand holding a cone.

(An interesting fact for New Yorkers is that two enterprising persons are producing "Bud's" ice cream from recipes bought from him at a dipping store about the size of a closet on West 4th Street known as **Mother Bucka's**.)

While we're still in S.F., there is a zany, typically untypical dipping shop called **Polly Ann's** owned by Ted, Lee & Bob Hansen. It is located not far from the Pacific Ocean on Noreiga Street and offers numberless inventive flavors of the Hansen's concocting. Things like Oasis (honey, coconut and dates), American Beauty (which tastes exactly like a rose smells), marvelously fruit-like Canteloupe, a fashionably "healthy" Vegetable which tastes like a salad of greens, carrots, corn, etc. My favorite in the unexpected-but-not-freakish category is a raspberry and licorice sherbet which would be wonderfully refreshing after a rich meal. The shop is very much a family affair with all kinds of crazy signs, hand painted by the Hansen's to illustrate the flavors available. They claim to be the only store in the world offering a dog his own cone. That is if he is "accompanied by a Human Being". The Hansen's have been happily at it since 1965.

**Old Uncle Gaylor's** is a newer series of "Homemade Ice Cream Parlours." About four years old with some amusing and attractive locations – an Art Deco shop on Market Street, an ex-filling station in San Rafael. **Rosita's** on Clement Street serves a delicious sweet called "It's It" (a cookie with ice cream dipped into chocolate sauce.) There are a series of **Shaw's** shops. There's a **King Cone** on Ocean. The **St. Francis Fountain**. **The Three Mills Creamery** has been "making their own" since 1936. An attractive sign reads **Ambrosia Ice Cream Parlour** on Shattuck in Berkeley. **Ghirardelli's** is highly regarded by many and has the added distinction of overlooking the chocolate-making process that has been going on at the famed manufactury for over 100 years. The Bay area is filled with favorites. Over in Oakland, **Fenton's**, an old-fashioned, family sort of place, dispenses scrumptiously ucky sundaes and milkshakes in a room that looks something like a college cafeteria in the 30's or "tourist class" on a ship going nowhere. Easy parking right next door. A chandelier shaped like an ice cream cone. No frills. It all goes into the goodies. *Women's Wear Daily* – a toughly written, highly critical trade paper, recently named San Francisco's **Red Poppy** as its quality choice (along with **Muldoon's** in Los Angeles, **Bertillon's** in Paris and **Bassett's** in Philadelphia).

Never underestimate the power of *The New York Times* (if I may be allowed to borrow a slogan once belonging to a national women's magazine). Not that the subject in question can't accomplish it all on its own quite extraordinary merits. But ever since that prestigious rag published a story headlined "At the End of the Quest Was Great Icre Cream" in 1972, which began by stating that the writer was out to "verify a frequently heard report that the nation's best ice cream was sold in Philadelphia, in the Reading Terminal Market, at L. D. Bassett, Inc.", the company has been singled out more and more as among the very best (note above). Ms. Howard hadn't yet been there in 1968 in New York City; Ms. Greene spoke of Wright's way out in L.A. but didn't mention nearby Bassett's in 1971; Mr. Dickson praised it in *The Great American Ice Cream Book* in '72 and has singled it out several times since. Friends were my reason for knowing about it.

So I went to that great collection of out-of-town directories in Grand Central Station and looked up Bassett in Philadelphia and dialed. None other than Mr. L. (for Lewis) L. (for Lafayette) Bassett himself answered. I arranged to call again and arrange a meeting and the following Wednesday found me enbused for Philadelphia. I had never been to the Reading Terminal Market (the "terminal" refers to a railway station and not the last of anything – although the market, sad to report, has a bit of that air about it). I found Market and 2nd Streets, purposely arriving early so as to "case the joint." The covered market is an extraordinary place. I wandered happily through fruiterers, green grocers, fish mongers, butchers, cheese and egg sellers. It was like being in Barcelona or one of these wonderful provincial English town markets. Bassett's ran along one wall: Old marble counter. Metal stools covered in red plastic. Fake wood formica wall. Seth Thomas Electric Clock. Fluorescent lights. Two overhead fans. Various signs. Sort of anti-decor. "Old fashioned sponge cake – 24¢ + 1¢ tax". "Sugar prices gone up (this in 1975) therefore prices up." Special flavors are not combined with regulars I learned (such as no dishes of Dutch Apple served with Chocolate Twirl). Steady flow of customers. All ages, sexes, races. Not a smoker in sight. Distinguished gentlemen with briefcases. Workman in caps.

Women with shopping bags. Slim lady in mink. Highschool kids. Decided to copy list of available flavors while waiting for single dish of French Vanilla (smooth, rich, dense, color of pale daffodils):

| | |
|---|---|
| Vanilla | Cherry Vanilla |
| French Vanilla | Pineapple |
| Dark Chocolate | Butterscotch Vanilla |
| Strawberry | Chocolate Mint Dip |
| Rum Raisin | Orange Ice |
| Coffee | Lime Ice |
| Irish Coffee | Apricot Ice |
| Butter Almond | Raspberry Ice |
| Peach | Egg Nog |
| Chocolate Twirl | Black Raspberry |

Followed the F.V. with single Dark Chocolate. Like something brewed for morning breakfast in Amsterdam – superb aftertaste. Not sweet. Best I've ever eaten. Only cones, dishes, take-home containers are sold. Cones offered beginning only five years ago. Servers used to pride themselves on being able to sling dishes along the counter so that they came to rest right in front of the customer much to the startled disbelief of newcomers. For a brief period banana splits were offered but people seemed to feel that such things as sauces, etc., were simply gilding flavors already solid gold.

When Mr. Bassett appeared in several sweaters, jacket and overcoat he looked very New England. He invited me upstairs to a Dickensian office where I met his daughter, Mrs. Ann Strange, newly representing the fourth generation in the business. Mrs. Strange had recently completed courses in ice cream manufacturing at Pennsylvania State University where her father had once studied after graduating from the University of Pennsylvania. Mr. Bassett was enthusiastic over some cheddar cheese from Massachusetts which he wanted me to taste. This I did, but my response wasn't much more than polite, bedazzled as I still was with French Vanilla and Dark Chocolate. (At an adjoining stand downstairs the Bassett's sell other dairy products as they still run a farm). There followed lively conversation and several tastings of other flavors – Rum Raisin and Orange Sherbet being two memorable ones. Something I tasted and thought super was not good enough for Mr. Bassett which made me feel like I was among wine tasters in Beaune.

Ice cream making for the Bassetts began on the family farm around 1861 with a horse walking in circles attached to a big boom in the yard. The family also made cheeses, stewed tomatoes, etc. In the 1890's they opened an ice cream stand on the corner of the Market. They used to exchange free samples of their chocolate for taste testing. Before that Mr. Bassett's grandfather, L. (for Lewis) D. (for Dubois) Bassett (what about those French middle names?), had done business on Market Street and then 2nd Street. The present Mr. Bassett looks much younger than his nearly seventy years. He joined the business when he was 22. He remembers that there was no set recipe for their mix (still a guarded secret) which was made in the basement of the Market. The refridgerant was chopped ice and salt – the old fashioned method. They made all their water ices the same way – "They were marvelous, but they didn't hold up as well as they do today. The flavor would come through." Bassett has the wry candor of New Englanders and has no special nostalgia for "the good old days". He recalls the plant as dirty and messy and that the makers were often drunk and chewed tobacco – some of which found its way into the mix (at this revelation his daughter cried, "Oh daddy, don't tell him that!) Sometimes salt would get mixed in with the ice cream as well. No left-over ice cream was sold the next day.

Understandably, Bassett began modernizing, continually improving equipment and methods. Recent changes at the Terminal Market have caused him to move manufacry to another location. As for his formulas, like any honestly creative person, when experts reacted to his using "too much of this or that" he responded by asking them to "Please let me do it my own way. It's our recipe. It's our formula, and it's crazy. You'd never think of a crazier formula." He claims many flavors now used by big manufacturers were invented by him. But not the shockers like yellow tomato, ginger mint, or licorice. "Our butterfat content is very high. You only have to hold some of ours in one hand and one of the commercial brands in the other to see which is heavier. We use Irish whiskey in our Irish coffee and real champagne, Great Western, in the champagne sherbet. Our overrun is low." There are popular holiday flavors like Plum Pudding, Dutch Apple, Egg Nog, and Champagne Ice. Alas, they were all out of the latter the day I was there. They use 18 bottles of champagne to make 50 gallons. Fifty gallons is the usual batch produced at any one time from any of their 100 flavors. There are several restaurants and other outlets in the Philadelphia area. The pun – titled Philly Mignon carries it in New York City. There are hopes for a possible foray into the European market. I think that many Europeans would be grateful.

L. S. Heath & Sons, Inc. was founded in 1915 (by yet *another* school teacher and carried on by yet *another* family through the generations). The candy bar that is now one of the half-dozen top sellers was introduced in the middle of what I'm coming to automatically call the "creative" Depression. In 1908 L. S. Heath gave up teaching (Latin and mathematics). He was 47, living in a town in Illinois named for his pioneer forefathers – Heathville. Not until he was well into his fifties in 1914 did he decide to buy a confectionary store

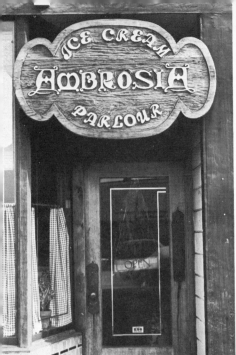

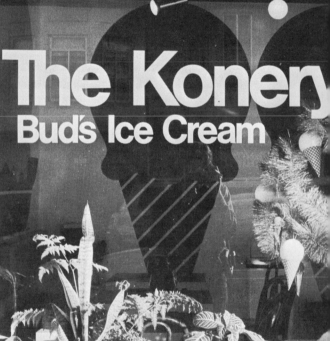

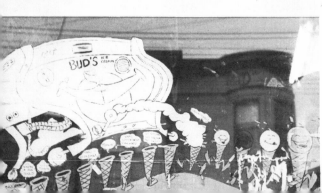

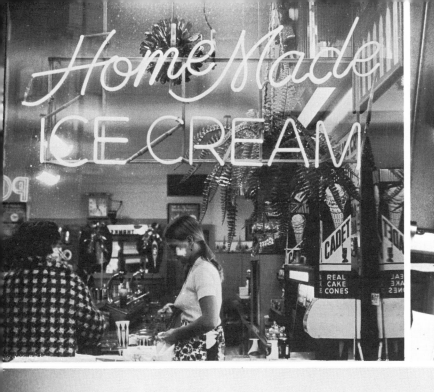

Enjoy a Cone... EAT-IT-ALL

Tastes Great!

FRANCIS *Fountain* THANKS YOU

SWENSEN'S ICE CREAM
MORE FOR YOUR MONEY
16 OZ PINT 32 OZ QUART

THREE MILLS CREAMERY

This is the PLACE that makes our own ICE CREAM and CANDY Since 1936

SWENSEN'S ICE CREAM

in neighboring Robinson. His sons joined him and the family sold fountain drinks, ice cream and homemade candy. Ice cream was made with a brine freezer; ice crusher; a two-horsepower steam boiler; 50 wooden tubs and 50 five-gallon cans; ice and salt. They prospered and bought a bottling plant in 1921 which later became part of a dairy business.

The first formula for their English toffee was developed in the back kitchen of the confectionary around 1928, but the famous candy bar was yet to emerge. The confectionary was sold in 1931 and, taking along only one copper kettle, one wooden stirring paddle, and a marble slab, the candy business was moved to its present location. 1932 saw the Heath Bar (milk chocolate, butter, sugar, almonds) launched on the national market. People thought they were crazy. The average candy bar at that time weighed four ounces and sold for a nickel. The Heaths had decided on a *one* ounce bar – the smallest on the market – to sell at the same price. Some thought it was a penny item. Others asked if it was a laxative. All couldn't have been more mistaken. From that Depression year on sales have continued to increase until there are more than 10,000 wholesale accounts – from supermarkets to theaters – in all 50 states and throughout the world.

Until 1941 things were still a matter of hand-dipping and hand-wrapping. In that year the plant was modernized. The dairy business grew too and was eventually sold to the American Dairy of Evansville, Indiana. In 1959 a highly successful ice cream candy bar was put on the market.

To read The *New Yorker* (24 June 1974) the Bud's of Boston is evidently **Steve's**. I should write more accurately, Steve's Ice Cream, Davis Square, Somerville. One waits in line – "naturally" (the ice cream is all "natural" of course). There is a hand-lettered sign to read while you wait. The *New Yorker* quotes it in full. I will edit it a bit:

When there is a line, please wait.
Help us move it along faster – and shorten your wait – by being ready with your exact order when you reach the front.
  Plain ice-cream flavors: vanilla, chocolate, strawberry, coffee, specials.
  With the 45¢ cone or dish only, we will mix in any fruits, nuts, candies, etc. displayed on the front counter . . .
  We do *not* mix in for 30¢ cone or dish, nor for pints and quarts, nor for the sundaes (see below).
THE SUNDAE INCLUDES:
  THE MINI SUNDAE is exactly the same, but every portion is smaller, and is only for skinny people on diets.
  IF YOU WANT A SUNDAE, please say something like "I . . .
  Please also specify for here or to go.
  WE WILL SPRINKLE EXTRA GOODIES ON TOP OF YOUR SUNDAE FOR 5¢ EACH

I'm afraid you have to go there to learn what I've omitted. I was happy to read that, along with raisins and granola, ground-up Heath bars are also used.

A very *grand* place to drop into in Boston, really, is the Marble Spa in **Gilchrist's** Department Store (133 years old) which has been noted for its ice cream since 1931 – "premium grade" and basic, classic flavors. Toppings are terrific and the "return of the Jumbo Banana split" has recently been announced. While you're there, you'd be a fool not to check out their legendary Golden Almond Macaroons.

**Bailey's** is another glory, especially its superb fountain on Boylston Street. (There are three stores altogether.) **Brigham's** in the city and suburbs is another place people recommend.

A "little giant" – the one-ounce candy bar appeared during
the Depression to become one of the all-time best-sellers.
The ice cream bar version emerged during the the 50's.

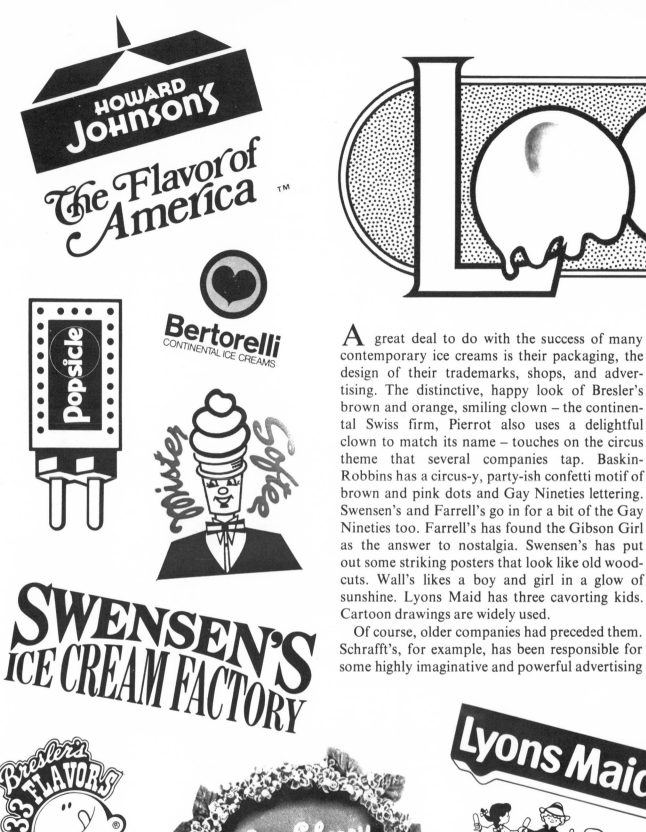

A great deal to do with the success of many contemporary ice creams is their packaging, the design of their trademarks, shops, and advertising. The distinctive, happy look of Bresler's brown and orange, smiling clown – the continental Swiss firm, Pierrot also uses a delightful clown to match its name – touches on the circus theme that several companies tap. Baskin-Robbins has a circus-y, party-ish confetti motif of brown and pink dots and Gay Nineties lettering. Swensen's and Farrell's go in for a bit of the Gay Nineties too. Farrell's has found the Gibson Girl as the answer to nostalgia. Swensen's has put out some striking posters that look like old wood-cuts. Wall's likes a boy and girl in a glow of sunshine. Lyons Maid has three cavorting kids. Cartoon drawings are widely used.

Of course, older companies had preceded them. Schrafft's, for example, has been responsible for some highly imaginative and powerful advertising

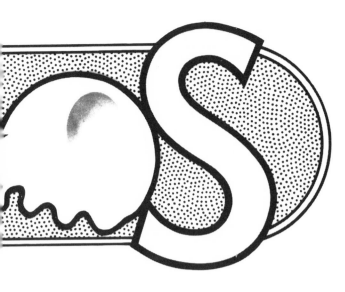

images (especially a series in which their container became a coffee pot or pineapple or basket of strawberries) and the TV ad they commissioned from Andy Warhol has become legendary.

In London, one of the finest and most subtle recent "looks" is Bertorelli's – a heart in a banded circle, in a series of purples and red. The symbol is cleanly modern while at the same time romantic: it suggests, obviously, love, but it also suggests the product itself – the layers of ice cream and sherbet that make up *bombes* and other frozen confections. The promotional pamphlets showing their line of "continental ice creams" are outstanding, visually connecting such things as fine wines with fine ices. Their containers have won a number of top design awards.

Of course, if you have an Elizabethan manor house to your name, along with a prize dairy herd, then you do well to emphasize both. As Loseley's does.

# Two Logo Legends

Every company "logo" or trademark obviously has a story behind it. Two more interesting than most belong to Carnation and Borden.

The origin of the rather romantic cluster of carnations that identify products of the Carnation Company was recorded by its founder E. A. Stuart. It seems that he wanted a flower as an emblem, realizing "that mothers send children to the store to get cans of milk," and that he needed something distinctive "whereby children could designate the brand even if they couldn't remember the name." He remembered "full well" a product which had a label he admired – Campell's Soup with its red and white label. "The next thing was to get a name. I thought of pansy, rose, poppy, pink and a few others. I had my attorney make inquiry in Washington to find out what names had been registered for milk and behold every name I had thought of had been taken. I began to get nervous. Manufacturing was going on. I couldn't delay going to the plant any longer so I started for Kent . . . and still had no name for our product." On September 6th, 1899, the first can of Carnation evaporated milk was processed. Within a short time they had piled up 2,000 cases of milk without any labels. "I didn't know what to do. I still wanted a flower. One day I was going down the street in Seattle when I passed the store of a

111

© BORDEN INC.

cigar jobber in whose window I saw a great pile of cigars and on the end of those cigar boxes I noticed the most absurd name I ever saw for a cigar – Carnation. The absurdity of calling a cigar Carnation struck me very forcibly but led me to know that I had at last found a name for my milk. My attorney immediately queried Washington to find out if that name had been taken. Word came back that it had not. I couldn't understand why I hadn't thought of the Carnation flower before because I had lived in California and they grew there by the acre."

The creation of Borden's "Elsie" has a very different history. In the 1930's there were ugly "milk wars" raging between farmers and dairy processors that caused the public to think very negatively of the companies involved. A rather oblique approach was taken to solving the problem: ads were placed in conservative medical journals emphasizing the health and quality of Borden's milk. The ads featured male and female animals and there were various names attached to them. A typical ad showed young heifers hanging on the words of a rather lazy, unimpressive-looking cow. Heifers: "And now tell us about the time you got kicked out by Borden's". Doctors were crazy about the ads and ordered reprints to hang in their offices. In 1938 a radio news commentator named Rush Hughes read one of the commercials prepared for his program himself, because he liked it. It involved a letter signed with the name "Elsie". Listeners wrote fan letters addressed to the cow rather than the commentator and Elsie became the "spokescow" for Borden's.

Great fame followed, involving a real cow – World's Fairs (14 million saw her in New York), nation-wide tours, etc. A husband was found – Elmer – and a daughter – Beulah. In the 1940's Elsie was co-starred with Kay Francis and Jack Oakie in *Little Men*. During World War II she was a popular pin-up in many Navy lockers. A B-25 bomber was dubbed "The Milk Run" and decorated with all-American Elsie.

She was used more and more by Borden's – for cheese, ice cream and even instant coffee. Things came a bit unstuck when Borden's came up with a milk-derived glue and realized Elsie just wouldn't do. Everyone knows the result: Elmer, her "husband", was loaned to the Chemical Division and "Elmer's Glue" was born.

Things looked bad in the 50's with magazine advertising in for real trouble from TV and Elsie just didn't "work" on the new medium. Her image began to disappear except for the "Elsie-Daisy" trademark developed in 1951. Various attempts were made to re-think, re-design, and retain the symbol – one contest to name Elsie's new twins resulted in 3 million entries! It was finally decided Elsie didn't fit the expanding activities of the company and she was put out to pasture in the 60's.

However, a nation-wide survey showed that consumers knew and loved the trademark more than any other similar symbol. So management relented somewhat reluctantly (after all, a daisy-collared, smiling cow doesn't exactly conjure up corporate connotations of "conglomerate"!) allowing Elsie to return – if only on dairy products and even then yoked with an utterly characterless, abstract logotype evocative of nothing.

Enter nostalgia. Animators tried again for TV ads. Borden's opened a turn-of-the-century ice cream parlor at Disney World (Disneyland's East Coast sister) in Orlando, Florida with Elsie opening it on October 4, 1971 – in person – the first live animal allowed to come face to face with a Disney animal (Mickey Mouse even presented her with a bouquet). And she's touring again (she led the Rose Bowl Parade on New Year's Day, 1974) – even if the glue generation sometimes asks, "Who's Elsie?" to be answered with "Elmer's wife".

# The Inventive 20's

As the 19th century turned into the 20th things evolved more and more rapidly in the United States. There took place a sequence of events which directly relate to the development of the ice cream industry. Not surprisingly, the first academic course in ice cream making was instituted in 1892 by Pennsylvania State College, followed not long afterward by Iowa State College. The dry milk industry began in 1906 and the homogenizer, invented in France, was patented in the U.S. (1899-1904). The parent organization of the present International Association of Ice Cream Manufacturers was formed in 1900 and its official organ, *Ice Cream Trade Journal,* chosen in 1905. The first state bulletins covering ice cream processing were issued between 1910 and 1912 by Vermont and Iowa. The horizontal circulating brine freezer was invented (1902), and the ice cream cone surfaced at the St. Louis World's Fair in 1904. Between 1910 and 1925, homogenization was applied to condensed or evaporated milk (1911); the continuous freezing process was patented and direct expansion freezing appeared (1911 and 1913); and textbooks began to be published on ice cream (1915-1917).

In the 20's ice cream began to be recognized as a "protective and essential food." Direct expansion refrigeration was adapted to freezers in 1922. Ice cream was delivered with the aid of dry ice for the first time by Christan Nelson, the inventor of Eskimo Pies (1925). In 1928 Henry Vogt of Louisville, Kentucky developed the continuous freezer named after him and there followed a series of improvements and variations.

The last major inventive streak, and the first since the entrance of the ice cream cone, occurred in the early 20's when the Eskimo Pie, Good Humor bar, and Popsicle were all invented in quick succession. Each has an interesting story connected with it.

Christian Nelson, the son of a dairyman, ran an ice cream and candy store in Onawa, Iowa – when he wasn't teaching high school.

*Eskimo Pie*

Advertisement for the "I-Scream-Bar" put out by Temptation Ice Cream in the 20's. The bar was the first Eskimo Pie.

OR SWELL GIFTS

One day in the spring of 1920 a youngster in his shop was torn between
his desire for an ice cream sandwich and a chocolate bar. Mr. Nelson
began to think about making something that was kin to a chocolate
sundae, but portable like a candy bar. He had a terrible time getting
the hot chocolate to adhere to the cold vanilla ice cream until a
resourceful salesman who had dropped in suggested he try cocoa
butter. He did. And things improved. One night he found the
necessary combination. He dipped a sub-zero slice of ice cream into a
coating of chocolate heated to 80-90 degrees and quickly placed it in a
home-made chill box. The coating solidified at once and stuck fast to
the ice cream. After Nelson established consistent results he named his
new delight the "I-Scream Bar." (The company claims this was the

117

inspiration for the Tin Pan Alley hit "I Scream – You Scream – We all Scream – For Ice Cream." The outcome was amazing: the financially depressed dairy industry was given a lift by the new product's help in popularizing ice cream as a year-round food. Cocoa bean-producing countries in South America and the chocolate-producing countries of Holland and Switzerland saw their economies rejuvenated. In its very first year of production, the Eskimo Pie Corp. (the name was changed to symbolize both ice cream and confectionery ingredients) averaged sales of a million bars a day.

The classic combination of candy-maker and ice cream-maker, in the person of Harry Burt, was the foundation for the emergence of the contemporary classic "Good Humor Bar." One January night in 1920, Mr. Burt was talking with his children about an experiment with a novelty ice cream product he'd been working on. He asked his son to get a sample from the freezer for them to taste and his daughter, while finding it delicious, complained that it was very messy to handle. His son suggested that he try inserting one of the candy lollipop sticks he used in making his "Good Humor Suckers." They got a supply of sticks and some covered ice cream and inserted the sticks, placing the result in the hardening room. The sticks stuck (it was later found it would take 64 pounds of pull to dislodge one). It was 2 A.M., but they took samples to the home of a Notary Public, woke him, and had him make out affadavits stating that they had created a new product. They applied for a patent, but none came through until three years later when Harry's son took a batch of "Good Humor Ice Cream Suckers" to Washington, D.C. and forced the lawyers to approve the patent.

From the beginning Burt used a distinctive white push cart, suggesting both coolness and sanitation. And, to let his customers know he was coming, he rigged up the pushcart with some bells taken from the family

Restocking an Eskimo Pie Counter Jug. Routemen serviced it daily and replenished the dry ice. Developed by the company's founder, it was placed in retail outlets lacking refrigerated cabinets to encourage the public to "help themselves."

sleigh. Trucks came next. And the first of a long long line of "Good Humor Men" dressed in snow white uniforms were photographed by newspapers ever year as among the first signs of spring.

Frank Epperson, a Californian, accidentally invented the Popsicle when he was 11 years old. He was staying with friends in New Jersey and he had mixed up some soda-water powder to make lemonade. The story goes that he left a glass of it on the porch overnight with the spoon still in it and that the February night temperature dropped to a

A painted wall bulletin advertising Eskimo Pies along Wiltshire Boulevard in Los Angeles. Photographed in the early 40's.

record low. The next morning young Frank found he had a lemon soda in the shape of a glass attached to a spoon. It wasn't until 18 years later, in 1923, that he recognized what his discovery might be worth. That year he patented what he called the "Epsicle," a name that never caught on. After his death in 1926, his company was sold to a group who went on to develop variations such as the famous Twin Popsicle, a double Popsicle with two sticks which sold for only a nickel.

# KING CONE

Americans are, you might say, cone-prone. Every year they buy hundreds of millions of ice cream cones to eat with their ice cream. Yet their invention is disputed and no claims made by any official body have been able completely to convince historians. But the focal point, all agree, is the Louisiana Purchase Exposition – or St. Louis World's Fair – opened in St. Louis, Missouri in 1904. That makes the cone over 70 years old. In the 19th century paper and metal "cones" were known in France; custard-type ice cream was sold in England in "cornets" – dough baked in the shape of sea shells – though edible containers are supposed to have existed in Germany. So we must give some space to several stories.

"Proper" ladies allowing themselves to be seen in public eating ice cream cones, certain sign that ice cream had truly "arrived."

May 11, 1937 – Coronation Day – and a man named Mr. Alfred is giving away ice cream "cornets" in the Paddington area. He anticipated handing out ice cream to 12,000 children.

One story has it that the cone was created by a Syrian named Ernest A. Hamwi, a concessionaire selling a crisp, waffle-like pastry made on a waffle iron, called *zalabia,* who rolled one into a cornucopia, let it cool, and added ice cream from a fellow-concessionaire's booth. The *New York Times* stated in its October 29, 1954 issue that Italo Marchiony had been making and selling cones as early as 1896 and, in fact, held a patent for the invention. (He did. It was issued December 13, 1904). An ice cream merchant named Menthes is also credited. The *New York Times* also mentioned in a 1965 obituary that David Avayou, a native of Turkey, had long claimed that *he* had invented the cone. Research by Paul Dickson has come up with a further claim: An August, 1947, Chicago *Sun* feature story tells of how a Mr. Goldberg "fretted over it, nursed it along, ate it, sold it and developed it over 44 years into a big manufacturing business [Goldberg was chairman of the board of the Illinois Baking Company at the time] and how he had first sold cones in 1903 having bought them earlier from a Brooklyn firm (un-named)."

As there were half-a-hundred waffle stands at the Fair and about the same number of ice cream concessions (selling 5,000 gallons of ice cream on some days) it isn't too surprising that several people may very well have come up with similar ideas. Anyway, after the Fair, Hamwi started the Cornucopia Waffle Co; a man named Doumar began operating in New Jersey; and Avayou set up business in Philadelphia.

The race was on. And by the mid-20's around 250 million cones were produced in one year! New designs sprang up all over the place, none of them more than variations on the original, and everyone tried to solve the melting problem with "dripless" inventions. Today we're pretty much back to the two classics: the molded cake cone and the still wrapped sugar cone. As Dickson rightly writes, the cone is now the "Volkswagen of the ice cream world." Perhaps the flat-bottomed "cup cone" is the only important variation that has evolved.

Nabisco sells millions of them. The giant firm (National Biscuit Company) has *its* version of the "St. Louis Story." According to them, two Fair employees, who realizing what others had failed to grasp, returned home to Cincinnati and began baking cones, turning out hand-rolled, sweet sugar cones along with the pressed or molded type. And in 1910 Frederick A. Bruckmann of Portland, Oregon invented a machine that could turn out 3,000 cones an hour. Nabisco entered the picture in 1928, buying the McLaren Consolidated Cone Corporation which had obtained certain rights from Mr. Bruckmann. The McLaren cone had an extra thickness around the outside near the top which allowed for

Schutzen Park, North Bergen, New Jersey awarded its ice cream cone concession to Abe Doumar who had, by 1910, taken on his three brothers.

five young ladies cooling off at a British beach. Notice there are six cones!

"nesting" – packing one cone inside another – greatly reducing one of the plagues of the industry: breakage. In the late 40's when "Soft Ice Cream" appeared the company came up with a flat-bottomed cone which enabled the dispensers to fill the cones faster, not having to hold them. This cone has had a huge success with mothers for similar reasons and accounts for over 70 per cent of Nabisco cone sales. One plant alone bakes over 300 million a year! The cup cones hold one to four ounces and come in several types including a "cuplet" which holds scoops side-by-side. Cones even come in green, yellow and chocolate colors.

As recently as January 1975 *The New Lebanese American Journal* retold the story that Abe Doumar's son Al has told quite well (in a family history called "The Saga of the Ice Cream Cone"). Abe was selling souvenirs in the Streets of Jerusalem section of the St. Louis Fair and one evening while talking to one of the waffle concessionaires he suggested that he could turn his penny waffle into a 10-cent one if he added ice cream. The man replied with a request for his help. Abe agreed and the cone was born. (Abe is credited in the files of the Institute of Ice Cream Manufacturers). When the Fair closed, Abe was given one of the waffle irons to take home.

Back home he worked out a four-iron machine and set up business at Coney Island with three partners in 1905. They did a nicely alliterative business in "corn on the cob and cornucopias" – at least after hiring some attractive young women to walk up and down the boardwalk eating ice cream cones. By 1906 Abe and his three brothers were all involved in the cone business. Abe's first move to Virginia was connected with the unsuccessful Jamestown Exposition in 1907 and he had his first experience at that time with the

OCEAN VIEW
PARK
1922

( GEO. E. ) ( ELMER ) JEO
DOUMAR HANDY BLAK

The Doumar stand at Ocean View Park near Norfolk, Virginia, in 1922. George Doumar is at the left operating the electrically powered iron cone machine.

127

ITEM NO: SS12

SCOOPY'S

24 BOXES
12 SUGAR CONES
IN EACH BOX

"SCOOPY"
The SAFE-T-CONE Clown

OLD FASHIONED
BROWN SUGAR CONES

© 19

Ocean View Amusement Park – a resort on the south shore of Chesapeake Bay. The Ocean View Hotel was the fashionable place to dine and people came from Washington, Memphis and Louisville to eat seafood there. Every Sunday the bath house behind the hotel rented three thousand bathing suits! There were band concerts and covered walks. Pavilions and a Japanese garden. There was dancing and terraces that overlooked the bay. There was fine fishing and sheltered picnic areas. Ice cream cones were the perfect addition.

The owners of the Park ran an open trolley car from the town to the Park and people often rode it for the view and a Doumar cone. Abe kept the concessions for over 25 years. He and his brothers also ran other concessions there along the East Coast as well as making visits to State Fairs.

In 1919 a semi-automatic cone machine was acquired. It was much faster than the hand irons. In 1921 a double-iron cone machine made it possible to produce 20 cones a minute. Crowds loved it and couldn't resist the marvelous odor of freshly baked cones. It was fun watching the "dipper" too. A good dipper could hold seven cones in one hand, fill the dipper with one pass of his dipper-hand, fill all the cones and then hand them to the server in next-to-no-time. One day in 1925 George Doumar and his staff sold 22,600 ice cream cones! Thus encouraged, the family went into the wholesale business but had to pull out when the National Biscuit Company was able to undersell them.

Then in 1933 a hurricane destroyed most of the wonderful old amusement park. George had been impressed by the curb service that Jes Maid's ice cream store was doing in Norfolk. On a Sunday waitresses were giving curb service for a block in both directions and on both sides of the street. George bought a store that provided off-street parking and opened his "drive-in". There was a ball park nearby. A dining room and dance floor was added in 1937. And, in 1949 an entirely new building was built. Today Doumar's still makes cones by hand on the original machine, still specialize in cones and barbecue after more than 40 years still serve no more than four or five kinds of ice cream.

# Little Orphan Ice Cream

If you look through the many volumes of the Subject Index housed in the exclusive London Library you will find nothing listed under the general heading "Ice Cream". "Mildew", yes, but not "Ice Cream". If you persist, or ask one of the librarians, you will discover that ice cream *is* listed – but as a sub-heading under such things as "Cookery". A *sub*-heading I ask you!

No, ice cream is conspicuously *not* written about. Where is it in Scott Fitzgerald? Where in Hemingway? Without re-reading half the works of English literature can you come up with ten quick references? Mark Twain (surely an obvious choice)? Agatha Christie maybe? Wodehouse? Marcel Proust? Drink? Yes. Food? Quite often (one thinks of Dickens or even Virginia Woolf – i.e. *To the Lighthouse*).

The only great poet I can name who dealt directly with ice cream is

Wallace Stevens (here included). Though no less a writer than T. S. Eliot touched upon it in "The Love Song of J. Alfred Prufrock":

Should I, after tea and cakes and ices,
Have the strength to face the moment
    to its crisis?

Giuseppe di Lampedusa, author of *The Leopard,* speaks of the "ice cream hour" in his native Sicily in *Two Stories and a Memory* (from which my poem on page 152 derives its scene, details and inspiration).

It's the same thing with songs.* Did Shirley Temple sing about a sundae? She did not. That was a lollipop. Sing your way through all of *Oklahoma* and you'll find everything from elephant's eyes to fringed surreys, but not a scoop of ice cream. Re-hum Noel Coward. Try Cole Porter. Not even in his "You're the Top." (Isn't it reasonable to expect somewhere in that endless list of comparisons something like, "You're the top/You're a hot fudge sundae/You're the top/You're a Paris parfait"?). Where is it in opera (*La Boheme* for example)? Operetta? Truth to tell, W. S. Gilbert did name it among his wonderful words for The Nightmare Song in *Iolanthe:*

And you're giving a treat (penny ice and cold meat)
to a party of friends and relations –
They're a ravenous horde – they all came on board
at Sloane Square and South Kensington Stations.

Did Fanny Brice ever spoof it? Bea Lilly? Jack Benny? Barbra Streisand?

In *A Streetcar Named Desire* why couldn't Tennessee Williams have Blanche say to Stella, "Some day I shall die from eating an impure *sorbay*?" instead of going on about grapes? And in summer-steamy New Orleans the two sisters go out for *cokes.* Of course Blanche is supposed to be watching her figure. I can think of no reference to the "flower of milk" in Hellman or Miller, Inge or Saroyan, Ionesco or Beckett, Osborn or Pinter (he gives an important scene to a cheese sandwich, but what about that birthday party?).

There *was* an English Music Hall song called "Oh! Oh! Antonio" that mentioned ice cream carts and was a big hit, especially as sung by Florrie Forde. It told of an Italian maid who, in deep distress, wandered the streets

"Searching in ev'ry part
For her false sweetheart
And his ice cream cart."
The chorus went:
"Oh! Oh! Antonio
He's gone away
Left me alone-i-o,
All on my own-i-o.
I want to meet him with his new sweet-heart,
Then up will go Antonio
And his ice cream cart."

A big hit show in South Africa and England in the late 60's also referred to ice cream – Jersey Taylor's "Wait a Minim." The first verse of the "Ballad of the Southern Suburbs" goes like this:

* With the exception of a very famous song about ice cream "I Scream – You Scream – We All Scream for Ice Cream". (see page 135).

An', pleeze daddie, won't you take us to the drive-in,
All six, seven of us – eight, nine ten.
We want to see a flick about Tarzan and the ape-man
An' when the show is over you can bring us back again
And the Chorus goes:
Popcorn, chewing-gum, peanuts and bubble-gum,
Ice-cream, candy-floss and Eskimo Pie.
O, daddie how we miss [dadda] balls and licorice
Pepsi-cola, ginger-beer and Canada Dry.

Broadway saw a musical in 1963 in which ice cream figures in a full-flavored manner in *She Loves Me* written by Joe Masteroff. Appropriately, it is set in Vienna (the source of the book is Molnar's *The Shop Around the Corner*) and Masteroff, together with his lyrist and composer, Jerry Bock and Sheldon Harmick, create an almost operatic *scena* leading to a long aria-like song:

GEORG: *I brought you something.*
AMALIA: *(Through her tears) What?*
GEORG *See for yourself.*
*(AMALIA sits up. SHE takes the brown paper bag and opens it)*
AMALIA: *What is it?*
GEORG: *Vanilla ice cream. It's the best thing in the world when you're sick. I'll get you a spoon.*
AMALIA: *In the little drawer. (SHE takes the container out of the bag) It's from Lindners! My mother works at Lindners! She may have waited on you!*
*(GEORG brings the spoon. AMALIA starts eating the ice cream)*
GEORG: *A small, stout woman?*
AMALIA: *Oh, no. The image of me – everyone says – only much younger-looking. (SHE stops eating) There's something wrong with this ice cream . . .*
GEORG: *There is?*
AMALIA: *So much salt –*
GEORG: *Are you surprised? All those tears falling into it –*
AMALIA: *Oh. I'd better cry in the other direction.*

A long scene leads up to GEORG's exit. Then AMALIA begins to write:

Dear Friend . . .
I am so sorry about last night –
It was a nightmare in every way.
But together you and I
Will laugh at last night some day.
    *(SHE stops writing and meditates)*
Ice cream –
He brought me ice cream –
Vanilla ice cream.
Imagine that!
Ice cream –
And for the first time
We were together
Without a spat.
Friendly –

133

He was so friendly –
That isn't like him.
I'm simply stunned.
Will wonders never cease?
Will wonders never cease?
It's been a most peculiar day.
Will wonders never cease?
Will wonders never cease . . .?

Where was I? Oh . . .
*(Re-reading the letter)*
*I am so sorry about last night it was a nightmare in every way but*
*together you and I will laugh at last night some day . . .*
I sat there waiting in that café
And never guessed that you were fat –
*(SHE crosses this out)*
That you were *near.*
You were outside looking bald . . .
Oh my . . .
*(SHE takes a new piece of paper)*
Dear Friend . . .
I am so sorry about last night –
*(Meditating)*
Last night I was so nasty –
Well, he deserved it –
But even so . . .
That Georg
Is not like this Georg.
This is a new Georg
That I don't know.
Somehow it all reminds me
Of Dr. Jekyll and Mr. Hyde –
For right before my eyes –
A man that I despise
Has turned into a man I like!
It's almost like a dream –
And strange as it may seem –
He came to offer me
Vanilla Ice Cream!

# I Scream-You Scream-We All Scream For
# ICE CREAM

By HOWARD JOHNSON,
BILLY MOLL and
ROBERT KING

Uke in B♭
With Piano
Tune Thus

F B♭ D G

Arr. by
A.J.Franchini

In the land of ice and snows
Col-le-ges may come and go

Up a-mong the Es-ki-mos
But the world will nev-er know

There's a col-lege known as Oo-gie-wa-wa
An-y oth-er place like Oo-gie-wa-wa

(WA - WA - WA)
(WA - WA - WA)

You should hear those
Har-vard, Prince-ton,

col - lege boys
Brown and Yale

Gee! they make an
Foot-ball teams would

aw-ful noise
all turn pale

When they sing an
When they played a

Es-ki-mo tra-
game with Oo-gie-

4

la - la _____ They've got a lead-er, big cheerlead-er, oh!what a guy He's
wa - wa _____ Those Es - ki-mos looked mighty tough when they took the field And

got a fro-zen face, just like an Es-ki-mo pie _ When he says "Come on, let's go"
peo-ple said "Ah! there's a team that nev-er will yield Then mid gore and fly-ing fur

Tho' it's for-ty - five be - low This is what those Es-ki-mos all hol-ler: _____
Just to show how tough they were All those Es-ki - mos be-gan to hol-ler: _____

CHORUS *Brightly*                                                            *optional*

1 I scream, you scream, We all scream for Ice Cream RAH!    RAH!    RAH! _____
2 I scream, you scream, We all scream for Ice Cream RAH!    RAH!    RAH! _____
3 (Greek) *Al - pha, Be - ta, A fro - zen to - may - tuh Yes!*   Oh!     Yes! _____

Ice Cream 3

I suppose the movies have done a bit better than the writers. Although, allowing my imagination free-rein, I regret that Carole Lombard didn't discover her "man Godfrey" at a corner drug store, that Claudette Colbert never shared a soda with Clark Gable, that the bitches of *The Women* didn't sneak off to attack mountainous sundaes, that, although they did a nation-wide promotion for milk shakes, Ginger Rogers and Fred Astaire never danced from stool-to-stool or through an enormous straw. (But Fred *did* treat Ginger to a sundae in *The Fleet's In.*)

Eddie Cantor did more justice to old frozen fun. In the mid-thirties he starred in a film called *Kid Millions,* a talkie in color, in which chorus girls cavorted through a giant ice cream factory – skating and coasting and observing small fry happily sipping from gigantic sodas – under the supervision of Cantor. The scene even boasted a cherry-spouting machine gun.

Just before World War II, Hollywood produced a series of small-town sagas, full of the girl-next-door next to the boy-next-door, usually enacted by stars like Mickey Rooney and Judy Garland. These established the local drug store as the meeting ground for Romance, the place to "get to know" someone and in which to make innocent confessions. The idea that the soda fountain was the place even in real life in which to be "discovered" by Hollywood was reinforced by George Montgomery's being spotted behind a fountain counter by Dinah Shore and by the sight of numberless young ladies imitating the expressions of Bette Davis or Jean Harlow in fountain mirrors. The famous Hollywood drug store, Schwab's, was even featured in a number of films and recreated on the lot of one of the big studios. So strong was its legend that it persisted well into the 50's and the days of James Dean and Natalie Wood.

Publicity shots of young hopefuls licking temptingly at cones were released by several studios (perhaps "ice" should have been the word used instead of "cheese" in the expression "cheesecake"). Even the trade journal *The Ice Cream Review* published a series of covers combining ice cream with the glamor of stars. A still from First National's *They Won't Forget* reveals a very mature (at 16!) Lana Turner sipping soulfully away accompanied by a girl friend – an image of the working girl at ease depicted by several painters of the same period. (See pages 76 and 77.)

Even the redoubtable Marx Brothers got into the act – using ice cream's connotation of good-for-you innocence as a cover-up for a betting racket in their hilarious *A Day at the Races.* Who, who has ever heard it, can forget Chico's cry, "Ice cream! Get your tutti-frutti ice cream!" Even the cliche connection of Italians with cart vending was seized upon in Chico's mock-Italian character dressed in a too-small but oddly elegant jacket and pointed Pinnochio hat.

Some famous and all-present was the Good Humor man in his white uniform and spotless truck that he was seen in one form or another in more than a hundred pictures and even given a film of his very own – *The Good Humor Man* which starred the comedian Jack Carson.

Perhaps the most unlikely figure ever to be seen spooning into an ice cream soda was the Great Boozer himself – W. C. Fields. (Perhaps proof to the never-proved theory that ice cream is a cure for a hangover.) In any case, the extended pinkie,

YOO-HOO....ICE CREAM MAN !

"Creature Feature" cards

An unlikely still of the Great
Boozer, W. C. Fields, battered
boater set at a cheerful angle,
pinkie poised, and mouth askew as
though about to make a
devastating crack about the
spoonful of whipped cream he is
lifting from a soda.

U.S.A. 1930. Director: Frank Tuttle. Prod. Co. Paramount

Hollywood's long love affair with the Navy. The unique Clara Bow, quite a dish herself, dishing up a sundae to an unidentified admirer in a flick called *True to the Navy*.

U.S.A. 1930. Director: Ray Enright. Prod. Co. Warner Bros./Vitaphone

Courtin' by Dixie Cup. Sue Carol being treated by Grant Withers in a tender moment from *Dancing Sweeties*.

U.S.A. 1929. Director: Leo McCarey. Prod. Co. Pathe Exchange

College tradition: The soda-with-two-straws date. Big stuff even into the 50's. Sally Withers and Eddie Quillan in *The Sophomore*.

U.S.A. 1937. Director: Mervyn Leroy. Prod. Co. First National

The young (only 16!) Lana Turner with Linda Perry in a soulful moment over a soda in *They Won't Forget*.

The poster designed by Jon Lopez for Bert Stern's superb 1958 film about the Newport Jazz Festival recently re-issued to great acclaim. A marvelous visual pun dealing with summer heat, a sweating "cornet" of ice cream, and the wet world of The America's Cup sailboat trials.

the battered boater, and the mouth askew, appear both anachronistic and faintly normal – like Wallace Stevens' "Emperor" (see page 97) calling up shadows in our memories and leading us into doubt, a little like that other emperor with his new clothes. It's fun to learn that Fields was once banned from Manhattan's H. Hicks for introducing "something more" into his ice cream dishes.

Recently, on the current wave of nostalgia, the California ice cream maker, Swensens, has tapped Hollywood's by-gone glamor with a delightful menu called "Scene Stealers" and decorated with pictorial paraphrases of Astaire and Rogers, the Keystone Cops, "leading players," and ending up with a witty portrait of Bert Lahr as the MGM lion.

LEFT: TOP TO
BOTTOM
Katharine Hepburn and
Spencer Tracy in
**Guess Who's Coming to
Dinner?**
*U.S.A. 1967, Director: Stanley
Kramer.*

Harpo Marx in
**A Day at the Races.**
*U.S.A. 1934, Director Sam
Wood.*

Carroll Baker and Karl
Malden in
**Baby Doll.**
*U.S.A. 1956, Director Elia
Kazan.*

RIGHT: TOP TO
BOTTOM
Chico and Groucho
Marx in
**A Day at the Races.**
*U.S.A. 1934, Director: Sam
Wood.*

Laurel and Hardy in
**Men O'War.**
*U.S.A. 1929, Director Lewis R.
Foster.
Copyright 1975 Feiner/Overseas
by permission of Hal Roach
Studios, Inc.*

Jack Carson in
**The Good Humor Man.**
*U.S.A. 1950, Director Lloyd
Bacon.*

Eddie Cantor in
**Kid Millions.**
*U.S.A. 1934, Director Roy del
Ruth.*

# FLAVORMANIA

**or More Flavors Than You Ever Wanted to Know (or, Perhaps, Care) About and Aren't Particularly Interested in Asking For**

Howard Johnsons has always emphasized its 28. Baskin-Robbins came up with their 31 (one for each day in the month, but what happens when February has only 28?). Bresler's boasts of 33. Good Humor has gone through more than 3,000. Swensen's offers at least 55 at any given store – "more than anybody else." I haven't counted the number produced or toyed-with by Haagen-Daz, or Wall's, or Bertorelli, or Dreyer's, or Lyons Maid.

Those numbers peering from posters and blaring from shop-signs don't tell all of the story either. Baskin-Robbins have come up with more than 500 flavors and there are usually 34 on tap at any given moment: vanilla, chocolate and strawberry besides the 31. Bresler's had topped the 300 mark by 1975. We seem to have an absolute fetish for flavors!

Puns, political overtones, alliterations, jokes abound in the naming of these delights. When we went to the moon, "Lunar Cheesecake" (Baskin-Robbins) and "Moon Shot" (Good Humor) were not long to follow. There's been "White House" (Swensen's), "Presidential Sweet" Bresler's) and, of course "Impeach Mint" (I can't remember whose). There have been notable disasters – Good Humor's "Chili-con-carne" (a mind-boggler) and noble successes – Baskin-Robbins' "Tanganilla". There are names such as Swensen's "Alice's Marble Fudge" (a reference to the great tennis champion Alice Marble) and Bresler's "Rambling Rose". Foremost lists Hop Scotch, San Francisco Mint, and Little Red Caboose. Eroticism has been touched upon: "Girlsenberry" and "Love" and "Never-on-Sundae" (banana and cherry). There's even something for the "heads" among us: "Acapulco Gold" (peach studded with "hash" which is flaked chocolate), "Panama Red" (Maraschino and Burgundy cherries plus more "hash").

Baskin-Robbins good humoredly admits to failing with a lovely idea: "Goody Goody Gumdrop". The bits of candy froze to such hardness that customers feared for their teeth. Back in 1961 Good Humor told the *New Yorker* that they'd not succeeded with prunes or licorice. Baskin-Robbins lists "Licorice" as one of its flavors and Bresler's makes a "Licorice Voo Doo".

There are monthly turnovers and seasonal flavors and specials to mark events and holidays. Thanksgiving means pumpkin and cranberry. Christmas brings out egg nog and champagne. The 4th of July is bound to find some, not always very successful, attempts to come up with a red-white-and-blue concoction (strawberry, vanilla and blueberry seems to be the most successful so far and *that* really means pink instead of red). For reasons which evade me our inventive inventors have mixed up batches of "Fickle Pickle" or "Dill Pickle" (for pregnant ice cream freaks?) and even "Chop Suey" (fruit, coconut, walnuts from Bresler's).

# SWENSEN'S ICE CREAM FACTORY

OF WESTWOOD VILLAGE
1051 Broxton Avenue    478-6785

*Outrageously rich ice cream* **menu** *made fresh here daily!*

## Swensen's Super-Sundaes

Delicious concoctions of vanilla ice cream, luscious toppings, whipped cream, toasted almonds and cherry.

HOT FUDGE 90¢    BUTTERSCOTCH 85¢

HOT CARAMEL 90¢    CHOCOLATE 85¢

STRAWBERRY 85¢    PINEAPPLE 85¢

BANANA SPLIT
Strawberry and chocolate ice cream, strawberry, pineapple and chocolate fudge topping . . . . . . . . . . . . . . . . . . . . . . . . 1.30

## Cable Carfaits

As you know, parfait in French means perfect. Merely-perfect. Such a tame name would insult these wild and wicked concoctions.

* **CHOCOLATE RING-A-DING:** Scoops and scoops of chocolate and vanilla ice cream in a sea of double-deep chocolate fudge. A cheery cherry sun shines over clouds of whipped cream on top. 1.00

* **STRAWBERRY STRIPES:** Rosy-red crushed strawberries cool their heels in dippers and dippers of vanilla, chocolate, and strawberry ice cream. Toasted almonds, a huge gloppffff of whipped cream, and a cherry with a stem top it off. 95¢

* **RED WHITE AND BLUEBERRIES:** You like blueberries? Be glad you're at Swensen's. They pour on the blueberries — BIG — and the vanilla ice cream, too. Lavish puffs of whipped cream and a red cherry aloft. 85¢

## Milk Shakes and Malts

Robust, rich and rambunctious with flavor, a meal in a glass. 20 oz. 80¢

**FLAVORS:**

| | |
|---|---|
| Fresh Banana | Pineapple |
| Vanilla | Root Beer |
| Chocolate | Cherry |
| Coffee | Chocolate Peppermint |
| Strawberry | |

Plus every other flavor on Swensen's Big Board.

## Swensen's Outrageous Sundaes

Think rich. Each one is incredibly creamy...a special production in itself.

* **THE ICE HOUSE:** Vanilla ice cream, butterscotch sauce, almonds, frosty chocolate fudge, whipped cream and a cherry. 75¢

**HOT FUDGE BONANZA SPLIT:** Hot fudge co-stars in this extravaganza with the noble banana, while vanilla ice cream, butterscotch sauce, nuggets of almonds, whipped cream and a cherry play supporting roles. Limit: One to a customer. 1.25

**IRISH COFFEE MACAROONEY:** Coffee ice cream, and plenty of it, is the nicest thing in this world when it's teamed with crushed macaroons, whipped cream, and a cherry. 65¢

* **BLACK BART:** With chocolate ice cream, frosty chocolate fudge, whitecaps of marshmallow topping, almonds, cookie. Black Bart held up stagecoaches. This will hold you up through a long, hard day. 75¢

* **GOLD RUSH:** With chocolate and coffee ice cream, golden butterscotch sauce, and frosty chocolate fudge. Almonds. Cookie. 75¢

**TWIN PEAKS:** Scoops of any two ice cream flavors on Swensen's long list, whipped cream and cherry. 55¢

**MR. SWENS SON:** Your choice of rich ice cream makes a face topped with an ice-cream-cone hat dipped in chocolate. Peppermint candies give the face a sweet expression. A whipped cream collar and a cherry on the hat will make you want this friend for dinner. 65¢

**THE EARTHQUAKE:** Your choice of eight scoops of ice cream, any flavor, with eight toppings, any flavor. Yes, we did say EIGHT. Almonds, whipped cream, and a whole gang of cherries. 2.95

**FIREHOUSE BIRTHDAY:** A celebration special with vanilla, chocolate, and strawberry ice cream with pineapple, chocolate fudge, and strawberry topping. AND: Fresh banana, a snowdrift of whipped cream, and cherries. AND: A plume of live fire on top. Note: Customers are only allowed one birthday per year. If you want to hear our firebell ring, order this one. 1.35

## Swensen's Super-Sodas

Crackling-cold, towering-tall, swamped with rich ice cream. Big, overgrown sodas— shamelessly luscious. 65¢

**FLAVORS:**

| | |
|---|---|
| Chocolate | Vanilla |
| Strawberry | Root Beer |
| Pineapple | Chocolate-Coffee Espresso |
| Cherry | Blueberry |
| Lemon | Chocolate Mint |
| Coffee | |

## Swensen's Cavalcade of Coolers

**FREEZES:** 60¢
BRR-RRRRR-R...R in 4 frosty flavors.

| | |
|---|---|
| Orange | Raspberry |
| Pineapple | Tangerine |

**TREASURE ISLAND FLOATS:** Root beer or cola, served in a beer mug with a bouncing ball of your favorite ice cream. 60¢

CHOCOLATE EGG CREAM    30¢

**SOFT DRINKS**

| | |
|---|---|
| Big | . . . . . . . . . . . . . . . . . . . .20¢ |
| Even Bigger | . . . . . . . . . . . .30¢ |
| COFFEE | . . . . . . . . . . . . . . . . .20¢ |
| TEA | . . . . . . . . . . . . . . . . . . . .20¢ |
| HOT CHOCOLATE | . . . . . . .25¢ |

* *No Substitutions Please*

**See Other Side for Sandwiches and Salads**

# SWENSEN'S

Strawberry
Road

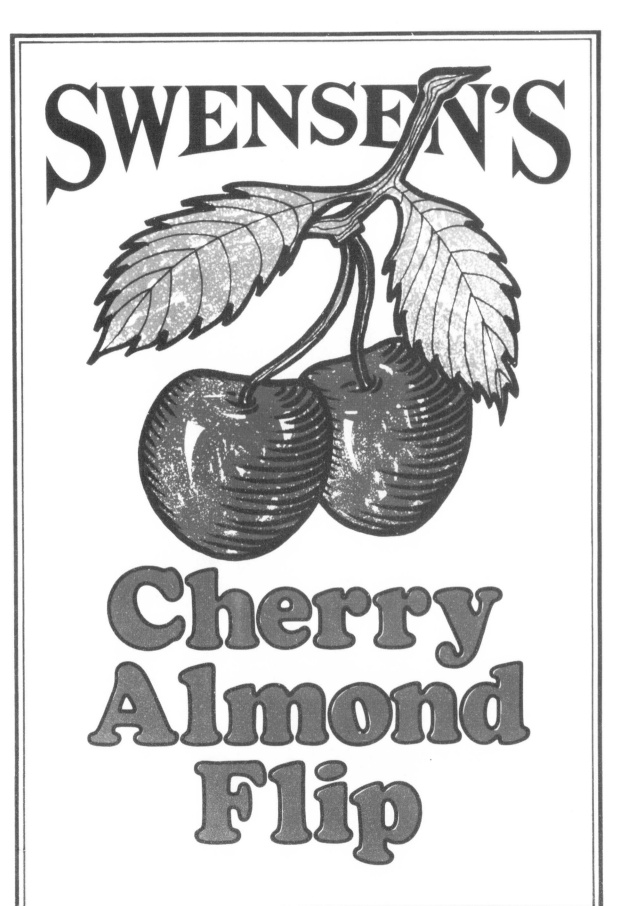

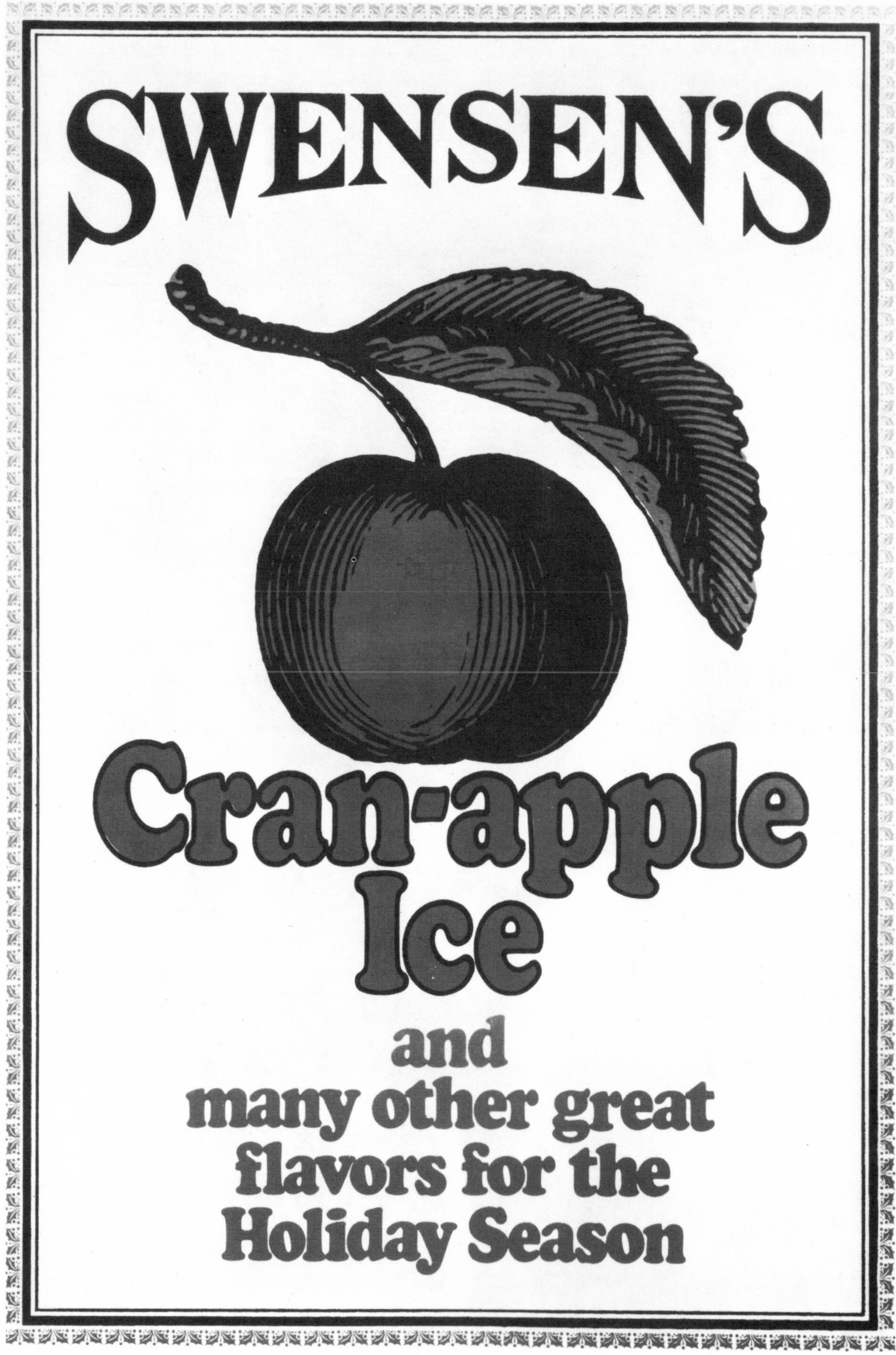

# SWENSEN'S

## Cran-apple Ice

and
many other great
flavors for the
Holiday Season

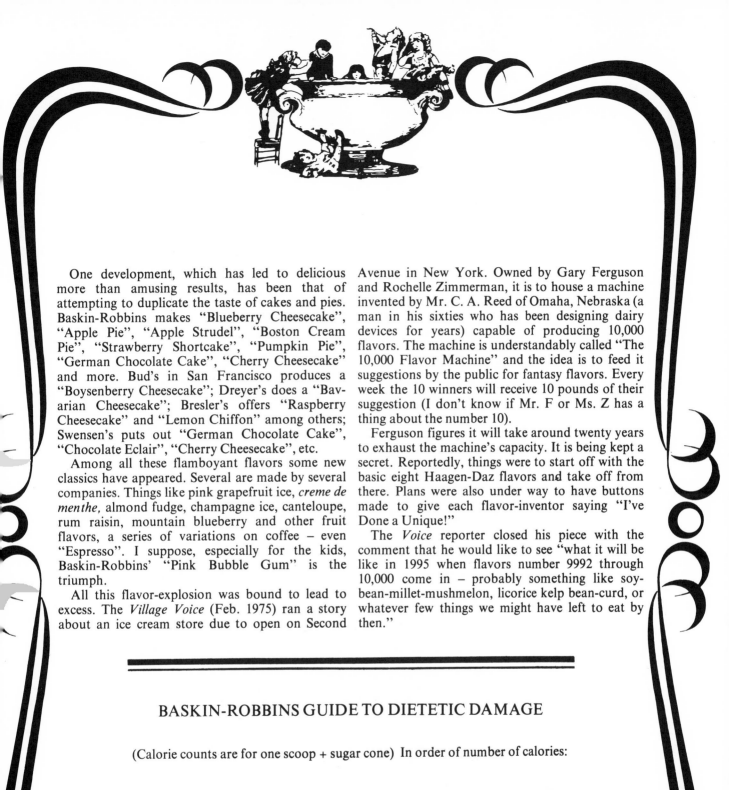

One development, which has led to delicious more than amusing results, has been that of attempting to duplicate the taste of cakes and pies. Baskin-Robbins makes "Blueberry Cheesecake", "Apple Pie", "Apple Strudel", "Boston Cream Pie", "Strawberry Shortcake", "Pumpkin Pie", "German Chocolate Cake", "Cherry Cheesecake" and more. Bud's in San Francisco produces a "Boysenberry Cheesecake"; Dreyer's does a "Bavarian Cheesecake"; Bresler's offers "Raspberry Cheesecake" and "Lemon Chiffon" among others; Swensen's puts out "German Chocolate Cake", "Chocolate Eclair", "Cherry Cheesecake", etc.

Among all these flamboyant flavors some new classics have appeared. Several are made by several companies. Things like pink grapefruit ice, *creme de menthe,* almond fudge, champagne ice, canteloupe, rum raisin, mountain blueberry and other fruit flavors, a series of variations on coffee – even "Espresso". I suppose, especially for the kids, Baskin-Robbins' "Pink Bubble Gum" is the triumph.

All this flavor-explosion was bound to lead to excess. The *Village Voice* (Feb. 1975) ran a story about an ice cream store due to open on Second Avenue in New York. Owned by Gary Ferguson and Rochelle Zimmerman, it is to house a machine invented by Mr. C. A. Reed of Omaha, Nebraska (a man in his sixties who has been designing dairy devices for years) capable of producing 10,000 flavors. The machine is understandably called "The 10,000 Flavor Machine" and the idea is to feed it suggestions by the public for fantasy flavors. Every week the 10 winners will receive 10 pounds of their suggestion (I don't know if Mr. F or Ms. Z has a thing about the number 10).

Ferguson figures it will take around twenty years to exhaust the machine's capacity. It is being kept a secret. Reportedly, things were to start off with the basic eight Haagen-Daz flavors and take off from there. Plans were also under way to have buttons made to give each flavor-inventor saying "I've Done a Unique!"

The *Voice* reporter closed his piece with the comment that he would like to see "what it will be like in 1995 when flavors number 9992 through 10,000 come in – probably something like soybean-millet-mushmelon, licorice kelp bean-curd, or whatever few things we might have left to eat by then."

## BASKIN-ROBBINS GUIDE TO DIETETIC DAMAGE

(Calorie counts are for one scoop + sugar cone)  In order of number of calories:

| | | | |
|---|---|---|---|
| Chocolate Fudge | 229 | Fresh Strawberry | 168 |
| French Vanilla | 217 | Fresh Peach | 165 |
| Rocky Road | 204 | Mango Sherbet | 132 |
| Here Come Da Fudge | 202 | Banana Daiquiri* | 129 |
| Butter Pecan | 195 | | |
| Jamoca Almond Fudge | 190 | | |

\* Irvine Robbins' own favorite for breakfast.

## THE ICE CREAM HOUR
Giuseppe di Lampedusa

*Les privilèges de la naissance
    sont des privilèges contre la
naissance.*

MANZONI

Outside Mazzaro's,
even now, carriages pause
at the Ice Cream Hour.
And waiters hustle out
hoisting trays of ices
to be eaten on the spot.

His shadow joins them,
but at a corner table,
in an inner room –
screened-off when there is
a family party going on.

To his table, from
morning into the dead hour
of Palermo afternoons,
would come what the Princess
called his 'pupils'.

He was forever reading or talking –
of 'eternal Sicily, *nature's* Sicily',
of his readings (with his wife,

in five languages),
of his ancient class with its 'low
consumption of general ideas'.

Often he talked with his cousin
the poet Luccio Piccolo
who wrote *Canti Barocchi,* living
at (what a name!) Capo d'Orlando.

Sometimes weighed down
by Sicilian sadness, the loss
of family palaces,
he sat and pined.
The Princess suggested he write
of what he loved that was gone.

He began.

So, *Il Gattopardo.* So
the 'memories of light',
of things more than people.
Places of his infancy,
meandering through a lost Earthly
   Paradise . . .

All written to the reader who,
he wrote, 'won't exist'.
Such positive use of the future!
That future – he couldn't imagine –
which was there, waiting to arrive,
filled with us.

RALPH POMEROY
from *In the Financial District*, Macmillan.

# GOODIES ARE GOOD (?) FOR YOU

Ice cream is high in calories. A six-ounce serving, three-quarters of a cup, totals 375 calories – okay for active children who burn up lots of calories, but to be watched by less active adults. An average cup contains 400 calories; sherbet contains 100 calories less per cup and water ices only 150 calories per fat-free cup. As far as protein is concerned, ice cream contains far more than most snacks and desserts – eight grams per six ounces – and the quality is higher: the amino acids, the components that make up protein, are in a ratio that can easily be used by the body. Calcium is somewhat neglected by both children and adults who don't drink enough milk. Six ounces of ice cream amounts to 257 milligrams of calcium – about one-fourth the daily requirement of 1,000 milligrams for children and more than that for the adult requirement of 800. Ideally, our daily intake of phosphorus should equal our calcium intake. Americans tend to eat an imbalance in the direction of phosphorus – about twice as much phos-

phorus as calcium. A small serving of apple pie can contain about one milligram of calcium to 35 milligrams of phosphorus and one ounce of potato chips has 11 milligrams of calcium to 39 milligrams of phosphorus. A six-ounce serving of ice cream contains 199 milligrams of phosphorus to 257 milligrams of calcium, which is a bit more in the right direction. Ice cream is about the same as most kinds of shakes and desserts in carbohydrate content and higher in fat. And the fat is saturated. Adults ought therefore to be careful about their fat intake, since they are not so active as children and therefore don't burn up fat as efficiently. Ice cream is also a source of vitamins A and B2, which contain riboflavin and thiamine and, because of its high fat content, exceeds milk in amount of thiamine which is a good source of protein.

Companies like Good Humor claim that one chocolate-covered vanilla ice cream stick supplies seven per cent of the Recommended Dietary Allowance of calcium for an adult (far more than

the average sweet), four per cent of the recommended protein, an advantageous calcium - phosphate ratio, 20 per cent saturated fat, and 230 calories which, they say, a careful ice cream fan can, "bicycle off in 30 minutes." Such firms would like us to believe that ice cream is the "major exception" to the "empty calorie" principle which deals with foods having a high calorie content in proportion to low protein, vitamins and minerals. They claim that ice cream has a "substantial nutritional edge" over such things as candy bars, cookies, colas, and the like.

Playing around with charts and measures is a tricky business. Almost anything can appear to be proved. It's not easy for the average person to envision a piece of pie described as one-eighth of a pie nine inches in diameter, or weighing 3.5 ounces as compared to 2 ounces of ice cream which *must* be much lighter, or to translate 6 ounces into an amount of dessert served on a dish. Quite naturally, the ice cream makers want to place their product in the best light. But to claim it as not fattening is a bit much. However, there are ways of slimming down on the fattening side. One way is to not eat too much ice cream which isn't that difficult as it tends to be very satisfying. Another way is to make your own where the use of the very best flavors allows you to decrease the fat content without diminishing quality. You can use milk, even skim milk, instead of cream. But beware of imitation products which are no good at all for dieters. They are usually made with coconut oil which, though it doesn't have the unpleasant taste of most vegetable oils, is high in saturated fat.

There is some sense in the claim that two ounces of ice cream, about a wineglass-worth, will seem more filling and therefore more satisfying than other food. But as far as milk benefits go, two ounces give you only a couple of grams each of protein and fat. The same two ounces contain 50 milligrams of calcium – approximately one-tenth of daily requirements.

Ice cream is easily digested too, as well as comforting, so that people who are ill or suffering from sore throats, are often fed it. If given *enough,* say 12 ounces spread over a day, it can supply quite a lot of nutrient at the same time, but would be death to a dieter.

As far as non-milk fat as opposed to milk fat is concerned the argument is complicated. Everyone these days talks of high quality ice cream in terms of its butterfat content, but the vitamin A missing in vegetable oil can be added to it and there are those who feel the cholesterol in animal fat is such a negative factor that they prefer ice cream made with vegetable oil.

Empty calories, the ones that give you energy-calories only, need, in order to be used up properly, to be taken in combination with B vitamins, protein and minerals – in other words, other nutrients. Ice cream

This diagram shows the proportions of calories in an average portion of each dessert.

156

includes several of these. Sugar and even honey, by comparison, are pretty much just calories, so that foods like candy or very sweet cake or cookies are quite high in empty calories.

When it comes to measuring ice cream against such things as jelly, canned fruit or puddings, everything depends on quantity. Normally, people eat larger amounts of things like pudding. Instant puddings are made with milk and usually add up to more than our two-ounce serving of ice cream. Canned fruit and jellies are largely sugar with some vitamin C and, in the case of jelly, gelatine-derived protein. Comparisons are difficult.

Wall's, the English ice cream makers, compare eight ounces of the average hard cheese containing 1,000 calories, to an "entire litre of rum-and-raisin ice cream" which contain "about the same number." They also compare an "average banana, providing 20 grams of carbohydrate" to the "average vanilla ice cream bar" which provides 10 grams of carbohydrate with both having the "same caloric value of 80 calories." They also provide two graphs dealing with protein and caloric content in their ice creams.

George W. Hennerich's *Let's Sell Ice Cream,* which covers nearly every aspect of the ice cream industry, also reproduces a food-value chart put out by the National Dairy Council in 1948.

This chart has a few surprises: 100 grams of vanilla ice cream contains 206 calories while the same quantity of apple pie contains 230, and 111 grams of angel cake will saddle the unwary dieter with 300 calories.

The same organization has more recently published a chart detailing the nutrient content of vanilla ice cream. This is for 100 grams (about a sixth of a quart). That means 206 calories – plus all the following:

Protein . . . . . . . . . . . . . 3.850 gm.
Fat . . . . . . . . . . . . . . . 12.060 gms.
Carbohydrates . . . . . . . 21.310 gm.
Total Mineral . . . . . . . . . 0.810 gm.
Calcium . . . . . . . . . . . . . 0.122 gm.
Phosphorus . . . . . . . . . 0.105 gm.
Iron . . . . . . . . . . . . . . . . 0.120 mg.
Vitamin A . . . . . . . . . . . . . 548 I.U.
Thiamine . . . . . . . . . . . . 0.038 mg.
Riboflavin . . . . . . . . . . . 0.236 mg.
Niacin . . . . . . . . . . . . . . 0.098 mg.
Ascorbic Acid . . . . . . . . . . 0 mg.

This diagram shows the amounts of protein you would gain by taking enough of these foods to get 100 calories from each.

# THE COLD RUSH

A modern drive-in. One of
Baskin-Robbins' dipping counters
with the usual row of one-armed
"school chairs."

How big is big enough? How big is too big? I suppose when the bigness can't carry its true size and weight. We are all familiar with this in our experience of, say, organizations we've belonged to, or in something like ordinary packaging where the container exceeds reasonable space requirements for the thing contained. In the world of ice cream this holds just as true. Lately, some of the finest makers of ice cream (and, let me repeat, related frozen products) have found it economically sensible and, they insist, technically possible to expand their operations greatly without compromising their standards. Thinking of some of the better California wine producers, involved in the very same thing, I'm inclined to believe them – *some* at least.

As I have brought up California let me begin there in this picture of a kind of Cold Rush, a Gold Rush in reverse.

Baskin-Robbins has numberless champions. It is an enormous operation (over 1,400 outlets as of early 1975), enormously successful. Gael Greene goes so far as to write, "If I have only one life to live. Let me live it next door to Baskin-Robbins and its incredible changing parade of 31 flavors." (For a discussion of flavors see page 146). She goes on to list some of them, using exalted adjectives like "beloved" and "noble". Rather endearing reporter's hyperbole. B-R was not yet in Manhattan at the time (1971) (it is now) and Ms. Greene drove to a Forest Hills place where she was a bit disillusioned. This is in New York don't forget. B-R does not have quite that high a reputation in San Francisco where companies like Swensen's and Dreyer's have tended to establish tasters' criteria. (Nor in Los Angeles evidently. Christy/Baldwin judged it worth only two stars and complained of its "clinical plastic scene" with one mere row of school desk chairs by way of seating facilities). This may not be quite fair as some of the very finest ice cream and sherbet is scooped-out at what the industry calls "dipping stores" – with not a chair in sight.

Truth to tell, Baskin-Robbins is an amazing organization. Burt Baskin was in charge of a PX in the New Hebrides during World War II and got the idea of trading a jeep for a big freezer from a visiting aircraft carrier. He also got the idea of trying some of the exotic local fruits for the first-ever time as flavors for ice cream. Irvine Robbins, the son of a Tacoma, Washington dairy owner, teamed up with Baskin after the war and the two opened their first store in Glendale, California. The company has grown steadily and now has stores in 39 states with new ones opening all the time. There are a goodly number in Canada as well and 22 have opened in Japan with 20 more scheduled. Until now the Japanese consumer has had few flavors to choose from beyond the Big Three. 1973 figures reveal total retail sales of over $80,000,000. The first European outlet has been opened in Brussels. In 1967 the United Fruit Company bought out Baskin-Robbins. In 1974 the company was bought by the English J. Lyons Group. It will be interesting to see if London and other parts of the United Kingdom will soon be enjoying "31 Flavors" in what *Time* Magazine described as "polka-dotted pleasure palaces".

Dreyer's has another of those colorful (flavorful?) beginnings that seem to be connected with makers of frozen desserts. William Dreyer was an 18-year-old pot washer on the S. S. Leviaton in 1905 when he was asked by the captain to invent something to celebrate the ship's arrival in New York harbor. He found some fresh fruit, sugar, gelatin and rock salt for freezing and came up with a dessert that was a pronounced success. Five years later he joined the National Ice Cream Company in San Francisco and later

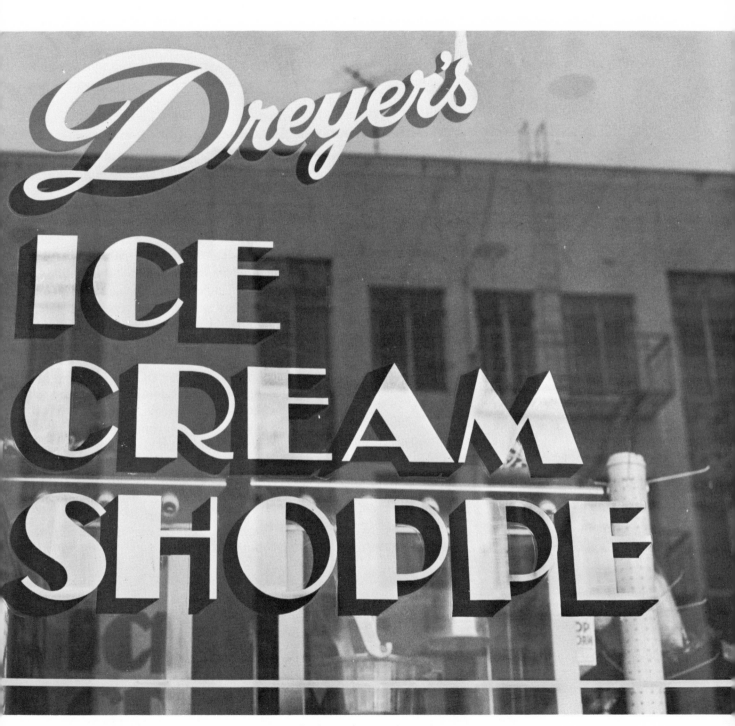

Window sign of Dreyer's home-office shop in Oakland, California with its Art Deco-type lettering.

A fun couple, 1920's style, cavorts on the cover of Dreyer's menu.

worked for the Peerless Ice Cream Company in Sacramento. In 1920 he was named Professor of Advanced Ice Cream Manufacturing at the University of California at Davis. He decided to open his own Grand Ice Cream Company in 1928 – the "grand" a pun on his location on Grand Avenue in Oakland (across the bay from San Francisco) and his estimation of his product. He went on to invent three famous flavors: Toasted Almond, Candy Mint (called peppermint stick by some), and Rocky Road. The last has a most domestic history. It seems the marshmallow part of it – the others are chocolate ice cream and nuts – was created with the aid of Mrs. Dreyer's scissors, which he borrowed to cut marshmallows into little pieces. Kenneth M. Cook is the present owner-president and rather charmingly maintains a desk for Mr. Dreyer who is in his late 80's. More than 30 flavors are now made and packaged in a spanking new plant. In 1973 one million gallons were produced and another 250,000 were expected to be added to that number in 1974.

Vanilla is the all-time favorite. Cook has come up with a successful Bavarian Cheese Cake: cream, cheese, almond crunch ice cream. Dreyer's superb ice cream is made from butterfat from 40 per cent cream and non-fat milk solids from skim milk. Percentage of butterfat differs (as ideally it should) from flavor to flavor: 16 per cent in vanilla, 14 per cent in chocolate, 12 per cent in

The Tricycle Man on his appointed rounds in London – the British equivalent of the Good Humor Man in the U.S. In the background, the Law Courts.

162

fruit flavors – altogether, "in excess of eight different blends." Sugar is a blend of liquid cane and corn. Again the degree of sweetness depends on the flavor – from 15 to 16½ per cent – they do not like to "over-use sugar." Only pure natural and fresh products (this admittedly includes an Americanism in the idea of "fresh frozen") are used. No imitation flavorings to increase flavor are introduced.

Dreyer's has hundreds of outlets in California (to my surprise I learned that these include the two remaining San Francisco Blums). Through Government Commissaries their ice cream is sent to Japan, Korea, the Marshall Islands, the Marianas. Franchised manufacturers distribute their frozen desserts to Taiwan and Hong Kong. You can even buy Dreyer's ice creams in Cape Town. For quite a number of years they have been providing frozen delights for shipping lines such as Pacific Far East, Royal Viking and the Trans-Pacific Transportation Co.

Another of the quality California companies busy expending is Swensen's, which didn't "happen" until 1948 – twenty years later than Dreyer's. Nothing late-comer about its ice cream though. Earle Swensen opened his first store (a "dipping shop") on the corner of Union and Hyde on Russian Hill in San Francisco and it's still going strong. When I first worked in San Francisco I remember *looking forward* to going to the dentist's because, to get home, I had to climb the steep hill along Union Street which took me right passed Swensen's. Naturally I would join the line to wait for a cone of Wild Mountain Blackberry or Fresh Banana. I learned early to ask only for a single dip because several times my receipt slip showed a red star – which meant a free cone of my choice (alas, the red stars have disappeared). For the last half-dozen years Swensen's has been opening what they call "ice cream factories" from Alaska to Mexico to the

District of Columbia. There are nearly a hundred franchises now and they are quite carefully controlled, from the manufacture of the ice creams and sherbets – on the premises – to their presentation, the menus, general decor (lazy-day ceiling fans, neo-Tiffany lamps, marble-topped tables). These are counter and sit-down parlors. Mr. Swensen still maintains four dipping shops on his own. The franchise operation, badly floundering on its first try, was saved and made successful by William A. Meyer who jumped at the chance to buy it in 1969. "It's very rare that you can own something that is the very best there is", is the way he enthusiastically and quite rightly puts it.

Swensen insisted from the very beginning on nothing but the very best – sweeteners, flavors, emulsifiers, stabilizers – and limited himself to making only 20 quarts at a time. Their butterfat content averages 14 per cent. One-scoop cones were, and are, a quarter-pound in weight. Two scoops measure at half a pound. Hand-packed quarts weigh two pounds – a half-pound more than "ordinary ice cream." Dipping out ice cream and sherbet (no necessity for sauces or other embellishments) to his connoisseur customers Swensen developed 150 flavors of his own. The franchises still mix only 20 quarts at a time and the flavors are all made from Swensen's formulae (Mr. Swensen remains thoroughly involved as a consultant). With winning purism only sandwiches and salads are offered in Swensen Ice Cream Factories. (There is argument that cooked food affects the taste of ice cream.)

Not surprisingly, Christy/Baldwin award Swensen's L. A. branch four stars for "delectable" ice cream, four more for "luscious" hot fudge sundaes – "the prettiest in town": glass dish on glass plate on lace-paper doily. It is reported that organic ice cream is "forthcoming" (fad gilding the already gloriously golden?)

Often companies with which a member of the founding family is still actively associated are noteworthy for the consistency of their character. Carnation is presided over by Dwight L. Stuart, the grandson of Elbridge A. Stuart who began it all in 1899.

Again there is a story. Stuart, with an associate, bought a bankrupt milk plant in Kent, Washington and hired a Swiss to evaporate milk. Cans were a major problem so they made their own – by hand. The cans were filled and nailed into cases. Another problem arose: no one wanted them: previously, the poor canning had often led to spoilage. Besides, people thought evaporated milk was something you took on a safari or up a mountain and bought when you couldn't get "real" milk. Mr. Stuart's partner bowed out. It took several years for the Swiss gentleman to perfect the evaporation and sterilizing process which Stuart then bought from him. Then began a long struggle to sell the new product. Orders were sometimes as small as six cans at a time. Of course today the company is selling its product worldwide and is the top selling brand in the United States. And in 1974 it celebrated its 75th Anniversary.

Carnation's entrance into the "cold sweets" field is relatively recent and restricted, so far, to restaurants in Arizona, Texas (12), Colorado, and California (6). The one in Los Angeles is rated three stars (on the C/B scale) for a smooth and creamy ice cream, not too heavy. Real whipped cream (a crucial test) tops a *four*-star hot fudge sundae with a "divinely textured" sauce. Thick sodas are the standard.

Still on the West Coast we come to Farrell's, started by Bob Farrell and Ken McCarthy in Portland, Oregon in 1963. Spreading fast throughout the U.S. and Canada, they are now part of the mammoth Marriott organization of hotels and restaurants and expect to nearly

Showbiz presentation by boatered and gartered waiters of a Farrell's super spectacular: Farrell's Zoo – eight ice creams, three sherbets, five toppings, whipped cream, cherries, almonds and bananas. "Serves one to ten."

double their number of "fun food parlours" to around 150 during 1975. Showmanship is the pitch, with emphasis on nostalgia and laughs. Jokey menus. Kids *do* love the free sundae offered on their birthdays and the exuberant, Gay 90's, bass-drum escorted, boater-hatted, two-man-delivered extravaganza named Farrell's Zoo: "EIGHT flavors of our famous ice cream; THREE natural fruit flavor sherbets; FIVE different and delicious toppings; whipped cream; cherries; almonds and bananas. (Serves one to ten)." C/B in *Los Angeles* award them two stars. Butterfat runs 14 per cent but results seem overly airy. Whipped cream is canned. The sherbets taste artificial.

Before moving to the Northwest Bob Farrell worked for Howard Johnson's on the East Coast. Howard Deering Johnson started making his own ice cream in the basement of his patent-medicine store in Wollaston, Massachusetts near Boston. The year was 1925 – making Johnson's another of the 50-year-olds. He also sold newspapers, tobacco, and other items (very much like his British counterparts today). From the start his ice cream contained "double the usual butterfat content" and was noted for its quality ingredients. Thus appeared the "Wonderful World of 28 Flavors." Johnson initiated a series of agreements in which he supplied his product and name to individuals for a fee – supposedly the beginning of the franchise concept. Today restaurants are either company operated or under license by independents. The chain has grown to include outlets in 42 states, Canada and Puerto Rico. I remember driving from New York to Los Angeles in the 50's, barreling along the superhighway (we were in a hurry) where the only places to eat seemed to be a succession of distinctive orange and aqua Howard Johnsons which appeared with rhythmic regularity like shrines in the Alps. I will not comment on the food (let me just pass on the found-to-be-sound advice given me by a number of foreign friends about *all* mass-produced food in U.S. restaurants: the safest things to order are breakfast, bacon-lettuce-and-tomato sandwiches, and hamburgers more or less in that order), but the ice cream was, and is, extremely good (three stars on the C/B scale in L.A.). Butterfat content is still "right." Flavorings are superior – Dutch-process chocolate from Holland; Bourbon vanilla beans from Madagascar; coffee from Brazil; pistachios from Afghanistan; Georgia peaches and pecans; Coconut from Hawaii; blueberries from Nova Scotia, etc. For years the delightful sign showing a little boy and his dog being served by Simple Simon was the *sure* sign for Howard Johnson's. These can still be seen here and there (there's a great one in New York City in the heart of the Broadway theater district), but renovated locations and all new sites have exchanged it for a more modern abstraction of the Johnson's roof-and-steeple motif.

The mid-western, Chicago-based company run by the Bresler family is one of the front runners in the numerical flavor race – something over 300 at present. It all began in that curiously creative and resourceful era known as The Depression when ice cream had just found its way onto the Stock Exchange and Prohibition had done wonders for business only to end with the repeal of Prohibition and a devastating drop in production from 1929 to 1933. For some reason, in the spring of 1930 two of Sam Bresler's sons – William and David – launched the Good Time Ice Cream Company. They were clever enough to peddle their ice cream – which they packaged themselves but didn't make – earlier in the season than their competitors. The success of that first effort led to a series of moves and changes until the family bought out a small company in Arlington Heights, Illinois and began wholesale

In 1925 Howard Johnson began making ice cream in this corner store in Wollaston, Massachusetts. "Flips, fizzes, cones and college ices" were among the goodies offered.

JOHNSON'S
SODA CANDY
Restaurant
SODA
HOWARD JOHNSON'S FAMOUS ICE CR
HOME MADE ICE CREAM
CIGARS
MAGAZINES
OFFICE

manufacture themselves. They took the name Paradise Ice Cream Co. and began distributing their product to drugstores, confectioners, delicatessens, lunch rooms and roadside stands. Electric freezer cabinets were very expensive in those days and the dealers' non-electric units had to be serviced daily. Bill Bresler got up every morning at four, drove 30 miles to Crystal Lake to buy 400-pound cakes of ice which were then taken back to the plant and cut into 50-pound cakes to be loaded back onto the truck and taken to the dealers. Another problem the brothers had to deal with was the ammonia ice machine which had to be constantly watched. Bill and Dave took turns sleeping in the truck and getting up hourly to check gauges and temperatures. Dave was even accidentally locked in the sub-zero hardening room one night; he luckily pounded a hole in the cement and cork wall with a metal container in time to get out.

The whole family was involved by now, including 11-year-old Charles, and it was decided that they had to enter the greater Chicago market. This they did by getting together with an independent group of 50 drugstores, and by 1932 they had moved to a larger facility and increased their staff. They also started their own chain of retail outlets called "Jack and Jill" which reached as many as 70 units during the summer months. The company moved to its present location on West Belden Avenue in 1942 and, with the return from the war of Fred and Charles in 1945, finally changed its name to the Bresler Ice Cream Company. Volume passed the one-million-gallon mark. That figure rose by 500,000 in 1956. Stanley Bresler brought the third generation into the picture that same year. The following year saw the purchase of the Legion Ice Cream Co. and a subsequent volume increase to two million gallons making the company the top independent

The Simple Simon motif seems to
have survived at this motor lodge
version of Howard Johnson's. It
can be seen both on the front of the
building to the right of the
entrance and, most delightfully, as
a weather vane atop the steeple.

Plant and retail store of the Carnation Company in Muskogee, Oklahoma.

in the Chicago area. The numbers game came next with the beginning of the 33 Flavors Ice Cream Shops franchise program in Bresler's 33rd year which has spread to 25 states and Canada with new stores being added weekly. Production figures are now *three* million gallons annually.

Yet another family-oriented company is Penn Dairies, Inc. of Lancaster, Pennsylvania, started 85 years ago when Eli L. Garber invested in a small creamery in Stevens, Pennsylvania. A series of mergers followed, including the Lancaster Sanitary Milk Corp., the Ideal Milk Products Corp., and the York Sanitary Milk Co. Two ice cream companies were also added – Breuninger Bros. and W. R. Smith & Sons. The present company was incorporated in 1929 and the trade name "Pensupreme" adopted. Previous trade names such as "Ideal" and "Purity" were being discontinued.

Over the course of the years Penn Dairies in its various forms produced pasteurized milk in 1900; ice cream, beginning in 1904; installed the first condensing plant in 1912; changed from ice to iceless cabinets in 1927; and installed the first freezing tunnel for quick freezing in 1937. The company also introduced tuberculin testing of cows well before it became mandatory.

Today, Eli Garber's grandson, John F. Garber Jr., is president of the recently expanded firm, now a completely automated plant of 160,000

The Carnation ice cream parlor at Disneyland, along with a marvelous old delivery truck.

square feet with an ice cream production of six million gallons a year. Products reach markets extending from Connecticut to North Carolina to Ohio. A chain of retail outlets has been opened – over thirty so far – called Grocerettes, "neighborhood convenience stores," open 7 A.M. to 11 P.M. seven days a week, which stock grocery items, magazines, soft drinks, and snacks along with Pensupreme products. Very much like the shops throughout Britain as a matter of fact. A number of "Ice Cream Shoppes" have also been opened which feature ice cream specialties, desserts, and a sandwich and platter menu.

In addition to the 12-pack and 6-pack cartons of things like fudge bars, ice cream sandwiches, "Penfrosties" which Pensupreme manufactures, to celebrate the 1976 Bicentenary are bringing out "Red Coats", "Spirit of '76", "Paul Revere's Rounds", "Boston TEA Party TWIN" – all forms of coated ice cream on sticks – under the over-all promotional title, "Revolutionary Treats".

Foremost Dairies Inc. was established in 1931 in Jacksonville, Florida. It was an outgrowth of a firm started by J. C. Penny in the late 20's and named for his prize Guernsey bulls, "Foremost." In 1951 the company combined with two others to become Foremost International. It has gone on merging ever since and is now known as Foremost-McKesson, a corporation distributing drugs, alcoholic beverages and chemicals. It also supplies whey by-products, processes water, and distributes fresh dairy products (in the western U.S.). The two companies date back to 1933 and reported sales of $1.7 billion for 1971. A curious thing about one or two names which appear on mimeographed "Flavor Parade" issued for January and February, 1975, and listed ice cream flavors produced in the San Francisco area, is

their connection with Foremost. Sara Lee, only just entering ice cream manufacturing.

By now Jane Howard's remark in *Life* magazine (see page 239) that if she were "being executed tomorrow morning, what I'd order for dessert tonight would be a dish of Coffee Haagen-Daz" has reportedly become their advertising slogan. Ms. Howard also comments on the *faux* Scandinavianism of it: it's made in the Bronx. But there's evidently more to say. Ms. Greene (*New York*) refers to Häagen-Daz (she puts in the two dots) fans as heads" – a supportive, not to say sporting, noun in the game of associating ice cream with addiction. She also tells of "periodic mainlining" by one Ali MacGraw while Ms. MacGraw was filming in New York. The heaviness of H-D evidently angers the competition. Heaviness means less air (overrun), which is unconventional and requires more of *other* things, like ingredients (a pint of Coffee H-D weighs $17\frac{3}{4}$ ounces for example). Not a great number of flavors (eight including "organic honey" and "organic carob" – a big brown peapod) but they're not in that race. Their Boysenberry sherbet is sure lavender but I love it.

Frankly I feel H-D should be included in another section I'm calling "Shepherds of Perfection" (as should one or two others like Swenson's), but I've only seen it in places like supermarkets and delicatessens. I *did* notice a pretty fake stained-glass sign reading *Haagen-Daz* over a tiny shop on Christopher Street in Greenwich Village and I read in the *New Yorker* a report dated August 19, 1974 about a Haagen-Daz dipping store opened on East 69th Street by a Gary Ferguson who is up to a couple of other things too. Like running the Cosmic Motorcycle Messenger Company and perfecting a machine for making 10,000 flavors.

The charming trademark long associated with Howard Johnso showing Simple Simon offering ice cream to a little boy and his d Examples of this sign can still be seen, but it is being replaced b modern image of the distinctive Johnson's roof & steeple symb

# BAR ROOM BAROQUE
## CONTEMPORARY Compromise

The new look in ice cream parlors (or, if you *must,* "parlours") usually manages to combine real marble, classic bentwood chairs, etched mirrors, Tiffany-inspired lighting fixtures; things like antique clocks, real flowers, truly old-fashioned candies, lazy-day overhead fans, and come up with a neo-nostalgia that is pseudo-revival and might as well *be* the merely formalized formica, real reproductions, lollipop Tiffany and movie marquee lighting they usually are. It would be stupid to hope for the authentically contemporary, the truly new. That would be like asking for clothes that don't keep harking-back. Or opera houses that don't. We seem to be living in a strange time filled with slightly-off recreations. Thanks anyway for the live flowers (when included), the often charming wallpaper or menu, and the honestly new ice cream.

Ice Cream Soda fountain at the Philadelphia Exhibition.

**ABOVE**
Helmbold's Drugstore on Broadway, New York City. It's hard to believe that this dates from the same period as Bailey's in Boston.
*The New York Historical Society.*

**RIGHT**
Doumar's soda fountain, Norfolk, Virginia in 1912. Leaning on the counter, Charles Doumar (disputed inventor of the ice cream cone). All set to serve from behind the high altar of goodies; John, his 16-year-old son.
*Doumar's*

**PAGES 180-181**
Original soda fountain built by Bailey's in Boston in 1873. The photograph dramatically proves that not everyone was going in for fantasy extravaganzas. The effect here is of visual coolness, distinctly "modern" in its lack of clutter.
*Baileys*

**PAGE 182**
A bit of barroom syndrome counterpoints the totally modern counter, stools, lighting fixtures, and floor of this fountain in Oakland, California – one of Carnation's first, acquired in 1929.
*Carnation Company*

**PAGE 183**
The Fortnum Fountain at Fortnum & Mason. A refreshingly contemporary place, full of pretty details.
*Fortnum & Mason*

**PAGE 184**
A Swensen's Ice Cream Factory. Note the tantalizing photograph of one of their concoctions.
*Swensen's*

**PAGE 185**
The old-fashioned sweet shop updated: Dreyer's ice cream store featuring ice cream, candies, gifts and sweets.
*Dreyer's Grand Ice Cream Company*

**PAGE 186 (TOP)**
A Bresler's "dipping shop" in a shopping complex – a mixture of functional modern and "gaslight" nostalgia.
*Bresler's 33 Flavors*

**PAGE 186 (BOTTOM)**
A typical Baskin-Robbins "dipping shop." Fresh, bright and designed to "keep the lines moving."
*Baskin-Robbins*

**PAGE 187**
Two ultra-modern Italian establishments, Veneta in Lucca and Grasso in Milan. Both outfitted by COF Refrigerazione of Lucca.

178

VENETA - LUC...

# Il gusto di arredare il freddo

GRASSO - MILA...

AN IMAGINARY SODA

In the 1930s Thorton Wilder was impatient with most of what he saw in the American Theatre. He wanted something sparer and more directly related to the lives of ordinary people. He readied himself as a playwright by writing a series of short plays – a number remarkably lasting only three minutes – without any limitations as to location, subject, number of performers, etc. This discipline of freedom led him to write his world-famous play "Our Town" in which he examined some of the inhabitants of a small town.

The play requires no scenery and the merest number of props. Its mood is that of sentiment, its form simplicity, but tempered by the abstraction of its setting and the universality of its theme of love and separation. Typical of its action are the scenes of a moonlit conversation from neighboring homes between a boy and a girl, their second-storey rooms represented by two stepladders some distance apart; the dead in the cemetery sitting on chairs and holding umbrellas against the rain; and the following scene in which the soda fountain is represented by some stools and a wooden plank, and the druggist by the character called The Stage Manager who assumes various roles and acts as a kind of chorus throughout the play. In one scene Emily tells George that she can now see that something they've been discussing isn't the truth and that she feels it isn't important. George responds by asking her if she would like an ice cream soda "or something." Emily says she would, and thanks him. Before they enter an imaginary drugstore, George exchanges remarks with several imaginary passers-by. Emily is emotionally upset and the Stage Manager – who has become Mr. Morgan the druggist – asks her what she's been crying about. George tries to explain by telling a fib about Emily's almost being run over. The Stage manager offers Emily a drink of water and remarks as how you have to look both ways before crossing the street nowadays. He asks her what she'll have and she politely orders an inexpensive strawberry phosphate. But George insists she join him in having an ice cream soda. The Stage manager talks on about the appearance of "auto-mo-biles" in Grover's Corners and the days when a dog could sleep all day in the middle of Main Street. Emily comments on how expensive their sodas are and George tells her they're celebrating – her election at school and something else as well: they're celebrating because he's got a friend who tells him everything. Emily protests (she had criticized him earlier), but George insists that she was right and that he is grateful. He then asks her if she'll write him "once in a while" while he's away at college. Emily says she will, but cleverly adds that maybe after a time, letters from Grover's Corners might not be "so interesting." George say that that could never happen to him. Whereupon Emily adds that she'll try to make her letters interesting.

Of course the whole "action" lies in the unspoken dialogue that passes between them, beneath the surface commonplaces and social gestures.

The scene ends with George telling Emily he wonders if it's so important to go to Agricultural School in order to become a farmer. His Uncle Luke is getting old and there are government pamphlets to tell farmers all they need to know and he guesses that "new people aren't any better than old ones". By the time he finishes – interrupted once by Emily – he has made up his mind not to go away and to tell his Pa about it that very night.

Collins Pharmacy, Islip, Long Island. c.1900

# SHEPHERDS OF

PART 2 – BRITAIN & THE CONTINENT

In England there have been similar stories of smaller, family-owned businesses which have flourished through insistence on the highest standards. Bertorelli's is one. Although part of the Lyons Maid group (housed in the delightfully named Glacier House in London) which includes such other names as Cornish Cream, Eldorado, Mister Softee, Tastee Freeze and Tonibell, it hasn't shown any signs of being "taken over" after ten years and indeed one suspects that it was added to the larger company just because of its high reputation (the highly praised Baskin-

Robbins has also become part of the Lyons organization recently).

Bertorelli began its ice cream life more than 25 years ago when Remo and Leo Bertorelli came out of the army. The brothers found themselves "surplus" as far as the family business went and, as Leo candidly tells it, "Someone had the bright idea of putting us into the ice cream trade. After all, we knew nothing about it." Hard to believe when one learns that by 1949 they were turning out hundreds of gallons of ice cream daily in an installation with a floor space measuring no more

# PERFECTION

than 18 x 12 feet.

After a brief hiatus of two years brought on by family differences, the brothers returned in 1952 determined to do things the right way. They both agreed that they could not compete with the big national firms and that the thing to do was to specialize in high quality ice cream for the London area. They reduced their staff by more than half and trimmed their retail trade to become primarily wholesalers. With the end of sugar rationing in 1953 they began making ice cream of ultra-high quality for use by caterers.

Since that time they have become a prize-winning firm – even for their packaging and advertising (their point-of-sales material captured the Gold Scoop International Award of America in 1968).

For years Bertorelli's was noted for its specials such as elaborate gateaux and sculptures. They even produced an ice cream Venus de Milo which nearly came to disaster after two freezing weeks of work (at 20 below zero) when newspaper photographer's lights nearly melted her away. They have fashioned everything from dogs to airplanes, football boots and foxes. For a charity party Leo came up with sausages (honey nut ice cream with a brown coloring), and eggs (pra line-coated ice cream with zabaglione) complete with salt (sugar) and pepper (ground nuts). They've even done fish-and-chips and spaghetti (Mama mia!). Tony Quinell, a member of the firm for years, even created a mauve Rolls Royce for a dinner party for the Shah of Persia, not to mention an oil tanker for an oil company and a model of a field gun for the Royal Tournament.

In 1956, Remo went to India along with one of the company's refrigeration engineers at the invitation of two owners of a restaurant chain who wanted to make ice cream in Bombay. The company was Kwality Ices, now the biggest in India. Remo had gone initially for six weeks, but ended up staying nearly 12 years. In 1967 Bertorelli launched a new luxury range. 1968 brought fire which badly damaged their factory and caused them to move to Kentish Town. That same year, Leo's wife Mary was made Sales Manager. They moved to Boreham Wood in Hertfordshire in 1970 and arranged with Midland Counties Ice Cream (another member of the Glacier Group) for wider distribution through their network of depots. They left Hertfordshire in early 1975 to establish headquarters at Glacier House.

Among the company's super specialities are Orange and Lemon "Surprises" – orange or lemon sherbet packed into fresh fruit skins. To help in the process of making the "Surprises" they recently bought one of the world's first fruit-scooping machines from Italy. The machine can scoop out 2,400 lemons or 3,000 oranges per hour which should help to satisfy customers at Harrods or any one of the many top stores and restaurants where Bertorelli's ice creams are sold.

Two very new companies are Loseley and The New England Ice Cream Company. Loseley's have been making dairy cream ices since 1969 on their 15,000 acre farm stocked with a prize Jersey herd of 800 cattle. The farm is part of an estate crowned by a beautiful Elizabethan Manor House built by Sir William More, a direct ancestor of the present owner, between 1562-1568. (The house, an official "stately home," is open to the public from June to September.) The farm is located in Guildford, Surrey and is the center from which live yoghourts, cream ices, cream, curd cheese, etc., are sent to outlets such as Harrods, Jacksons of Piccadilly, Fenwick's in Bond Street, Moore Bros. of Sloane Street; The Army and Navy Stores; Grants of Croydon; Fortnum & Mason; Justin de Blank; Habitat Restaurants; Selfridges, etc. – about 300 outlets, mainly in London. But routes also go to the South Coast, as far as East Grinstead, and west to Alton, Chichester, Reading, Henley and Great Missenden, "and all stops in between."

No artificial colors or flavors are used and only original recipes are followed. Because only rich cream and milk from the Jersey herd, along with other pure ingredients, including raw brown sugar, are used, Loseley's ice creams have found favor with many health-food shops such as Cranks and Wholefood in London. Available flavors are Old Fashioned Vanilla, Montezuma Chocolate, Brazilian Mocha, Fresh Orange, and Acacia Honey & Stem Ginger. Ice cream gateaux and sherbets have been announced as upcoming at the time of this writing.

The New England Ice Cream Company has been selling ice cream only since 1973 and is the brainchild of an American named William Blackburn. Mr. Blackburn, an advertising man in London for the past dozen years, doesn't believe in British ice creams, which he has been quoted in The Financial Times as saying "wouldn't be allowed on the U.S. market because of their high vegetable fat content." N.E.I.C. is made from plenty of real cream by a dairy in Devon* and sold at over 80 outlets including Harrods, Jacksons of Piccadilly, Cullens, Fortnum & Mason, Selfridges, and is inching out into the London suburbs: Waitrose in East Sheen,

---

* Pollard Confections Limited of Newton Abbot, ice cream makers for nearly 50 years. Donald Ollard told a reporter on the *Western Plymouth Independent* that the ice cream is quite unlike the usual British type. "We took a chance when we started manufacturing it. But now we're very proud of our 'American' ice cream. It's made with a high content of real cream . . ."

Bertorelli

Diana Dors, three feet high and dressed in a mink bikini – *all* made of ice cream by Bertorelli's in the star-struck 50's.

Bentalls in Kingston, Buylate in Putney, and so on. At least two fine restaurants – Carrier's and Leith's – are enthusiastic about it. The packaging is charming: a drawing of a cottage. Colors: red, white and blue of course.

The lack of any "intense pleasure" on the part of the British when it comes to ice cream is, according to Blackburn, understandable given what they're used to. This is of course highly debatable. But the low British consumption, one-eighth of that of Americans, may well change once they try N.E.I.C. vanilla, or Dutch chocolate, green peppermint, wild blueberry or Vermont maple pecan. The chocolate comes from Holland. Colombia coffee beans enrich the coffee. From the U.S. come the blueberries (Maine), pecans (South Carolina), and maple syrup (Vermont).

Blackburn may be attempting to carry fineness to France, but he intends to tackle Paris (where the splendid ice cream is splendidly expensive) and after that Copenhagen and certain German cities.

Fortnum's Fountain is one of the very few actual ice cream parlors in London. It is located on the ground floor of the famous specialty store which made its bow in Piccadilly 250 years ago. The Fountain serves delicious food and some marvelous fountain drinks and sundaes. Their fruit syrups, fudge sauces, etc. are their own, but the ice cream is Bertorelli's. In the store proper one can buy in bulk such premium ice creams as the aforementioned Bertorelli, Loseley, and New England. Among the exoticisms are "Bracers" – ice cream whipped with egg; "Peg's Fancy" – a frappe blend of raspberry and strawberry ice cream; numerous superior sundaes. Among them:

San Tropez – vanilla ice cream, pineapple and orange sorbet, with mandarin oranges, pineapple and banana

Knickerbocker Glory – vanilla and strawberry ices with raspberries, and chunky pineapple, cherries and whipped cream

Fortnum's Fancy – mandarin oranges, orange sorbet and vanilla ice cream and ginger syrup

193

A sculptor at Bertorelli's putting the finishing touches on a curious-looking warrior. The company's been known to sculpt everything from Rolls Royces to sausages and eggs.

Happy Pair – vanilla ice cream and raspberry sorbet, raspberries and whipped cream

Black Velvet – blackcurrent and vanilla ice cream, blackcurrants in heavy syrup and whipped cream topped with broken meringue

In 1974, *Nova,* as is such fashionable magazine's wont, did a sort of "nice ice" guide which dealt mostly with London. Fortnum & Mason are praised particularly for their "Knickerbocker Glory" (see above), Harrods' black current sorbet and port-and-melon water ice are singled out. Also praised: Bertorelli (see page 191); Bernigra Ices, Tottenham Court Road– "a most delicious find," who make 20 varieties on the premises (walnut and zabaglione singled out); Hard Rock Cafe, Piccadilly – a "divinely rich" Hard Rock Old Time County Ice Cream, "double-quantity egg yolk and butter"; Marine Ices "takes a lot of beating" – recommended especially: their fruit water ices; and G. Coletta – "top of the trade ice cream polls". In far-away Scotland, Luca's of Musselburgh is highly

recommended for their vanilla and strawberry.

A leading English sculptor and an even more leading British writer both join a number of the *cognoscenti* in claiming Marine Ices as the best ice cream made in the U.K. The firm is adamant about serving only the central London area. Two of the few ice cream parlors in London serve their ice cream – their own, at Chalk Farm near the Round House, and The Ice Dream Parlour on Fulham Road. In 1974 Marine Ices won the international ice cream competition in Milan. Eighty samples were entered from a number of countries – thirty-five from Britain. Besides the gold medal, Marine Ices won a cup presented by the *Gelaterie Italiani*, a trade journal. Bernigra and Gallone also were prizewinners.

In the summer of 1973 The Times Diary (London) added its voice, reporting the findings of Mirabel Cecil in her search for "the sensuous ice cream." The Dusty Road and Banana Boat at Fortnum & Mason's upstairs Patio bar came up to "expectations" and would be "perfect for a secret eater in search of consolation." "Immobilizing and satisfying." Bertorelli's restaurant (a different branch of the family) provided "good but unmemorable" Zabaglione and Melastrega. And their Bomba Sophia "tasted like nothing and nobody asked for more." (The ice cream Bertorellis supply Fortnum & Mason.) Marine Ices at Chalk Farm was found to be an "unadorned haven" with its "Vesuvius" — chocolate, vanilla, sponge cake soaked in marsala, morello cherries, marrons glace, crushed meringue, and whipped cream – a "rich, light, amazing kaleidoscope of delights – a glutton's dream." Their *Bombes* were smothered in too much whipped cream. Their creme de menthe was a vivid green. Rum and butter was "rose-pink with a lingering after-taste." Tangerine ice was "straight" and the grapefruit ice, "unalloyed purity."

A taste of Loseley Farm's Acacia Honey and Stem Ginger was "delicious, dreamy while not too heavy." Yogice (Fordhall's organic farm) wild blackberry liqueur and honey turned out to have "no trace of any liqueur." The ice cream at a Wimpy Bar was reportedly a disaster. The ungenerous portion of coffee granita served at the Ice Dream Parlour tasted "fine and refreshing," but was "ruined by tasteless whipped cream." New England Ice Cream, only just beginning in 1973, was found to sell a vanilla that was

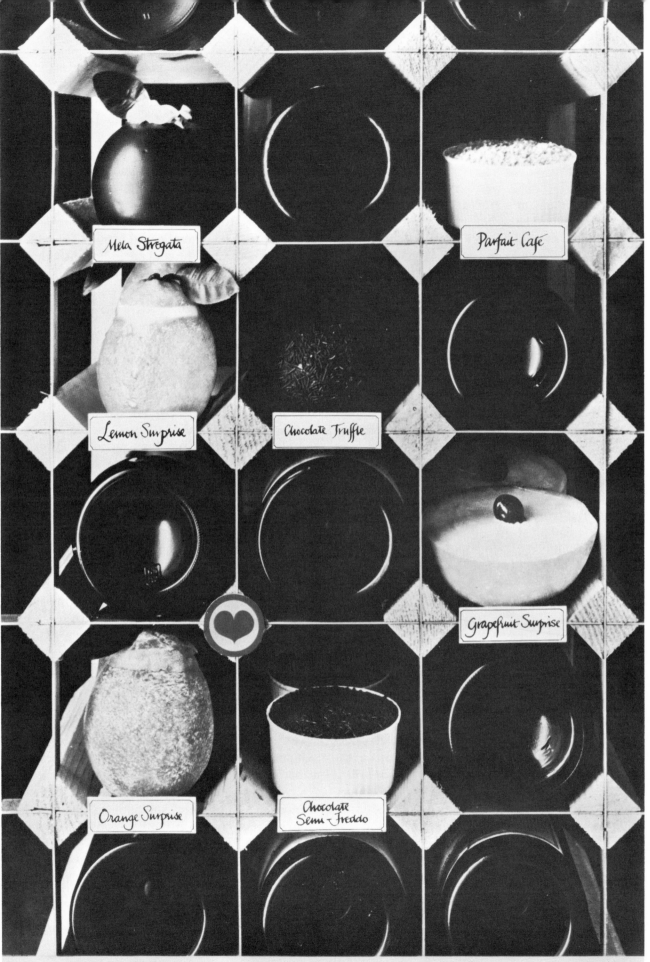

Mela Stregata

Parfait Café

Lemon Surprise

Chocolate Truffle

Grapefruit Surprise

Orange Surprise

Chocolate
Semi-Freddo

# Bertorelli

individual ice creams

"sensuous, nay, positively voluptuous, but lacking in flavor – not a thriller." Justin de Blank's bitter lemon cream was "absolutely yum yum." Borza's near the seafront at Eastbourne wasn't bad, especially the vanilla, but on the whole, heavy in flavor and "unharmonious." Marcari's had a "delicious sorbet" – refreshing, colorful, and natural. Things were very bad at Brighton with the ice cream served at Forte's "tasteless." Lorier strawberry sherbet imported from France was "quite superb" – packed with a light fresh fruit, pretty in color, and with a fine after-taste. *The Times* found Olympic Cafe in Musselburgh, Scotland "generally poor" and judged it "not worth a detour." A Q.C. was quoted as recommending Annabel's marmalade and bitter chocolate ice creams as was the champagne sherbet at the Capital Hotel in Basil Street.

Robert Carrier, who should know, mentions nostalgically how Gunters used to make their own fresh fruit ice cream in London and many Paris shops still do. He believes that perfection can be achieved only if you make your own ice cream. I'm not so sure. The do-it-yourself school tends to overstate its case. If by "you" you mean Paul Bocuse or Mme. Poiret, by all means go ahead. But it seems to me the "yourself" doing it has a great deal to do with the degree of perfection that can be achieved. I've suffered an awful lot of lousy home cooking – including desserts.

But let's not quibble. Mr. Carrier is a dream of a food writer and I've tended to trust him ever since reading a piece he did for the London *Sunday Times* in which he praised some Paris bistros, then little known – including one I'd eaten in daily for months. As could also be expected from a non-victim of fashion – how could one think of going to St. Tropez in the summer! – Mr. Carrier surprises us. He describes the place that produces the "best ices in the world" in his classic *Great Dishes of the World* as follows: "In a side turning at the end of the port, Mme. Lamponi makes ice cream of such perfection that her customers have been down on bended knees, begging her to open in Paris. They have promised her backing ... a clientele, but nothing will budge her. As the last yacht leaves the harbor in the autumn, she puts up her shutters and firmly remains closed until spring ... Then she opens again and all summer long a procession of people can be seen leaving her shop, bearing

the round cylinders in which the best ice cream in the world is packed. Mme. Lamponi is wise. By opening during the summer months only, she need use nothing but fresh fruit purées in her confections. ...

"Experiment yourself with different flavors. Quince and tangerine, fresh lime or bananas will amaze you in this new setting. Almost anything will work ... I had heard of a legendary ice served by Gunter's at garden parties before the war – a grape ice cream. When I asked Mme. Lamponi to make some for me, she told me indignantly that it could not be done – the flavor was too subtle to be captured. Disappointed, I gave up; but she did not. Behind her closed shutters she worked away all winter, experimenting, until she had perfected the new flavor. And when I visited St. Tropez the next year, Grape Ice Cream was her top seller!"

Parisians seem in uncharacteristic agreement that *the* place to buy ice cream in Paris is Bertillon's on the Rue Saint-Louis-en-l'Isle (even *Women's Wear Daily* says so). Noble sherbets (*sorbet*) and flavors like rhum-raisin, banana and Camembert (!). Expensive and, in all but dietary cases, the best possible gift to take to your hostess.

In Italy, go to Florian's fabulous café in Venice (Henry James has the heroine of *The Aspern Papers* taken there) haunted by the ghosts of Proust, the Brownings, Stravinsky. The Café Greco in Rome has its haunters too – poets, artists, composers, "tutti Roma", along with today's nostalgic tourist. Waverly Root in his super book *The Food of Italy* gives us a kind of geography of quality confections: *semifreddo* in Bologna, ice cream with custard, a thick chocolate sauce, like an English trifle; Bologna's favorite, strawberry ice cream "incomparably light"; Parma for the "lightest, most luscious ice cream imaginable"; Lombardy, famed for its whipped cream (*lattemiele*). In Root's "personal experience" the best ice cream he has ever eaten "was served me in the Galleria of Milan." "*Spumone,* misspelled spumoni in the United States," has gotten around too; but such local varieties as *stracchini* and *mattonelle* are found only on the spot. The quality of Neapolitan ice cream results from the subtlety with which its ingredients are mixed. Elsewhere it might be considered sufficient to use strawberries to flavor strawberry ice cream; but *gelato di fragole alla napoletana* contradictorily but successfully adds

One of the most delightful "bill-board" buses in London: Bertorelli's double-decker moving advertisement, on its way home at the end of a run.

tartness to the crushed strawberries with lemon juice and balminess with vanilla; only then are they considered worthy to go into the cream." ("Neapolitan" ice cream, by the way, was invented outside Italy.) In Sicily the marvelous *frutta candita* – candied fruit – are candied whole and cut into tiny pieces to mix into ice cream. Sicily, which still, "at its best, outdoes even Naples, and is often credited with making the best ice cream in the world."

"A Sicilian ice-cream parlor would strike no visiting American as foreign. Here are rows of great canisters of ice cream of all flavors . . . here are fancifully named mixtures like American sundaes: Cardinal's Cup . . . Misto Umberto (a variant of *cassata*), and dozens of others, crowned with whipped cream, chopped nuts, fruit and fruit syrups, maraschino cherries. Instead of soda you have *granita,* a frozen drink, of which lemon and coffee seem to be the most popular flavors . . ." Perhaps this visiting American would be quite startled to find "Chocolate ice cream frozen into the shape of truffles, [and] apples," orange sherbet served in "chilled, hollowed-out oranges; different-colored ice creams used to produce elaborate pyramids, erupting volcanos, imitation bouquets, or foliage." These are sold in shiningly modern shops, "while humbler kinds are sold at street corners from brilliantly painted vendors' carts – not so very humble, for even the simplest of Sicilian ice creams are likely to contain morsels of fresh fruit, or of candied fruit, like the *cassata gelata,* sold from carts as brick ice cream, with a light-colored (perhaps vanilla or

hazelnut) center studded with fruit and perhaps flavored with liqueurs, and a surrounding border of sherbet (currant or strawberry)."

Sylvia Vaughn Thompson, in a charmingly written article on *granite* (Vogue, January 1, 1968) tells of experiencing an ice on day in Portofino. An Italian friend told her that the little stall opposite the quay sold "the best ice on the

ENGLAND
CREAM

NEW ENGLAND
ICE CREAM
A DAIRY RECIPE FROM OLD AMERICA

...TH FRESH CREAM

entire Ligurian Gulf." She had always felt that "ice was nothing but a poor man's substitute for ice cream." That is, until she tasted this one: "An ice of lemon, clear and crisp and quenching . . . almost better than the true flavor was the coarse texture . . . crystals that tinkle on the tongue and give a little crunch before they're by. . . . Orsina was right. This was the best ice I'd ever eaten."

Newly in England: New England Ice Cream. Begun in London in 1973 by an American advertising man homesick for what the British call "dairy ice cream."

199

# EXERCISE NUMBER 5

In her helpful and often hilarious bestseller *The Sensuous Woman,* "J", as she styles herself, instructs the reader in "Sensuality Exercise Number Five" as follows:

For this one you will need a truly delicious prop – a double dip ice cream cone. Remember that erotic eating scene in the movie *Tom Jones*? Well, you can do a great deal with your tongue on that cone in the way of sensuous action. Make circle and swirling patterns with your tongue on the ice cream, lap at it delicately like a kitten with milk, put all of your mouth over the ball of ice cream, sliding down until your lips touch the cone and then s-l-o-w-l-y withdraw it. When the ice cream starts to melt in rivulets down the side of the cone, catch the drops on the tip of your tongue. Linger over each morsel of ice cream, letting your taste buds fully savor the flavor, texture and cold.

*A later section called "The Whipped Cream Wriggle" substitutes ice cream for whipped cream.*
If you have a sweet tooth, this is the one for you. Take some freshly whipped cream, to which you have added a dash of vanilla [in the case of ice cream, chocolate sauce?] . . . and spread the concoction evenly so that the whole area is covered with a quarter-inch layer of cream. Then lap it all up with your tongue. He'll wriggle with delight and you'll have the fun of an extra dessert . . .

*Fox Photos*

Morecambe, 1938

200

"Girl With Ice Cream Cone", by Wayne Thiebaud. Date: 1963

Over these many years, by cart, pushed or horse-drawn; by tricycle, trundled; or, more modernly, by gaily painted van – the ice cream vendors return like swallows to Capistrano. Newspapers dutifully photograph them as first signs of spring. Children hop impatiently with hope at the first tinkle of their bells. They flourish in Scandinavia and Russia, in India and Hong Kong, they are an integral part of the scene on every Riviera.

But there have been problems: the often unsavory sanitary conditions – complained of in the days of "hokey-pokey" – are still complained about; mothers often militantly oppose them because of the danger to their youngsters of being run over while dashing across the street. In the U.S. the famed Good Humor man (selling as many as 90 million stick-bars a year) is carefully instructed to drive slowly and cautiously and to try to avoid children having to cross the street. (Even so, the company, the largest in the field, has been brought to court many times, paying out damages for as much as $100,000.) In recent years dozens of communities have passed ordinances against vendors. Mothers complain of bad timing – just when a child is napping – and spoiled appetites. The violinist Jascha Heifetz even went to his lawyer about the sour sound of music alive in *his* hills (Beverly). There's a certain amount of litter too. Children being what they often are, lawns and walks of a neighborhood recently visited by a vendor have been known to resemble sticky-paper dumps. *The New York Times* reported in its Brooklyn - Queens - Long Island section for Sunday, July 8, 1973: "Suffolk County is considering a total ban on ice-cream trucks on its streets because of the deaths of two children ... killed when they darted from behind trucks and were killed by passing vehicles." Nearby Nassau County was also reported as preparing preventive measures. Among several new proposals to increase safety the

most helpful seemed to be flashing lights, front and rear, when a truck has stopped (similar to those on school buses) and a flip-out sign on the driver's side which would warn motorists to proceed with caution. It is an unhappy situation. Surely no driver can dampen the exultant mood, accompanied by total heedlessness, of a child involved in eating, showing, and generally celebrating his happy purchase, all more-or-less simultaneously. All he/she can do is try.

On a happier note, vendors are still very much with us, a new flavor ("Secret") introduced each week, and vendors in many countries are thought of as friends. *Newsweek* (May 8, 1961) wrote that the G.H.M. "is not adverse to putting commerce on a neighborly basis (one young customer successfully proffered a live snake as security for Good Humor credit; another borrowed a Good Humor man's white coat for his confirmation.)" *Time* magazine once described him as a folk hero "better known than the fire chief, more welcome than the mailman, more respected than the corner cop." Neighborhood kids have even been known to get up petitions when a popular vendor's route has been changed.

In Britain one of the last tricycle-carts can be seen in the summer streets of Gloucester, but there are numberless vans. Tartaglia's of Gloucester is among the independents who operate vans (their "Gloucester Maid" ice cream is a continuous prize-winner). Many small companies operate in London and other cities. Santelli's (to be found, February to October, outside Bishop's Park in London) is considered a local landmark. One of the very few licensed street trader/ice cream manufacturers – on a really hot day they've been known to sell as much as 40 gallons – they began in 1878. The founder's son, Joseph Santelli, owns other vans but limits himself to the one at Bishop's Park where his wife and sister help out at the same spot they've been at for nearly 40 years.

THE
MAN

A sea-going salesman

# ICE (CREAM COMETH

...aves at Brighton in 1939.

Stop me and buy one.

Radio Times Hulton Picture Library

The young film star Belinda Lee celebrates her 21st birthday by giving away ice cream to children in the East End of London.

Gloucester Journal

One of the vans belonging to Tartaglia's, makers of "Gloucester Maid" ice c

Hokey-Pokey amid the hopfields in war-time Britain, September, 1941.

Unrationed

Even during the war, the Good Humor truck (Humor*s* here) made its appointed rounds. The year is 1942 and the customers are patriotically reminded to "Buy Defense Bonds".

Typical British ice cream van.

Radio Times Hulton Picture Library

A pretty girl posing at the British sea-side in the pre-war days when the tricycle vendor numbered in the thousands.

Photo by Donovan Brown.

Territory Manager checking ice cream vendors' stock and cash receipts in Leningrad.

Photo by Donovan Brown

End-of-the-day cash-in and stock-taking in Leningrad. The word for ice cream (*Morozhenoyeh*) can be seen clearly along with the attractive snowflake symbol.

# NEWS

## A Party Picasso

John Bertolini, a sculptor who uses ice cream instead of stone, creates works of edible art that would cheer the heart of the most conceptual of current anti-object "artists." He is one of the last of a rare race and has been sculpting ice cream for more than 40 years as head of the "fancy forms" department of the Louis Sherry Ice Cream Company. Mr. Bertolini estimates he has made over 100,000 sculptures, from simple molded forms to which slight details are added, to elaborate concoctions for people like Queen Elizabeth, President Eisenhower, Jack Benny (750 violins for a testimonial dinner honoring the comic), and Princess Grace of Monaco. He has made Easter bunnies, Santa Clauses, turkeys, and portrait busts. Once he fashioned 500 devils for a Faust Society dinner. The larger forms require a mixture of different flavors – and colors – decorated with ices and sherbets and painstakingly etched with sculpting tools.

Busts are sculpted in clay first, then covered with plaster of paris from which rubber molds are made. The molds are then packed with ice cream and the details added after removal. Work can be done only a few minutes at a time as the busts have to be constantly returned to the dry ice to reharden. A normal-sized portrait takes about 50 hours of work.

According to Mr. Bertolini, who was born in 1910, ice cream sculpting appeared around 1900 when the New York social set wanted elaborate frozen creations for their banquets. There still seems to be a demand for similar – primarily molded – frozen fancies with quite a few ice cream makers producing them. Wil Wright in Los Angeles, Zendler's in Philadelphia, and Bertorelli's in London (they once did a purple Rolls Royce for the Shah of Persia) are only three that come readily to mind.

# ITEMS

FROM THE TIMES (LONDON), FEBRUARY 26, 1975

According to a report from Paris by Charles Hargrove: on the occasion of his investiture with the Cross of a Chavalier of the Legion of Honour by the French President, Giscard d'Estaing, M. Paul Bocuse – one of the outstanding younger chefs in France – invited a dozen of his colleagues to help him create a luncheon at the Elysée Palace: "M. Michel Guerard, of Amélie-les-Bains in the Pyrenees; M. Pierre and M. Jean Troisgros, of Roanne; M. Jean-Pierre Haeberlin, of Illhaeusern in Alsace; M. Charles Barrier, of Tours . . .; M. Pierre Laporte, of Biarritz; M. Alan Chapel, of Mionnay, in the Ain; M. Roger Verges, of Mougins; M. Louis Outhier, of La Napoule; M. Delaveyne, of Bougival, near Paris; M. Jean-Jacques Bernardet, of the Landes, the best French apprentice chef of 1974 . . . [and] M. Marcel Le Servot, the chef of the Prime Minister for 11 years, and of the President for seven, who, for the first time in the annals of the presidency, both cooked a meal and sat down to eat it with his employer. . . ."

In the new style of "light" meals the menu consisted of truffle soup, "a vegetable broth in which the humble potato is replaced by sliced truffles and diced *foie gras*" (invented by M. Bocuse and named in honor of the President), Loire salmon with a sorrel sauce, cold duck Margaux, a selection of salads, goat cheeses from Lyonnais, and a dessert described as "wild strawberries, and chocolate cake with vanilla ice cream", but which actually consisted of vanilla ice cream topped with wild strawberries and a fresh raspberry sauce and genoise cake of cream, chocolate and cherries covered with shaved chocolate to look like a giant truffle. The meal was accompanied by five wines.

# UNTOUCHED

The "Things to Come" are here. The world of computers and automation was bound to encompass the industrial manufacture of frozen desserts. In gleaming rooms filled with intricate and equally gleaming machines, workers watch dials and gauges like a new breed of machine-minders. Formulae (recipes) are translated into coded punch cards which control the flow of ingredients through valves accurate within a fraction of one per cent, handling as many as seven or eight ingredients for any particular flavor. Packaging and sealing are also automated. Lines, vats and tanks are cleaned after each production day – again automatically. A company like Pensupreme prefers quick freezing its product at 35 degrees below zero in a space with a wind velocity equal to 40 miles per hour.

In the United States the basic mix consists "largely" of cream, milk and milk solids. After a quality check, these are fed into large refrigerated tanks; a weighed amount goes into other tanks and the mix is then blended in proportions of around 80 to 85 per cent cream and milk to 15 per cent other ingredients – about six quarts of whole milk to the gallon of product, a small amount of stabilizer, sweetener, flavoring, and sometimes eggs. Pasteurization follows for "safety" and to add to "keeping quality" and flavor. Next comes homogenization which spreads the ingredients

# BY

photo Maurice Broomfi

# HUMAN

evenly, improving whipping ability and eventual digestion. The hot mix next goes to the cooler where its temperature is reduced to 40 degrees Fahrenheit and held for three to four hours to "age." The fat becomes solid and the mix sets. Next it is frozen quickly "for smoothness." Air is incorporated into the mix, improving its texture and increasing its volume (this process is called "overrun"). At this point, fruits, nuts, and flavoring of various kinds are added – *before* freezing when the batch method is used, *after* freezing has begun for the continuous freezing method.

The ice cream is then fed into containers in a semi-flaccid state and put in the hardening room, where sub-zero temperatures do the rest.

(In continuous method, the mix is continually pumped into one end of the machine, then whipped, frozen, injected with fruits, nuts, etc., all under pressure. It is mechanically packaged and sent to the hardening room and then to refrigerated trucks for distribution.)

# HANDS

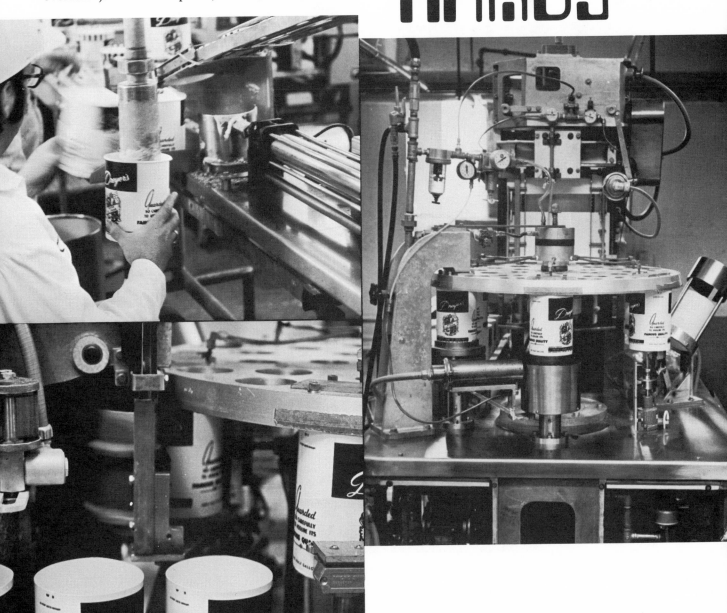

A "gourmet" ice cream producer like Dreyer's usually has the "candor" to give quite a number of details about manufacturing methods. Dreyer's uses higher butterfat content than most – up to a point. Beyond certain levels butterfat contributes nothing to the ice cream and can, in fact, impair its quality. Percentage of butterfat varies depending on the flavor. Sweetness is supplied by a blend of liquid cane and corn sugar and runs 15 to 16½ per cent, again dependent on flavor. You can, it seems, overuse sugar. Flavoring comes from pure, natural, fresh products and is never augmented by imitation flavoring. Pasteurization is achieved in a "unique way": instead of heating the mix to 184 degrees for 15 seconds "as most major companies do," Dreyer's heats it at 165 degrees for 15 *minutes*. They believe that this leads to a finer mix even through the cost is higher.

The people at Dreyer's prefer continuous flow freezers which handle about 300 gallons an hour. These produce the texture the company wants. They also prefer to freeze in the hardening room

for up to 24 hours instead of the more usual tempering time of only a few hours.

Aside from their vanilla and chocolate ice creams they list their fruit ice creams as made up of the basic mix to which 8 to 10 per cent "fresh fruit or its equivalent" is added. Candy and nut ice creams contain three to four pounds of same for each 10 gallons of product.

Dreyer's doesn't use egg products in its regular mixes. Their stabilizer is either animal (gelatin) or plant (pectin, agar, dariloid) used in very small amounts of less than ½ of 1 per cent. No sodium chloride is used. Some manufacturers add salt for bulk and to aid in stabilizing the solution. Some of them also believe it helps the flavor. As much as one per cent can be added without damaging flavor, according to Dreyer's, but they do not use it in any of their mixes.

A line of vanilla and chocolate sugar-free "Frozen Desserts" is also produced by Dreyer's for diabetics and those on reducing diets. These products consist of butterfat, milk carbohydrates, sorbitol, protein and saccharin.

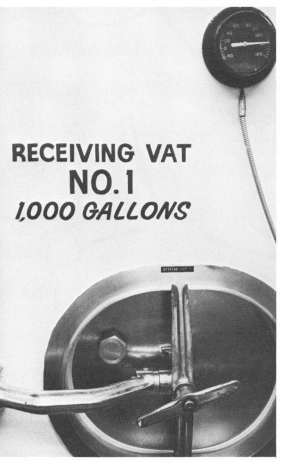

Fast freezing improves the flavor of ice cream, so the temperature in the freezing room is 40° below zero.

*from a coloring book* Pensupreme

After a few minutes in here . . . I'm not pink anymore . . . I turned blue with the cold.

## A SIMPLE GUIDE TO ICE CREAM MANUFACTURING

*Most of the big ice cream makers put out promotional material aimed at children. There are coloring books and minute histories, games and definitions. Some of them are quite delightful. One of the most attractive is sponsored by the National Dairy Council. It's called "Ice Cream for You and Me" and the following is an abridged version of the text:*

Most of the ice cream we eat is frozen at ice cream plants
Let's find out how ice cream is made at the ice cream plant

What dairy foods are used to make ice cream?
Skim milk and cream
They come to the ice cream plant from a milk processing plant
Milk is separated into skim milk and cream
The separator is a machine that takes the cream from milk quickly

Cream separates from milk slowly without a separator

Skim milk, cream, sweetener and flavoring are mixed together.
This liquid ice cream mixture is called mix.

Next the ice cream is pasteurized.
It is heated very carefully [71. C – 160. F]
The milk you drink is pasteurized too

Then the hot ice cream mix is homogenized
Milk fat in the mix breaks into tiny bits
The bits of fat spread evenly through the mix

This helps to make the ice cream smooth
The ice cream is cooled quickly
Flavoring and color are added

The mix goes into the freezer

The ice cream must freeze fast
Inside, special blades whip the mix

Whipping mixes air into the cream
Whipping air into ice cream is called overrun
The right amount of overrun is needed to make the ice cream smooth
    and good to eat

As the mix freezes, tiny ice crystals form, the ice cream gets thicker
Have you ever seen ice crystals?

If the ice crysals are very tiny, the ice cream will be smooth

Soft-frozen ice cream is piped from the freezers to machines that
    package ice cream
They package ice cream in many ways
Look at an ice cream package
What does it say? *

The ice cream packages go on moving belts called conveyors to the
    hardening room
The hardening room is a big refrigerator
People who work in the hardening room must wear warm clothes
It is very cold in the hardening room
It is 20 degrees below zero

---

* A good question. The labeling of ice cream is important.

# O! MY ESKIMO PIE

WORDS AND MUSIC BY
## DALE WIMBROW
POPULAR
SINGING SONG WRITER

Al Barbelle
N.Y.

# New Eskimo Pie On A Stick

By DALE WIMBROW

All the girls___ are now eat - ing     All the boys___ are now
There's no both - er for moth - er     It's good for fa - ther and

treat - ing     NEW ES - KI - MO PIE CREAM - Y
broth - er     NEW ES - KI - MO PIE CREAM - Y

PIE     ON A STICK___     Go in a - ny di -
PIE     ON A STICK___     Lit - tle Bil - ly and

rec - tion    You can buy____ this con - fec - tion
Ma - bel    Eat it all____ but the La - bel

NEW ES - KI - MO PIE ON A STICK_____
And they're sor - ry they can't eat the stick_____

In the heat of sum - mer it will
Rich and cream - y food for eve - ry

cool your day_____    In win - ter time it
girl and boy_____    You on - ly spend a

New Eskimo Pie On A Stick-3

218

New Eskimo Pie On A Stick-3

## COOL CONTAINERS

I've always found the glassware, silver, china, and other impedimenta having to do with the serving and presentation of ice cream especially attractive – the special shapes, all that glisten and shine! "Boats" for banana splits. Tall fluted glasses for sodas. Splendid parfaits. Metal dishes, looking like morning glories, to hold sundaes. The wonderful holders into which tumblers are slipped.

Old fountainware can be found in antique shops. Contemporary ware, in the old shapes, can be found through Sears & Roebuck in the U.S. or Habitat in England. And there are restaurant supply houses. The Indiana Glass Co., 717 E. Street in Dunkirk, Indiana, manufactures a very handsome line of traditional shapes and sizes and the Anchor Hocking Corporation in Lancaster, Ohio has been producing pressed glass for 70 years.

And of course any lovely bowl will do for serving, any beautiful or amusing dish or plate will do to eat from, and, in fact, will greatly add to the delight of the whole experience. The French serve ices in champagne glasses. I think I like glass above all because I like to see all of the confection.

Typical catalogue illustrations showing soda fountain ware available wholesale to drugstores, parlors and restaurants.

The forms of the classic glass ice cream dishes are preserved in these containers made by the Indiana Glass Company.

Mayor Collection. Liverpool City Museum. Photo: Wedgwood.

A superb covered *glacier* made by Josiah Wedgwood in 1803. It is in Queen's Ware (ivory or cream colored earthenware), gilded and with pink enameling. The decorative crest shows a hand grasping a thistle issuing from clouds. Ice was kept in the lower part while food kept cool in the upper.

Wedgwood

Contemporary *pots de creme* on a matching tray made in bone china by Coalport, part of the Wedgwood Group since 1967.

Wedgwood custard cups with matching tray in **Black Basalt** (fine-grained, unglazed black stoneware developed in 1768 and still produced). Engine-turned, late 18th century. In the Wedgwood Museum, Barlaston, Staffordshire.

A shallow ice cream bowl *(Coup à Glaces)* by **Baccarat**, the famous French crystal makers. Ten inches in diameter, two and one-half inches high, with the flat cutting for which the firm is noted.

It's fun to imagine what kind of frozen delicacy might have been served in this enchanting cream cooler made by Wedgwood c.1800. Queen's Ware enameled in brown with a cow filial on the cover.

WAFER BISCUITS 1

STOP ME
AND
BUY ONE

LARGE BRICKS 1'-
SMALL BRICKS 6ᴰ
TUBS 4ᴰ
CHOC BARS 3ᴰ
BRICKETTES 2ᴰ
SNOFRUTES 1ᴰ

# THE GOLD Rush

## Part 2

Wall's famous tricycle. By the 30s
there were 8,500 of them all over
the land. Obviously, it was no
longer considered questionable for
a lady to be seen buying ice cream
in the street.

The English picture (perhaps British picture would be better) is an interesting one. The consumption of ice cream and related frozen sweets is far less than that in the United States but at least two companies are in very big business indeed. There is considerable disagreement about ice cream. The British call our ice cream – which has milk fat while theirs does not (or not necessarily) – "*dairy* ice cream". There are exceptions to this difference which I will discuss elsewhere. At present the basic retail outlets are "corner shops" – confectioners, tobacconists and newsagents, "CTNs" as they are called by the industry – about 50,000 of them. In 1973 40 per cent of the British market was accounted for by these small shops as compared to eight per cent in supermarkets and 19 per cent in vans. About 6,000 of the CTNs belong to "multiple groups" ("chains" to Americans), the rest are independent. People are found to be loyal to their local shop and children to prefer them to the bigger stores. They are usually open longer and more often too – 7 a.m. to 9 p.m., six to seven days a week, is not uncommon. There are no social or economic categorizations either. Things are rather difficult for the owners these days: rents steadily rising, developments moving in, etc. There has been a decline of about 10 per cent in their number but turnover has been reported at around 30 per cent higher. 1973 sales totalled £48 million.

Changes are occurring. First the increase in home refrigerators, more central heating, and a new emphasis in advertising on take-home frozen desserts as well as market distribution, has caused a rise in sales for home consumption. More ice cream is being eaten as a dessert than as a snack. The grocery "multiples" sold dessert ice cream worth £9 million in 1965, £19.2 million in 1970. Since 1970 the figure has dramatically increased to £35 million and multi-packs can now be kept up to a week in "three-star" fridges. 1971 saw the appearance of litre packs for the average fridge. One-half gallon packs came out the following year.

The home freezer market is growing and the potential market for frozen desserts is increasingly important. Home freezer owners eat over twice as much ice creams as non-owners. New ideas and outlets are constantly being considered. Many stately homes now offer frozen confections along with souvenirs, maps, local crafts, etc. Restaurants are being approached in an effort to make menus listing ice cream more evocative with descriptions similar to those of other courses instead of the usual "ice cream – various" business. The Martins chain has introduced "Rest-a-while" areas where customers can sit down for a coffee and hopefully an ice cream. Strategically placed signs just outside shops call attention to the fact that more than cigarettes, magazines or candy are for sale inside.

Most British ice cream makers feel the tax situation has been somewhat arbitrary. A purchase tax of 10 per cent in 1962 resulted in the closing or merger of a number of companies. Still, the tax was just one of those things. The companies rallied and improved during the 60's – partly because of a general trend in favor of ice cream. Then in 1973 the Value Added Tax was applied and, happily, ice cream was rated zero. Sales soared by 22 per cent. Only a year later the rating was changed and a 10 per cent VAT levied. The industry is presently trying to have the tax removed and ice cream treated as an ordinary food.

Lyons Maid, now in its 50th year, is one of Britain's biggest makers of ice cream – over 1,500 *million* ice lollies and portions of ice cream. Back in 1925 J. Lyons and Co., Ltd. began selling – mostly in its own tea shops – "bricks, choc ices and kups." The tea shops go much further back, to 1894 when the first one opened in Piccadilly with an attractive color scheme of white and gold. Food was inexpensive and people liked it.

National sales of ice cream began in earnest in the 20's with delivery by van, the wrapped ice cream packed in zinc containers surrounded by salt and ice. This presented many servicing problems and things finally improved in 1927 when low temperature refrigeration made its debut. Dry ice and mechanical refrigeration sped up expansion throughout the United Kingdom. In the early 30's distribution was accomplished mostly by passenger train. In May, 1933 a major heatwave created havoc – insufficient goods and means of distribution, enormous demand on the part of the public – and woke management up to the true importance of ice cream in terms of production schedules. Shifting emphasis, the company increased sales, advertising, and its range of products. In 1934 ice cream was offered in cinemas and theaters, where it is still very much in evidence. This new move resulted in the public's acceptance of ice cream as an all-year-round treat. Things were about to really take off when 1939 brought the Second World War and a halt in production for six years.

Although things started up again when the war ended in 1944, there were many frustrations: sugar and fat were still rationed and dealers' refrigerators had stood unused for a long time. Not until two years later did bureaucratic development ease the situation somewhat. A "permit-transfer scheme" allowed a caterer to surrender his fat and sugar to a manufacturer *if* the ice cream produced was eaten as part of a meal, *not* off the premises. As a result cafes, restaurants and what the British call "canteens" were able to serve ice cream as a sweet.

During the 50's ice lollies and ice cream on sticks were introduced – a good 30 years after the Good Humor was invented. Lyons created two now-classic variations: Orange Maid, the first "drink-on-a-stick", and Mivvi, ice cream in a fruit jacket. Soft ice cream was added in the early 60's. The same period saw the establishment of the first sterile canned ice cream mix plant in the United Kingdom.

Continuing efforts to turn ice cream into an all-year food were aided further by the significant growth in home refrigeration. Something like 85 per cent of homes can keep ice cream for several days with about 10 per cent of that number owning deep freezers. By 1974 the company, now known as Lyons Maid (a rather nice British association of "made" with "maid" – as in "dairymaid"), accounted for 43 per cent of the British market. They had opened the first automatic ice cream plant in Britain and developed a fleet of refrigerated trucks delivering, via depots, to 70,000 trade customers: shops, caterers, hospitals, cinemas, theaters, beach sites, cash-and-carries and mobiles. Typical of British habits, over 50 per cent of Lyons Maid business is still done through confectioneries, tobacconists and newsagents. Like Louis Sherry, they have recently brought out individual *bombes,* as well as something called "Triple Glories," a new "turn-out dessert." They have also acquired the American giant Baskin-Robbins with results one can only wonder about.

A famous firm of meat pie and sausage makers run by Thomas Wall wanted to find a "summer product" to keep things going on a less seasonal basis, so in 1922 began the large-scale manufacture of Wall's ice cream – the other British "biggie." From the start they hit upon a super idea (like "Mr. Humor" and his Good Humor van): a tricycle-driven cart bearing the slogan "Stop Me and Buy One." The first "trike" cost them £6. By 1939 there were 8,500 of them being peddled around the United Kingdom ringing their announcing carillons (playing Beethoven's "Pastoral Symphony"!) and – the company claims – making Wall's the leading ice cream manufacturer in the world.

All of which ground to a dead stop two years later in 1941. With the ending of the war in 1945 and as soon as some of the rationing problems could be dealt with, Wall's was hard at it once again. Sales had reached an annual £6 million by 1939. In the ten years following 1950 sales rose from £14 million to £46 million a year. To compete with the great variety of candies, etc. offered by the CTN's new products and methods have been evolved. A new logo has been created,

adding a sunny glow to the boy-and-girl symbol. New flavors are being introduced such as the "Cornish" series augmenting the very popular Cornish dairy ice cream. Fizz Bangs are a combination of a shell of tangy lemon-and-lime-flavored water ice with a sherbet center. A Feast is caramel ice cream on a crisp biscuit, "the first ice cream snack bar." There are Jelly Jumbos, Super Stars and Count Dracula's Deadly Secret. The *Evening Standard* ran a story in February 1975 about Wall's Soft Scoop – the first ice cream especially for home freezers. The method is a secret (a world patent is being sought) but Wall's say ingredients are unchanged and they have not added lots of air or more chemicals. Supposedly you can scoop the ice cream out of the economy-size container while it is still in the freezer – no thawing is necessary. And "the flavor is better because taste buds don't get frozen while you try to melt a mouthful." It is pointed out that no other food can be eaten directly from a freezer and that once removed from the freezer Soft Scoop doesn't melt any faster than conventional ice cream. Long planning because of melting is also no longer necessary. Early tests were reported as "so successful that Wall's may bring forward their national launch date planned for June." Since 1973 Wall's and Lyon's have introduced over 80 new products. The Cold Rush of the 70's speeds on.

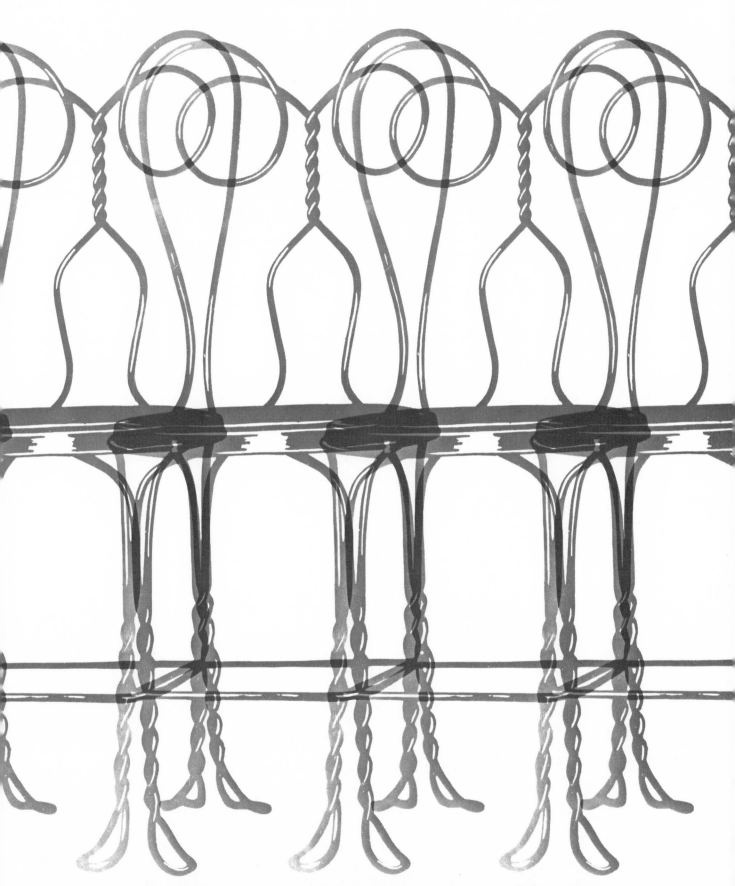

A CHAIR FOR ALL FLAVORS

The Ice Cream Chair (yes, all capitals) is really a classic piece of furniture. At least to Americans. To real lovers of "antiques" it conjures up lazy afternoons gazing through Victorian bricabrac bentwood rockers ("Pray it's a real Thonet!"), empty frames and bits of old glass. Time was — it definitely isn't anymore — when you could take home the real thing for a couple of dollars or less.

Ironically, the Ice Cream Chair was not originally made by some great cabinet maker or designed by an architect. It was designed in 1905 — and I think this fact is enchanting — by a man who made handlebars for bicycles. Six of its seven parts consisted of twisted wire and it sold for $1.25. The man who made it was a Chicago metal finisher named J. Silverman and his company was called the Great Northern Plating Works. He was determined from the start to supplant the wooden chairs that were all the rage in ice cream parlors with his "Heart Design" (the back of the chair is bent into the shape of a heart) and he hoped that it would one day become the "most famous furniture of the world".

By 1911 he was making tall chairs for soda fountains, tables, stools, models with arms, models for pool parlors, and barber shop shoe shine stands. He was shipping a boxcar at a time — 1,200 chairs worth — in every direction. But a curious phenomenon, which even today plagues contemporary designers working with humble materials such as laminated cardboard or certain plastics, took place: though the chairs sold by the thousands, furniture stores would have nothing to do with them. People had to search them out second-hand as I mentioned before. Like all great designs they have a quality outside of time and can "go" with any decor — next to a period couch, a steel-and-glass table or out on the terrace. Amazingly enough the chairs are being made to-day, in Chicago (by the Simpson Bosworth Co. of North Ashworth Street) by a hand process, and with the original machinery. Where they were once only copper-plated they now come in other metals as well as in paint finishes. There are still wooden seats and perforated seats along with upholstered ones. Arm chairs, stools, tables, and one-armed "cafeteria chairs" are still available. There are attached "love-seats" and tall bar stools with or without arms. There are even chairs and tables for children.

Similar Thoughts About Chairs By Two Professionals

"Chairs are a good thing, when resting, customers drink slowly. This means looking about seeing other things to buy."

– "Thoughts After 10 p.m."
from *The American Soda Book*
by Tufts, 1863.

*"Chairs and Benches.* Where trade is the transient kind, and comes and goes quickly, it is not advisable to have chairs or benches at the fountain. In family neighborhoods, on the other hand, people like to linger and take their ease, and here there should be sufficient seating capacity. A good plan is to have some nice, light stools at the counter, and, in close proximity at convenient points, some nice benches. It is the customers who are inclined to linger just a little who may cast their eyes about and observe other things to purchase."

– from *The Standard Manual of Soada and Other Beverages,*
by A. Emil Hiss, Chicago, 1906.

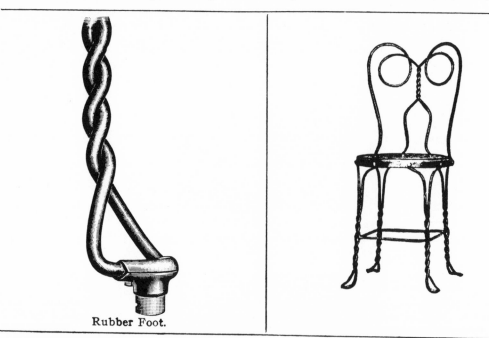

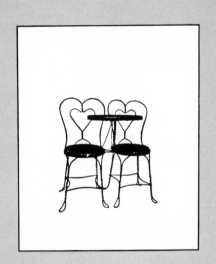

A tradesman's horse named Kitty who was in the habit of stopping for an ice cream cone on her daily round along the front at Margate in 1938.

# Animal and Aerial Gourmets

A dog's best friend sharing his Dixie Cup at New York's Coney Island in July, 1939.

Polly, an Australian cockatoo who lived at the Whipsnade Zoo in the 1930's, was a great favorite with ice cream men.

"We needed a bear for the film, and I heard that a store-keeper in a neighboring village owned a tame one . . . It was remarkably greedy. We drove it about in a van, and whenever we passed a shop selling ice-cream it roared, so that we had to stop and buy some."

– Jean Renoir, *MY LIFE AND MY FILMS*

Maytime in 1936 – a little boy offering some of his ice cream to one of his Irish Setters while the other manages to get a bit of something from the vendor.

This seems to be a good place to pause to read a short essay by Jane
Howard, another of that half-handful of writers on ice cream
and a self-confessed ''unregenerate ice cream fetishist'':

I heard a rumor the other day that somebody's about to make a new kind of ice cream you spray, like hair lacquer, from a can. This technological breakthrough may gladden some hearts but it strikes me the same way news does about the tearing down of the redwoods. I am an unregenerate ice cream fetishist. In my hierarchy of the pleasures of this world, good ice cream – not the kind you spray, or the brick-shaped kind that tastes like cardboard, or the roadside stand kind that tastes like soap – ranks right up there with Mozart and sea heather and Armagnac. I'd drive five hours, and recently did, for a dish of Maple Pecan. In fact I've been obsessed of late with seeking out sources of uncompromisingly good homemade ice cream, and the men, nearly as anachronistic as shepherds, who make it.

If I were being executed tomorrow morning, what I'd order for dessert tonight would be a dish of Coffee Haagen-Dazs. Haagen-Dazs, which also comes in Boysenberry Sherbet, Rum Raisin, Chocolate and Vanilla, is a delight available only through the "better delicatessens" of New York City. A friend of Reuben Mattus, the man who makes it, thought up the name because it sounded like "an Old World Scandinavian delicacy." Never mind that it is in fact a New World delicacy concocted in the Bronx. Never mind that at 85¢ a pint it isn't exactly a bargain – it doesn't taste like a bargain, either. (Not that fine ice cream has to be costly. I had an occasion recently to buy eight cones, seven of them for others, at an estimable little store in Albuquerque called Fitzgerald's. The whole bill came to $1.04.)

San Francisco is a fine town for hedonism in general and ice cream in particular. The late Senator Robert Kennedy chose to stay there instead of in Los Angeles one night during his campaign just for the ice cream. Lynda Johnson Robb and some friends, earlier, were ordered off a cable car because they wouldn't give up their Butterscotch cones. Since the cones in question came from a justly famed local chain called Swensen's, I could sympathize. I too would rather climb Nob Hill than relinquish such a cone, though my own Swensen preferences are Mocha Chip and Lime Sherbet. And I'm thankful to the friend who introduced me to a magnificent Coffee dispensed across the Bay in Berkeley at an unassuming store called Botts'.

240

I've discovered two excellent and unrelated ice cream parlors called Petersen's. One, in Oak Park, Ill., Offers a Mocha with an embarrassingly fine aftertaste, an assertive little Peppermint Stick and a legendary Lemon Custard. The other, in Marion, Mass., has booths that look like church pews and a clientele positively reverent – as well they should be – about the Butter Crunch and the Raspberry Sherbet. The great thing about the Massachusetts Petersen's is that they'll pack you a pint container in layers, allowing you to dig like a euphoric geologist from, say, a topsoil of impudent Ginger to a substratum of Chocolate Chip so good it outsells even the Vanilla to a bedrock layer of even more remarkable Blueberry.

I have yet to visit the ice cream parlors of Philadelphia, which say used to be and maybe still is the ice cream capital of the nation, or a much touted place in Kalamazoo called the Chocolate Shop, but so far my favorite ice cream connection of all is a humble store in Cedar Rapids, Iowa called Dysart's. Hugh Daggett, who manages Dysart's for his mother keeps fresh roses from his own garden on his marble topped tables and Fresh Gooseberry, among other superb flavors, in his deep frosty cylinders. "We figure on using the best," he says. "They can get the other stuff somewhere else. Anyway a lot of people don't care what kind of ice cream they put in their stomachs. Things aren't the same. People used to stay in here until three in the morning and be much more sociable before television and deep freezes. Now we close at ten. I don't know who'll take over this store when I'm gone."

Fortunately Mr. Daggett is only 49, and looks healthy. I wish long life and prosperity to him and his scattered soulmates. May more establishments like theirs erupt among the Trading Stamp Redemption Centers and Karate Instruction Parlors and Gypsy Reader & Advisor studios that seem to dominate the streets of America. May their tribe – as admirable and unsung a tribe as I know of – somehow increase.

– from 'LIFE', 27 September 1968
Copyright Time, Inc,
Reprinted with permission

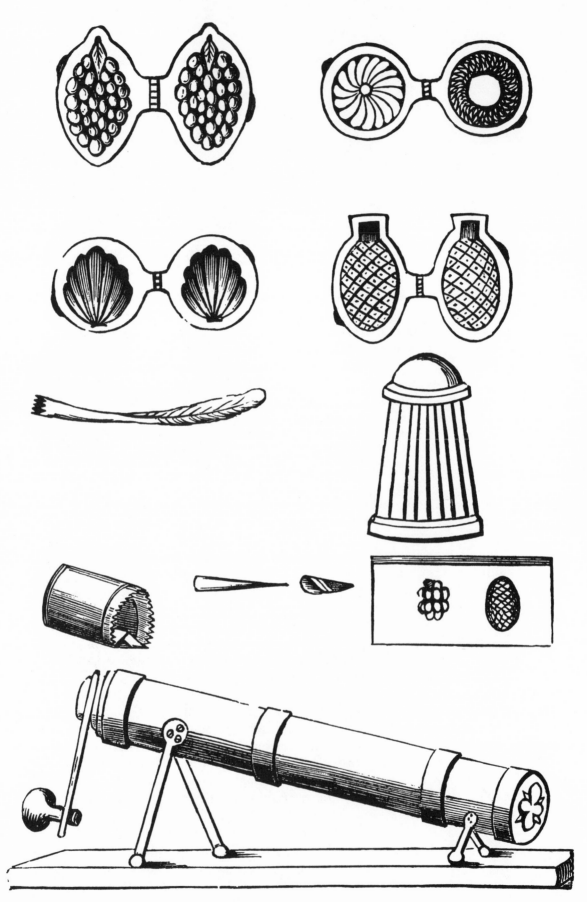

According to Escoffier, molded ices – or *Glaces Moulees* – are made in large or small molds. The large ones are made of tin and have hinged covers "ornamented with some design." Small ones are similar and are usually used to garnish larger ices in the shape of "flowers, fruit, birds, leaf-sprays, etc." Any ice preparation may be used, "But, as a rule, the preparation should have something in keeping with the design of the mold used."

*Gunter's Modern Confectioner* writes of them thus: "They are made of pewter, and fastened by a hinge. They may be procured of almost any shape suitable for ices – fruits, shell-nuts, ornaments, etc. If you desire to represent a fruit, mold accordingly, giving the Ice the proper flavor. Get your Ice ready, open and clean the mold, fill it, and insert, in the small hole at the end, a stem or a couple of leaves belonging to the fruit; or well-made artificial leaves will do. Close the mold at once, the stem and leaves being outside. Put some paper around, and bury it amongst the Ice and salt in the tub. See that the Ice covers it. In about one hour and a half it will be ready." Amusing to compare these instructions, written in the 19th century by William Jeanes, Gunter's Chief Confectioner, with those written by J. & C. Dueker (*The Old Fashioned Homemade Ice Cream Cookbook*) in this – especially the length of time for freezing (see below).

Molds are not that easy to find, but they are still being made, especially in France, and gourmet cookery shops and departments of large stores may carry them. You can also use jello molds. When filling them be sure to pack the semi-hard ice cream into every "corner" so that the shape comes out complete. When using jello molds cover the open end with foil or plastic wrap. "Proper" molds are not leak-proof at the seams so work speedily in packing them and cover the seams with plastic wrap. It will help too if you chill the molds beforehand. Freezing should take about 24 hours in a refrigerator freezing compartment.

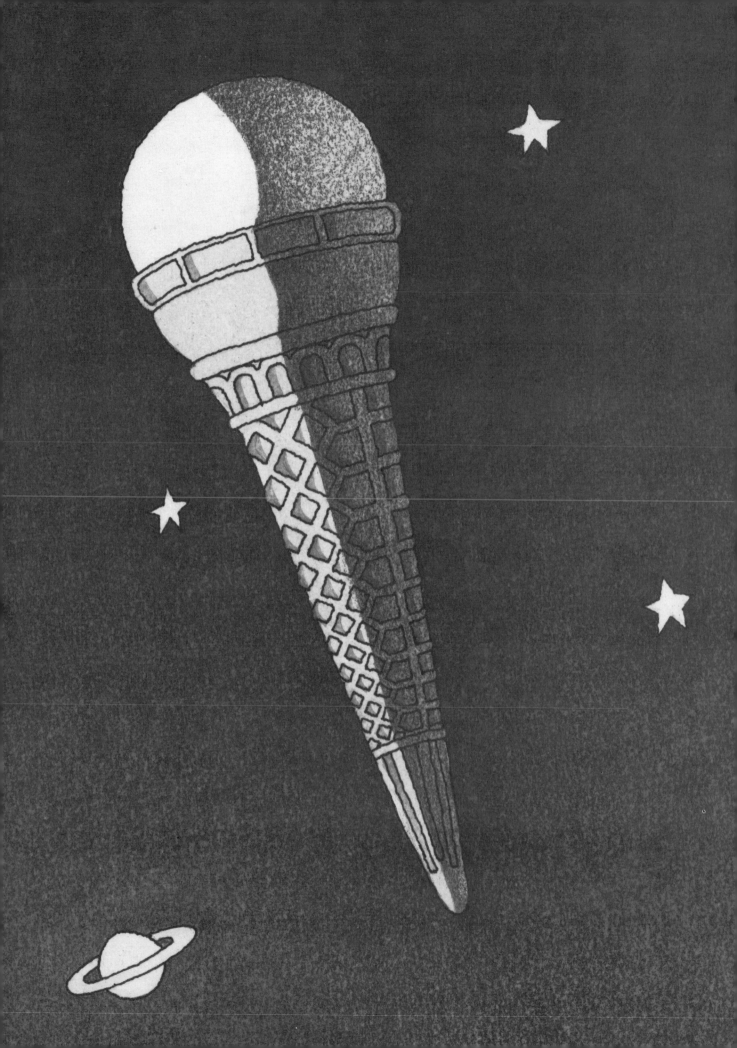

# THE DARK SIDE OF THE CONE

So much of today's so-called ice cream isn't. Instead it is a combination of everything from artificial flavors to plain air. In America, something like 1,200 chemical stabilizers and emulsifiers – things with names like sodium carboxy, methylcellulose, glycerin, mono-glycerides, propylene glycol, dioctyl sodium sulfosuccinate – are legally allowed. So are artificial flavorings and colorings. Seaweed and gum acacia, bean gum, etc., are some of the ingredients introduced into ice cream's make up. And there's quite a bit of deceit too. One manufacturer told me that some (manufacturers) do such things as using bits of inferior peaches, adding fig seeds and dying the whole thing with a nice pink to produce "strawberry" ice cream! Cheap super-market ice cream sometimes contains as much as 60 per cent air although the legal limit is set at 50.

The public hasn't helped. From Japan to Jamaica (New York) they don't seem to care much more about the quality of the ice cream they gulp down than they do about the wine they drink or the TV dinners they eat. The highest sales figures deal with near "plastic" frozen desserts. And we have the recently patented process that makes "ice cream," "ice milk," and "sherbet" that can be sprayed into a dish like those ghastly ready-whips.

There are no comprehensive guides to good ice cream as yet. No commercial product is required to list all its ingredients – although that is supposed to change by 1976. And you can't always tell by price. Expensive but poor as opposed to inexpensive but good often turns out to be the case. One rule you *can* follow concerns the weight of the ice cream you buy. The less air there is in it the more it will weigh. If you go by weight instead of volume an expensive brand can actually prove to be cheaper. Premium quality brands like Swensen's brag about producing "heavyweights." Their single cone weighs $\frac{1}{4}$

pound, a double, $\frac{1}{4}$ pound. Hand-packed quarts weigh 2 pounds. They claim their products weigh 33 1/3 more than their "middleweight competition."(see below).

Other problems beset the ice cream world. All through the 50's soda fountains and ice cream parlors were closing at the sad rate of more than 1,000 a year. As with some endangered species efforts *have* been made to reverse the process, but most of the now-existing fountains and parlors are very much a new breed. In the 70's, increases in the cost of raw materials have been horrendous. In 1973 the cost of sugar alone rose 16 per cent in the third quarter and prices were not allowed to rise.

A 1972 article in *Consumer Report* checked out three Midwestern states – Missouri, Illinois and Kansas – representing about 10 per cent of all U.S. ice cream sales. They tested 34 brands of ice cream and other frozen desserts for flavor, body, texture, melting characteristics, bacteria count, etc. They found some surprising things. They found some ice cream Very Good at only 57¢ a half-gallon and some Not Acceptable at 99¢ a half-gallon. Packaging information was practically nonexistent. In 1960 the U.S. Food and Drug Administration finally got around to establishing a Standard of Identity which barred things like "acid neutralizers," but ten years later they allowed "balancing salts" which can help in disguising inferior dairy ingredients as well as thicken the product.

The testers found "reworked" ice cream – making one flavor from another that has failed to turn out or is beginning to go bad or has even been returned from retail stores. Federal controls apply only to ice cream made in one state and sold in another. And, at the time of the article, there were no Federal regulations limiting bacteria in ice cream and similar frozen products! Bacteria levels found in some samples were so high that they couldn't be counted.

Of the chocolate flavors tested only three Excellents were found: *Lucerne's* "Party Pride Dutch" was one. Interestingly, *Lucerne* is sold by Safeway supermarkets and it also rated as one of the two Goods awarded ice milk.

Sherbets scored lowest, getting only *one* Good. That was given to *Meadow Gold's* "Orange" (*Meadow Gold* was the other one given a Good for ice milk).

Judges complained in all categories about lack of flavor, unnatural flavor, lack of freshness, crumbly, coarse or soggy body; too-sweet or too-acid sherbets. They found metallic flavors and unnatural color.

In melt-down tests, *Baskin-Robbins'* "Vanilla" came closest to the mix they started out with. Again, Meadow Gold rated high, being among the few which "wept" a small amount of watery liquid (*Howard Johnson's* was another.) Unfortunately, *Meadow Gold's* "Magic Freeze Vegetable Frozen Dessert" chocolate was highly contaminated. All the sherbets scored low in bacteria count.

The report concluded with several warnings and suggestions.

Weight losers were told to shun ice cream as a $3\frac{1}{2}$-ounce serving contains 200 calories, mostly fat and carbohydrates. It *does* contain complete protein derived from milk but they figured it would cost about $9.00 a pound derived from milk bought at 85¢ a half gallon. Ice cream *is* a good source of calcium, phosphorous and vitamins A and B2. And they admitted it was a "satisfying food in many respects" although not "nutritionally complete."

Watch out for coconut oil, a vegetable fat as highly saturated as most animal fats. It is cheap and as labels do not have to qualify whether the fat content is saturated or unsaturated there is the unhappy likelihood that coconut oil is being used.

The best way to check ice cream is to weigh it. It should weigh at least $2\frac{1}{2}$ pounds per $\frac{1}{2}$-gallon. Buy it last and choose the hardest. Try to get it wrapped separately – ideally in an insulated bag. Keep it out of the sun as much as possible on your way home. Wrap it in a plastic bag to minimize evaporation and store it in the area of your freezer which has the least temperature fluctuation. Eat it within two weeks.

*Ice Cream & Frozen Confectionery,* the official journal of the British Ice Cream Alliance, gives a hint of the conflict that exists between Britain and the rest of the world as to what constitutes "ice cream": "Scoop", the journal's columnist, suggests to Mr. J. D. O. Knowles – Chairman of Wall's and President of the European Association of Ice Cream Manufacturers ("Euroglace") – that "he must in no way bow to the European blackmail to have us call our vegetable fat product by some ludicrous name such as 'non dairy fat ice cream type product' ".

Professor Arnold Bender, Professor of Nutrition, Queen Elizabeth College, London, in a most candid interview published *by* Wall's, remarks at one point to a question as to why certain Continental countries don't make non-fat ice cream: "Well, I think this is just national habit. *We* started by calling the material that we now call ice cream 'ice cream'. We are not being misled in any way because everybody [in Britain] knows what ice cream is. On the Continent, the cream part is the vital part of the word, and they are horrified at the thought that we do not have milk fat. So are the Americans. What we call *dairy* ice cream, which has a quite clear designation, they will accept . . . a problem which is occurring with all Common Market foods. We like what we have been eating and they like what they have been eating. We all want to keep to the food we have been eating, and the argument is: let us try and standardize in some way. Well, we are not getting standardization; people will continue to eat the kind of food that they have liked for generations. Now we have accepted that the stuff we call ice cream is something that we like to eat, and whether or not it's got dairy fat in it doesn't bother most people."

"Scoop" also received a letter supporting the clear differentiation between dairy and non-dairy fat ice cream. A Mr. H. T. Sheldon of Derbyshire wrote asking that "it not be thought that your membership (of the Ice Cream Alliance) is unanimously against the EEC proposal that dairy ice cream alone should be called ice cream. As a producer of dairy ice cream I am entirely in favor of it."

The Marcantonio family opened an ice cream parlour in Surrey Street in Croydon in 1936, later opening a small factory in Whitehorse Road which Mrs. Marcantonio's son Lou managed (Mr. Marcantonio had died some years before), supplying the shop, a few mobiles and some wholesale. In 1964 a new parlour was opened in Surrey Street Market and is run, since Mrs. Marcantonio's death, by Lou and his wife Maria.

Mrs. Marcantonio was the daughter of Giuseppe and Addolorata Mancini who were artists' models as well as ice cream makers. In fact, Addolorata was the model for the maternal group on the Victoria Memorial opposite Buckingham Palace, and the baby in her arms is none other than her son Alf, the international boxer who was never knocked out.

(Culled from an obituary in *Ice Cream & Frozen Confectionery,* January, 1975)

In 1935 the then U.S. Treasury Representative attached to the American Consulate in Kobe, Japan, E. W. Dalen, was so homesick for Bassett's ice cream that he wrote Philadelphia asking that some be sent by ship "in time for Christmas". The ice cream was duly sent via the refrigerators of the Dollar Line which sailed from New Jersey. The ice cream kept for three months and Mr. Bassett received letters of praise not only from Mr. Dalen but from several of his dinner guests.

ON THE SODA JERK:

"He became as much a particularly American figure as the cowboy or the lumberjack and was honored in song, poem, short story, joke, and film. His epic was a film serial of 1932 called *Fighting Blood,* starring George O'Hare as a tender but tough soda jerk who defends the honor of the innocent, becomes a champion prize fighter, and goes on to make a fortune with a drink he invents at his fountain."

–*The Great American Ice Cream Book* by Paul Dickson

". . . when the Woolworth's-hot-fudge-sundae switch goes on, then I know I really have something."

"My favorite restaurant atmosphere has always been the atmosphere of the good, plain, American lunchroom or counter – the old-style Schrafft's and old-style Chock full o'Nuts are absolutely the only things in the world that I'm nostalgic for. The days were carefree in the 1940's and 1950's . . ."

*The Philosophy of Andy Warhol,*
by Andy Warhol.

According to David Soanier, Diplomatic Correspondent for the *London Times* (February 24, 1975), lunching with a noted representative of the capitalist block – in this case Dr. Kissinger – can be traumatic: "You start with a couple of powerful martinis, ice cold. Then you sit down and have, in order, a glass of iced water, a frozen salad, a plate of cold warmed-over roast beef, a slice of cold apple pie, all washed down with coffee."

Contrast this with his further description of a luncheon in the Soviet Union as a member of the press: "Vodka comes first of all, with a dollop of caviar on bread, smoked fish, cold veal and mushrooms en croute, followed by trout, then a steak, then ice cream, all washed down with a selection of Georgian wines and Russian champagne."

DEFINITIONS

Professor W. S. Arbuckle of the Department of Dairy Science, University of Maryland, discusses the classification of ice cream in his important book *Ice Cream.* He mentions attempts by various text book writers and leading authorities to classify ice cream over the years, but without any success in achieving and adopting a standard. He also speaks of the confusion that surrounds efforts to make specific rules for the definite classification of ice cream.

The following definitions are culled from Dr. Arbuckle's attempts as well as two or three other sources.

Plain ice cream: Made from milk or cream, sweetening, flavoring, and stabilizer. Highest frozen food in milk fat and milk solids. Color and flavoring less than five per cent of volume – as in vanilla, coffee, maple, caramel, etc. Basis into which variations are introduced such as candy, chocolate, fruit, nuts, etc.

Bisque: ice cream containing suitable flavorings and particles of bakery products such as cookies and cake.

Custard ice cream: Also French ice cream or Frozen custard. Highest egg-yolk content.

Ice milk: Lower in milk solids. Contains more sugar,

non-fat milk solids. Flavored. Sweetened.

Parfait: Custard with high fat content. Served in layers in tall glass.

Mousse: Whipped cream, sugar, color, flavoring. Not churned during freezing. Sometimes contains condensed milk.

Granite: Coarse-textured water ice.

Frappe: Ice made from mixture of fruit juices. Slushy. Served as drink.

Sherbet: Made from milk or cream in lower proportion than ice cream. Fruit juices (tart taste due to fruit acids), sugar, color, stabilizer (eggs whites or gelatin).

Water ices: Made from sweetened fruit puree or juice thinned with water. No dairy products.

According to scientists, there are only four flavors: sweet, sour, bitter and salt. According to the gourmet, the greatest of these is, indisputably, sweet. We are inclined to sympathize with those who consider a meal merely the straightest line to dessert, and see great logic in that one avoid the dreadful dilemma of being too full to enjoy dessert by having dessert first, and proceeding backward to soup or hors' d'oeuvre!

– *The Gourmet Cookbook,* Vol. II

"Winnie Manders, who works at the Clark St. store [Baskin-Robbins in Chicago], designs special ice cream creations: she's made three and four-tiered wedding cakes, hamburgers and hot dogs, and even some X-rated creations: a champagne grape ice penis and a vanilla ice cream breast. For approximately 11¢ an ounce, she'll try to duplicate your wildest fantasy."

– from *The Scoop on Chicago's Ice Cream* by Sari Staver Sheldon in *Chicago,* March, 1975.

In 1972 freezer ownership in the following countries stood at (in declining percentages): USA – 60 per cent; Sweden – 55 per cent; Denmark – 45 per cent; West Germany – 28 per cent; Austria – 25 per cent; Finland – 15 per cent; Switzerland – 15 per cent; Holland – 14 per cent; Belgium – 13 per cent; United Kingdom – 8 per cent; France – 6 per cent; Italy – 5 per cent.

In the ten years from 1960 to 1970 the consumption of ice cream in litres per capita increased by: 3.1 to 4.7 in West Germany; 1.1 to 3.1 in Belgium; 2.1 to 2.7 in

France; 2.2 to 4.6 in Italy; and 3.4 to 6.9 in Holland. But it *decreased* by 0.1 to 4.6 in the Unitd Kingdom. In 1970, by comparison, the USA consumed 23.0 litres per head.

A. C. Thayer quoted in *Ice Cream & Frozen Confectionery,* London, December, 1974.

Pre-war radio had its Popsicle Parade of Stars featuring Milton Berle, Martha Ray, Arthur Godfrey and Fanny Brice. Fred Allen told a joke about "Ripley who knows a cannibal chief with a sweet tooth. For dessert, he always eats a Good Humor man."

On first tasting ice cream, Stendahl quipped, "What a pity this isn't a sin!"

In the 19th Century clipper ships sailed from North America with precious cargos of ice, preserved in holds insulated with sawdust, which they delivered to cities all over the world.

Dreyer's use a "Peek-a-Boo" lid on their containers so that buyer and seller can see what's inside, and a round shape which they prefer for a "better air flow around the ice cream while it's tempering in the hardening room." They also prefer paper to plastic as it allows the ice cream to breathe."

*A posey of posers*: clues from Barbara Hall, Crossword Puzzle Editor for the *London Sunday Times*:

Mice care for it = Ice cream.

They may be sucked or blown = Cornets.

Ice cream cornets just about right for old ladies = Crones.

(All examples of "cryptic framework", i.e. not straight, synonymous clues.)

There's nothing in the ice cream container that will go to your head = Coronet.

(A lovely example, with zero, or naught – which is "nothing" – set in the very center of the word.)

And the most difficult kind of all: the "Mephisto":

This fruit should be soft when served, with plenty of whipped cream ice, so it's said.

From which, if you are clever, you are expected to work out "ample mousse" plus the letter P for "soft" (as in *piano*), to come up with "pamplemousse" which is a fruit, and the word required.

In the 1920's ice cream was served on airplanes and Pullman cars and companies which sold it first appeared on the Stock Market.

"Ah, but you haven't seen the ice pudding," said Cook. "Come along." Why was she being so nice, thought Sun as she gave them each a hand. And they looked into the refrigerator.

Oh! Oh! Oh! It was a little house. It was a little pink house with white snow on the roof and green windows and a brown door and stuck in the door there was a nut for a handle.

"Let me touch it. Just let me put my finger on the roof," said Moon, dancing. She always wanted to touch all the food. Sun didn't . . .

. . . And the little pink house with the snow roof and the green windows was broken – broken – half melted away in the centre of the table.

"Come on, Sun," said Father, pretending not to notice . . .

. . . "Daddy, Daddy," shrieked Moon. "The little handle's left. The little nut. Kin I eat it?" And she ran across and picked it out of the door and scrunched it up, biting hard and blinking . . .

*Sun and Moon,* Katherine Mansfield.

During the Second World War there were attempts made to can ice cream – none of which succeeded, and the Eighth Air Force Squadron chose the Popsicle as their symbol for The American Way of Life.

According to the GUINNESS BOOK OF WORLD RECORDS, 1974 edition, the eating record for ice cream is "7 lbs. 13 ozs. (50 2½ oz. scoops) in 16 min. by Archie Leggatt, 22, in Hamilton, Scotland, Feb. 9, 1973."

249

A revealing association emerges as one reads the definition of Hokey-Pokey given in *The American Thesaurus of Slang* by Berrey and Van den Bark. After "Cheap ice-cream sold by peddlers," there follows several sub-definitions: "1. General heading: Foolishness. Sub-heading: Nonsense. 2. Deception; deceit. 5. Fraud; deceit." Fuel for the anti-ices folk.

The best time for street vendors, according to the Good Humor people is: 3 to 5 P.M. for children, 7 to 9 P.M. for adults.

According to the GUINNESS BOOK OF WORLD RECORDS, 1974 edition, "The most Monstrous ice cream sundae ever concocted is one of 1,551 lbs. by Bob Bercaw of Wooster, Ohio, built on July 4, 1972. It contained 67 flavors and 144 lbs. of chocolate fudge syrup. It far surpassed the sundae built on Mike Douglas' TV program during 1972."

During the Second World War a Good Humor man was stopped by an M.P. at Chesapeake Bay dock and told to "drive out onto that barge!" The barge duly pushed off and tied up at a troopship until the entire Good Humor "cargo" was swung aloft to waiting G.I.s.

from a story in the *Readers' Digest* in the 1950's

Harry was enjoying his dinner. It was part of his – well, not his nature, exactly, and certainly not his pose – his – something or other – to talk about food and to glory in his "shameless passion for the white flesh of lobster" and "the green of pistachio ices – green and cold like the eyelids of Egyptian dancers."

– *Bliss,* Katherine Mansfield

"Every year brings its quota of tales of soda water 'winks', which are published in the daily press, but it is gratifying to know that very few pharmacists stoop to the contemptible habit of serving intoxicating drinks at the counter. The serving of liquors belongs to the saloon, and should not be countenanced outside of saloons. For this reason, formulas for soda syrups containing wines or liquors are not given in this work, except in a few instances where the formula is one so well established that it could not be omitted."

– from *The Standard Manual of Soda and Other Beverages* by A. Emil Hiss, Chicago, 1906.

In his book *Ices & Soda Fountain Drinks,* published in London before the war, P. Michael writes that in London there were ice cream scandals in 1901 resulting from a tour of inspection by two of the best analytical chemists in the busiest ice cream centers. They published two reports, one on ice cream, the other on the water used to wash glasses in. Through "microscopical examination ... all sorts of undesirable matter were found ... including human hair, coal dust, fragments of bed straw, hair of dogs and cats, sour crusts, fleas, bugs and many other nauseating articles! ...

"The water used for washing the glasses used by the street vendors (the 'washing' merely consisted in a dip in the pail, a tap-tap-tap movement, and, very rarely, a touch with the dirty towel hanging over the vendor's shoulder or tied to one of the blind supports at one end of the corners and used for other purposes, such as drying the moist container lid, the spoon, and sometimes the face of a not too clean urchin when 'Jack' was not looking) was found to be ... an evil-smelling, thickish and slimy liquid, full of bacteria and sediments, including, of course, saliva from the many mouths that had touched the glasses during the day!"

A public scandal resulted and a great drop in sales which affected even the best-kept shops. The London County Council set up new regulations to try to control contamination and fined the offenders 40 shillings. Mr. Michael goes on to say that, "Perhaps the first thing brought about by this scandal was the breaking up of the 'boss system' in the various Italian quarters throughout the kingdom, where poor agricultural and very ignorant and illiterate lads, fresh from Italy, lived under cruel bosses and under nauseating conditions at a very miserable wage, which was often replaced by kicks and bullying, especially if the day's takings had been very low, in spite of the weather being bad!" Shades of Charles Dickens! No wonder Mr. Michael is given to exclamation marks!

Frozen soufflé: Sherbet with eggs or egg yolks.
Soft ice cream: Ice cream drawn from freezer without hardening. Most are ice milks.

Sweeteners: Primarily cane and beet sugar. Also corn syrup, maple sugar, honey. Aids flavor.

Stabilizers: Egg yolks in richest ice cream. Gelatin from animals. Agar-agar from vegetables. Aids texture. Prevents formation of coarse ice crystals.

Emulsifiers: Eggs, cornstarch, gelatin, corn sirup, etc. Cause fat to combine with non-fat. Improves whipping and texture.

Overrun: Air incorporated into mix and the volume of ice cream obtained in excess of volume of mix.

Rural Ice Cream: In the Trough of Bowland on the Lancashire-Yorkshire border.

*Saturday Evening Post*, 1908 September
"About half-past eight Johnny ambled up, decorated with a blue coat, white vest an' ice cream pants, an' his hair all slicked down."

*MILNOR (OKLA.) Teller* 1884
"An ice cream parlor where the dudes and dudines sip . . . congealed milk and sugar"

*A Dictionary of Americanisms* by Mitford M. Mathews.

"Do not allow flirting, long conversations, appointments, etc. at the fountain. The last two should only be tolerated at the tables, and hardly concern you;

the first does, and will make your profits flit away."
– from *Ices and Soda Fountain Drinks* by P. Michael published in London in the twenties (no date given)

French – *glace*   Italian – *gelate*   Spanish – *helado*   German – *eis*   Portuguese – *gelado*   Dutch (and Flemish) – *ijs*   Chinese (and Japanese) – no word for it*   Danish, Swedish, Icelandic – *is*

\* the Japanese have bastardized it into "a-i-su kur-ri-mu (in the Katakana alphabet). More a kind of fruit bar.

The Russian word is MOPOXEHOE – which because P is really R and H is N and E is YE, and O before a consonant is often A – is pronounced MAROZHNY or MAROZHNYE (MAROZH is frost, ice is LYOD)

According to H. L. Mencken's *The American Language* – the loan-word in Polish for ice-cream-soda is "ajskimsoda."

When Nikita Khrushchev visited the United States, Dave Basset (of the Philadelphia ice cream family) and George Stuempfig (son of the painter Walter Stuempfig) got through a battery of security agents at Blair House and the Russian Embassy in time to deliver six quarts of borscht ice cream for the Eisenhower-Khrushchev dinner that evening.

In 1972 when Nixon served Baked Alaska to Brezhnev for the first time, the Soviet leader referred to it laughingly as "Hot ice cream."

"Ice creams of the market always contain a variety of ingredients, such as condensed milk, cottonseed oil, artificial flavors, etc. Hence they are liable to be of suspicious character, and every one who has occasion to dispense ice cream should prepare it himself."
– from *The Standard Manual of Soda and Other Beverages* by A. Emil Hiss, Chicago, 1906.

In H. L. Mencken's *The American Language*, Supplement II under the heading "Carpenters", "Ice-cream, or scap" is the slang term for overtime.

A promotional photograph showing the "first Americans" refreshing themselves at a slightly different kind of watering hole.

It's impossible to glean anything like more than a day-or-two's findings from a wander along some beach or boulevard; more would require much geography and time. Herewith, then an imbalanced, incomplete, necessarily partial notebook of jottings about ice cream in various parts of the world.

Any person now entering the United States would not be caught by the same surprise expressed by immigrants disembarking at Ellis Island in the 1920s when they were met by something "truly American", i.e. ice cream. Their reaction then was to think of this unknown cool substance as a kind of butter or cheese and to promptly spread it on their bread. Nowadays pretty much the whole world knows about ice cream.

We think of the world as round, but apparently there isn't all that much, if any, ice cream in reactions to ice cream of some touring members of the Peking Opera would also seem to suggest its absence in China. (They politely refused to eat any on a tour of Canada, saying it might affect their performance.) Evidently not true in the 20's: Paul Dickson writes in *The Great American Ice Cream Book* that a Paul S. Crawley is known to have sold ice cream in his shop in Shanghai during that time, selling "nine thousand gallons of ice cream and over a million Eskimo Pies."

Even though entire soda fountains were exported to Japan in the 20's (as well as countries in South America and places like Kuwait) and those resourceful people even came up with a way to deep-fry it, they apparently have no really *Japanese* word for ice cream (see page 251). A report in the November 1974 issue of *Ice Cream & Frozen Confectionery* says that "Wherever you

contemporary China. Curious this, because it all is supposed to have started there more than 3,000 years ago when the Chinese were known to mix snow with lemons, oranges, and pomegranates. And, of course, it was from China that Marco Polo brought ices to Italy when he returned from representing Venice as Ambassador to China and Japan. After his death in 1323 his memoirs were found to mention his having seen frozen milk and water being sold in the streets in summer. Efforts made through at least one Chinese embassy have led to polite but useless responses. The suspicious

walk in Tokyo you see the words written up in English." Even on otherwise all-Japanese menus. Over 40 per cent of total sales occur in July and August when temperatures run in the 90's. Alas, pure ice cream – with "8 per cent or more fat content" – doesn't account for more than 10 per cent of "ice cream product" sales. Most popular items seem to be imitation ice cream, sherbet, water ice and ice milk "in that order." Ice creams are not usually eaten while walking along. Cones are surprisingly inexpensive. There are usually a variety of flavors. Scoops are "meticulously clean" and the ice cream is served in "crispy" cones wrapped in paper. The ice cream was found to be "good in both texture and flavor, without being remarkable ... [and] the portions adequate."

Something referred to by the reporter as "a slush-type product" seems to be the most popular of all. As described, it sounds like a very classic Italian ice: "A block of ice, about a foot square, is placed on a small turntable inside a machine and clamped into place. The turntable revolves and a blade scrapes away little slithers of ice ... When the dish, about four inches across and three deep, is piled high, the machine is turned off and the ice block returned to the cold cabinet below. Flavored syrup is poured over the ice and it is eaten with a spoon." Although it was found to be "rather too sweet," the writer had to admit "it was easy to see just why the product is so popular in Japan. On a hot and humid day it was cooling and refreshing." Again, there are many flavors and it is cheap.

Moving on to Hong Kong perhaps the English reporter was unaware of Dreyer's exclusive market for premium quality American ice cream. In any case his or her first "encounter with ice cream" was in the form of a Mister Softee sales van. It was in a small back street among craft and curio shops; "I could hardly believe my ears when I heard those familiar chimes. The van, which would not have looked out of place at a British garden fete, came into view and pulled up right outside a traditional apothecary shop where dried snake skins, sea-horses and a thousand different herbs were on sale ..." It seems there's no way of getting away from that drugstore connection!

"Little ice cream barrows, such as one sees in London's Oxford Street, were everywhere ... and the Chinese have no such inhibitions about walking while enjoying an ice cream as the formal Japanese have. I saw more ice cream being eaten on the ferry boats than anywhere else ... And what could be more pleasant after working all through a hot and humid day than to return home on a ferry-boat with a refreshing ice cream? Little kiosks near the entrance to the ferry do a roaring trade with scoop-served ice cream in a small

(about six) variety of flavors. I tried the mango ... and found it delicious. About 5p [12¢], but a small portion."

In Hawaii there is a chain of ice cream and confectioners called "Ed & Don's" with outlets at the Ala Moana shopping center in Honolulu's Kahala Mall, Kailua-Kona, Lahaina, and Windward City. The Maui Soda & Ice Works Ltd. on Lower Main Street, Wailuku, Maui, has been in operation since the 1870's. The "Tasaka Guri-Guri" in the new shopping mall, Kahalui, has been a family business for at least 20 years. They serve delicious raspberry and strawberry ices and a "Guri-Guri" sherbet – a bean sprout base topped with preserved bean sprouts. Macadamia nut ice cream was flown from Hawaii to former President Richard Nixon from the Kahala Hilton.

Early in 1975 the BBC televised a portrait of Iqbal Ghai in its "Larger Than Life" series. Ghai was born in Pakistan and rose from a filling-station attendant to ownership of Asia's biggest ice cream factory and a chain of restaurants called Gaylord's with branches in London, Chicago and cities in Japan. He has no formal office – "My office is where I am" – and uses his restaurant in the center of Delhi as the place to meet with people. Perhaps one person in 200 can afford to eat in one of his restaurants, but his ice cream, called Kwality, is much to be seen. He is admittedly a ruthless employer – or was: "You can't kick people anymore – you have to move with the times." He and his partner started about 35 years ago with about $250. Their slogan was "A Dream With Cream." At night they slept on the roof of their parlor. The influx of troops during World War II, particularly Americans, gave the business its push to fortune. Some years ago the older brother of L. B. D. Bertorelli (of the noted British ice cream making family) went to India to help set up modern production methods and found himself staying for a dozen years. During the broadcast, the interior of one of Mr. Ghai's factories was shown. The rotary machine for stick confections was modern enough, but

Theater Square, Moscow, April 1957. A young boy trying to decide which flavor to choose from an ice cream barrow. The Bolshoi Theater stands in the background.

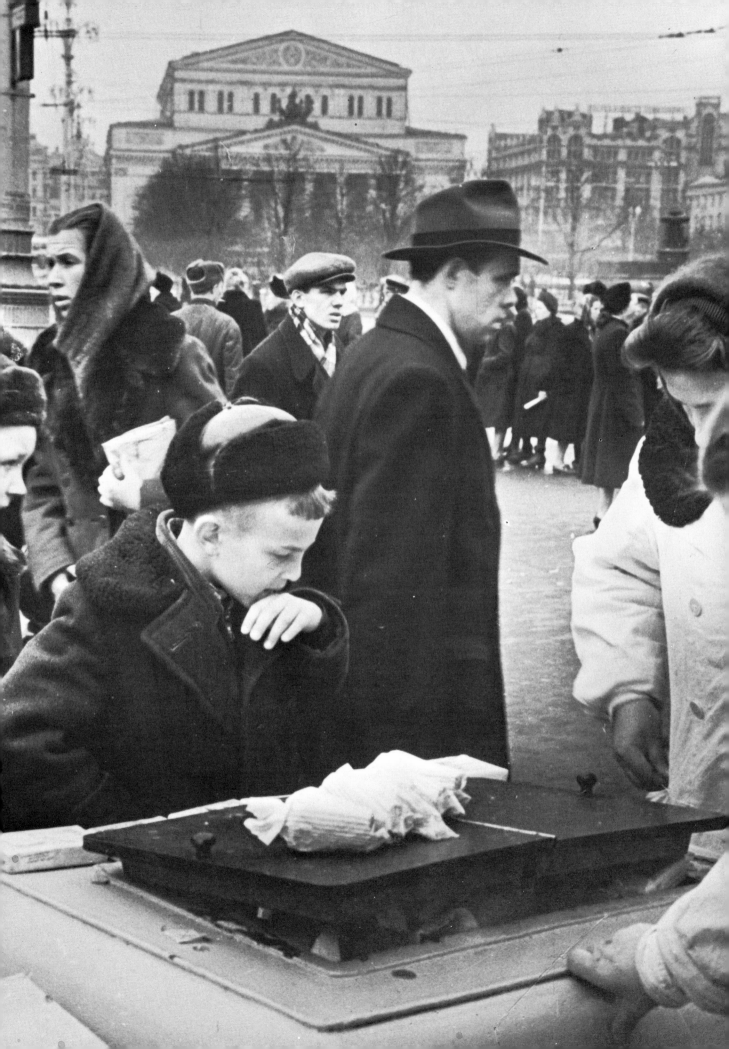

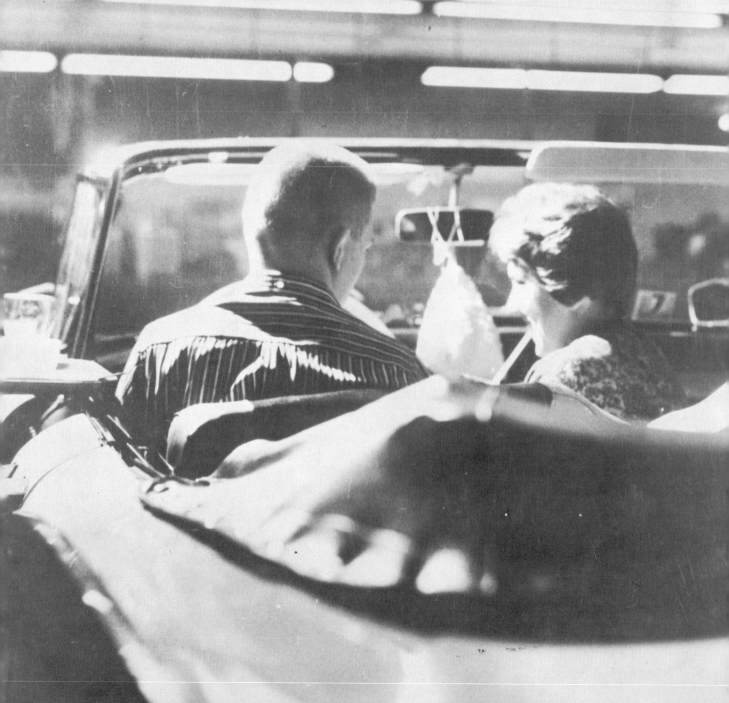

wrapping was done by hand.

During the BBC interview the slightly hostile reporter got Mr. Ghai's son to admit that his father's "agressive" control and supervision once earned him the nickname of "Hitler." In recent years, semi-retired (and no doubt influenced by his deeply religious wife) Mr. Ghai spends much of his time under the tutelage of the guru Sai Baba and seems somewhat subdued and even melancholy. Irresistibly, he has been called "The Maharaja of Ice Cream".

"Scoops" notes on India (*Ice Cream & Frozen Confectionery,* Nov., 74) include the following:

"As for the street vendors, there are plenty of them, particularly in the fetid and overcrowded streets of Old Delhi. Many of them push carts with the name Kwality on the side ... What was the ice cream like? I'm afraid I can't tell you. Devotion to duty can go so far ... but no further."

Some doubts are also expressed as to sanitation methods in production as compared to "whatever it is that our backroom boys at home do to protect our tums – but really one of the most delicious ice creams I had during my whole trip to the Far East was eaten in a small hotel in Delhi: its texture was smooth, its color good, it was creamy without being cloying, and its flavor – which I can only describe as being a sort of perfumed vanilla – was out of this world. A day or two later, in Agra, I tried another, strawberry this time, but though it was nice, it was not up to the standard of the first ..." What a pity the name of the "out of this world" ice cream isn't given!

In the Soviet Union – according to information generously supplied me by Donovan Brown of the *Soviet Weekly,* London – ice cream has always been a great favorite. "It is sold in vast quantities, winter and summer. It is sold in restaurants and cafes, in theaters, circuses, football matches (football is a summer game) and, most of all, from small mobile cold boxes in the streets – placed at strategic street corners and staffed sometimes by men but more usually by women in white overalls and compulsory white cap or kerchief.

"It is universally good, and must contain no adulteration. It is made centrally in each town or city and then delivered to the distribution points. The largest manufactury is perhaps the Kikoyan Factory in Moscow. The street barrows carry a price card and a colored picture of each variety, and list the weight of each pack. There are usually four sorts – plain vanilla, chocolate covered vanilla (what we call 'choc-ice' here), chocolate covered and rolled in chopped nuts, and two-flavor/two-color – vanilla/chocolate (cream and pale brown). The cheaper is a long cylindrical block wrapped in foil. There are also 'wagons' selling tubs only. Some places have waxed paper tubs, others have biscuit tubs. There are plenty of street receptacles for the empty papers as all packs are paper-wrapped. There are cones as well – the biscuit of which is thicker and less tasty than those in Britain – but undoubtedly hygienic.

"In hotel restaurants ice cream is served in the usual stemmed metal dishes and in the usual semi-spherical lumps. The National Hotel in Moscow has an expensive concoction called 'Ice Plombiere' in which the ice cream sits on a meringue, and is crowned with a hooped handle of biscuit pastry, and floated in black cherry jam!

"A great place for ice cream is the circus. People pour out into the large foyers at the interval and line up for the same sort of ice creams sold from the barrows. In the theaters (I speak of the Kirov in Leningrad, the Bolshoi and Palace of Congressers in the Kremlin in Moscow) one can get ice cream in the refreshment halls, or line up for it on the landings. The lines are long and slow, however, because the ice cream is weighed out – 100 grams – into stemmed metal dishes for each customer. One would think they'd get a good batch ready. But perhaps this would be unhygienic! So one waits whilst each dish is filled on shop scales ... I don't recall tubs anywhere.

"Another good sales point is outside football grounds after the match, when fans can buy ice-gateau in their club colors!"

257

Luigi Valente first made ice cream in Belfast in 1890. He sold it from handcarts in the area around Little Patrick Street – amusingly expropriated by the Italian community into Little Italy. The area was the first port of call in Northern Ireland for arriving Italian immigrants and no doubt some of today's figures in the ice cream industry can trace their beginnings back to a handcart rented from Luigi. Vittorio Antori Cerefice (a name as beautiful as the opening words of an aria by Monteverdi!) married Valente's daughter and they produced five sons – all involved with ice cream. The family owns the Russell Cafe and a "smart stand" on Rhyl promenade. Mr. Valente opened the Dolphin Cafe in Rhyl and his brother Tony, Nino's Restaurant in Colwyn Bay.

The Belgians eat lots of ice cream but, to some minds, without much imagination – all vanilla, chocolate and strawberry. There is a great deal of commercial stuff that runs from very average to down right bad. There is a fine fantasy called *cafe liegeois,* after the city of Liege, which consists of coffee ice cream swimming in cold coffee with a dollop of whipped cream on top. The chocolate version is considered the "better thing" to order in chic cafés. Quite surprisingly it is even known by the same name in France which usually prefers to name its own foods.

In Flemish Belguim where Dutch is spoken, ice cream is known as *ijs* (which sounds like "ace" in English). A single portion is called by the diminutive, becoming *ijsje* (which sounds like "Asia" ). An Eskimo Pie is known as *een ijsko.* French-speaking Belgians say *glace.*

There are many ice cream parlors in Brussels. Two outstanding ones are "Au Buquet Romain," an old-fashioned shopper's haven on the Rue Neuve which looks like it has been there forever, and "Chez Pol," one of the best modern drugstore-type "glitterdives" near the Arch of Triumph and the museums of art and archaeology.

Ice cream is a great favorite at banquets, where it shows up in all kinds of appropriate shapes – a

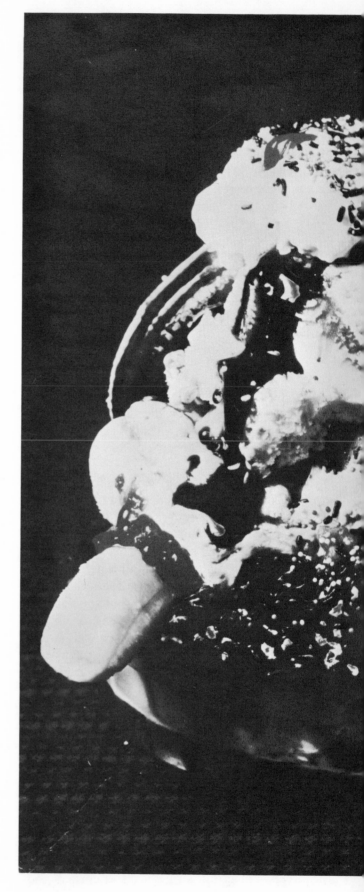

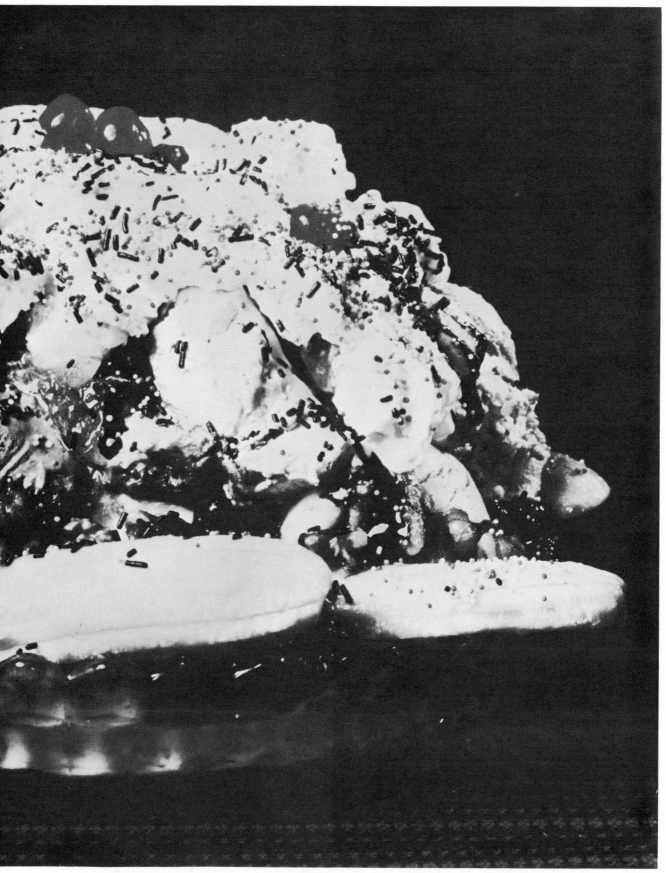

*From a story about jigsaw puzzles in* The San Francisco Chronicle, *Friday, October 18, 1974.*

"Perhaps the pièce de résistance among the latest crop of jigsaw puzzles is something called 'Dieter's Delight' which comes in two 500-piece versions – French pastry and banana split."

vanilla lamb for first communion, a yule log for Christmas, a three-tier *pièce montée* for a wedding. There is a superb *orange givrés* too – an orange shell filled with orange sherbet.

During the Second World War ice cream in Belgium had little to do with cream and wasn't allowed to be called "ijsroom" ("room" is Dutch for cream). Instead it was hideously dubbed *consumptieijs,* which sounds like a disease and means "ice for consumption." But even during the Occupation there was always some sort of frozen water for kids to enjoy.

The Dutch in Holland are a bit more inventive than the Belgians and like to use liqueurs in their "ijsbekers." One favorite is "advokaat," a very yellow egg liqueur. Sherbet is *sorbet* the same as in France.

Ways of eating ice cream and methods of distribution are not very different from those in Great Britain. The ratio of industrially produced ice cream to trade-produced being about 70 to 30. Interestingly, the production of powdered mix is large – 26,031 (1,000 kilogrammes) in 1973, as compared with exports of ice cream itself which were 2.693 (1,000 kilogrammes) for the same year while *imports* of ice cream stood at 9.922 (1,000 kilograms).

In Germany the best ice cream parlors are run by Italians and are called "Italienische Eisdiele." Preference seems to be for mixtures with sugarcoated fruit – what the French call *fruits confits.* Ice cream on a stick is called "Eis am Stiel" which the French have always referred to as "un eskimo."

One would expect Vienna and ice cream to be synonymous: they prepare the perfect *Poire Josephine* (a sublime combination of hazelnut ice cream, half a pear, nougat and chocolate sauce *mit schlag* (the ubiquitous Viennese whipped cream). Places like Demel's, Sacher's and Zu den 3 Husaren are legendary sweet-dispensaries. Yet *Newsweek* reported back in 1966 that Sealtest, "a division of the National Dairy Products Corp. and America's largest manufacturer of ice cream," was trying to crack Vienna. Evidently they were trying to create a market in a country which thought of ice cream, at least at that time,

as a hot-weather luxury and only consumed an average two pints per year per person!

I'm told the Norwegians eat ice cream all year round (so much for those myths about cold food in cold countries!) and I'm *also* told a great day for youngsters is May 17th, Constitution Day, which heralds the new ice cream eating season (somewhat confusingly I should think).

The word for ice cream in Iceland is *is* and the chief manufacturers are Mjolkursamsalan, Reykjavik Milk Distribution Centre, Kjöris, and Dairy Queen.

In February 1975 the BBC telly-magazine produced at Pebble Mill told of an English company which exports iced lollies to Iceland.

In Yugoslavia ice cream production only began on the industrial level in 1956 in Beograd. Before that time it was made by "artisans" beginning around 1910. There are now several modern, Danish equipped factories producing around 15,000 tons a year. The factories all belong to dairies.

Yugoslavs prefer eating ice cream while strolling along the streets or at a sporting event or in a café. Home consumption has not yet caught on very much. Ice cream is usually eaten in the summertime when there is also a surplus in milk production. Annual per capita consumption is 1 kg. Bars on sticks, cones, and cups are the most popular forms of ice cream accounting for 80 per cent of all consumption.

There are Federal standards and the major categories produced are: ice cream made with cream (12 per cent milk fat, 16 per cent sugar, 35 per cent total solids), with milk (2.8 per cent milk fat, 18 per cent sugar, 32 per cent total solids), and fruit ices (30 per cent sugar, 32 per cent total solids). Maximum use of stabilizers runs 0.5 per cent. No artificial flavors are allowed and only milk fat is permitted (no animal or vegetable fats). Overrun allowed is 100 per cent (which is really 50 per cent – the same as in the U.S.).

All refrigeration equipment from factory to vending vehicles belongs to the factories. Most sales still occur through the street vendors although there is an increase in the sale of ice creams in shops and the larger self-service stores.

A detail of a fabric used in children's sportswear by the New York firm Coming Thing and their designer Lucille Bertorello. A Russell printed cord of Kodel polyester and cotton in pink, yellow, green, and white.

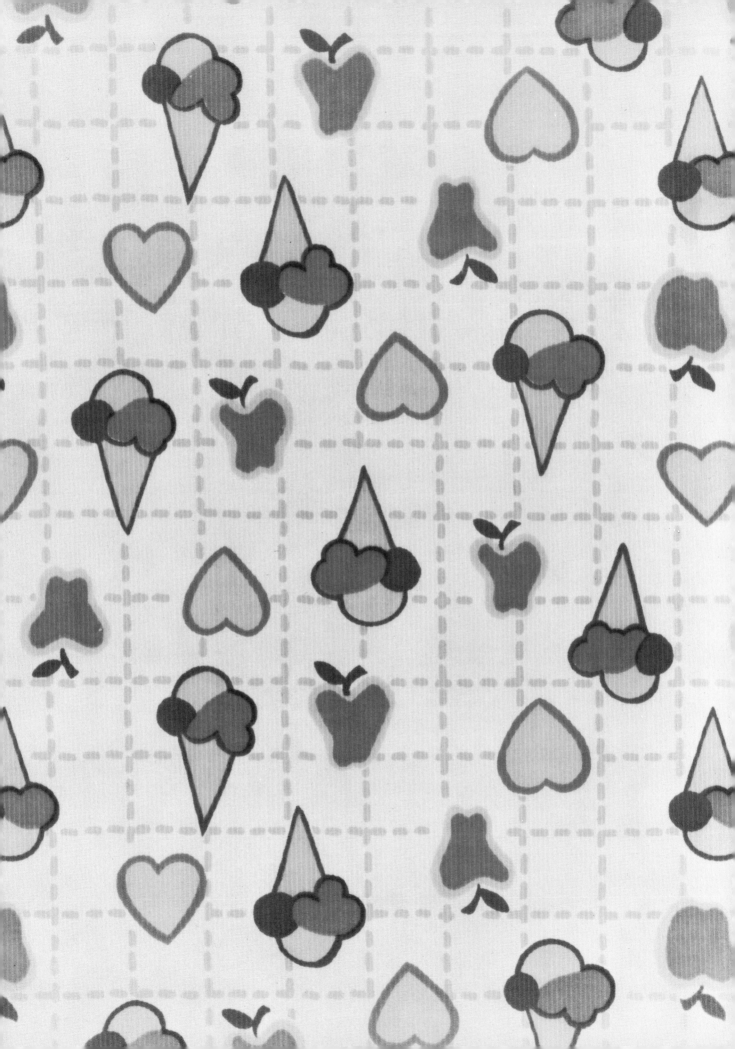

# A LITTLE ANTHOLOGY OF RECIPES

All recipes in this anthology are given as published – in the form, style and measurements of the originals. A table of equivalents will be found on page 283.

# VANILLA EXTRACTS

Among the many "delectable mountains" of frozen sweets, vanilla is surely the Everest. It is in fact the parent of all ice creams, the basis for most other flavors which it outsells by 50 per cent or more. It is the major measure against which all talent and excellence in the making of ice cream can be weighed.

Here, then, are several ways of making it – 13 in fact – culled from several sources.

Let me start off by quoting from Mrs. Mary F. Henderson's 1888 *Practical Cooking and Dinner Giving* because of its wonderfully easy and direct style and very "New England" elegance-mixed-with-commonsense. (Alas the prices given are redolent of other days.)

It is as cheap and easy to make ices in summer as almost any other kind of dessert. If one has cream, the expense is very little, as a cream-whipper costs but twenty-five cents. A simple cream, sweetened, flavored, whipped, and then frozen, is one of the most delicious of ice creams. By having the cream quite cold, a pint can be whipped, with this cream-whipper, in five or ten minutes. It will require ten cents' worth of ice – half of it to freeze the preparation, to keep it frozen until the time of serving. Salt is not proverbially expensive; a half-barrel or bushel of coarse salt will last a long time, especially as a portion of it can be used a second time. . . . The devices of form for creams served at handsome dinners in large cities are very beautiful; for instance, one sees a hen surrounded by her chickens; or a hen sitting on the side of a spun-glass nest, looking sideways at her eyes; or a fine collection of fruits in colors. One may see also a perfect imitation of asparagus with a cream-dressing, the asparagus being made of the *pistache* cream, and the dressing simply a whipped cream. These fancy displays are, of course, generally arranged by the confectioner. It is a convenience of course, when giving dinner companies, to have the dessert or any other course made outside of the house; but for ordinary occasions, ices are no more troublesome to prepare than any thing else, especially when they can be made early in the day or even the day before serving."

Mrs. Henderson then gives her recipe for vanilla ice cream along with another called Delmonico Vanilla Cream.

## Vanilla Ice Cream

Beat the yolks of eight eggs with three-quarters of a pound of sugar until very light. Put one and a half pints of rich milk on the fire to scald, highly flavored with the powdered vanilla-bean (say, one heaping tablespoonful). When the milk is well scalded, stir it into the eggs as soon as it is cool enough not to curdle. Now stir the mixture constantly (the custard pan or pail being set in a vessel of boiling water) until it has slightly thickened. Do not let it remain too long too curdle, or it will be spoiled. When taken off the fire again, mix in a quarter of a box of gelatine, which has been soaked half an hour in two tablespoonfuls of lukewarm water near the fire. The heat of the custard will be sufficient to dissolve it, if it is not already sufficiently dissolved. Cool the custard well before putting it into the freezer, as this saves time and ice. When it is in the freezer, however, stir it almost constantly until it begins to set; then stir in lightly a pint of cream, whipped. Stir it for two or three minutes longer, put it into a mold, and return it to a second relay of ice and salt. The powdered vanilla can be purchased at drug-stores or at confectioners. It is much better than the extract for any purpose, and is used by all the best *restaurateurs*.

## Delmonico Vanilla Cream*

*Ingredients:* One and a half pints of cream, one ounce of isinglass, one pound of sugar, yolks of eight eggs, half a pint of milk, vanilla powder. *Scald* the cream only; then add the isinglass dissolved in the milk, and pour it on the sugar and eggs beaten together to a froth; add the flavoring. Strain, cool and freeze it; then pack it for at least three hours and a half.

---

\* Famous confectioners and restaurants often find their names – very much as chef's – "entering the language" of superior food.

Irma S. Rombauer and Marion Rombauer print modern directions for Delmonico ice cream in their *Joy of Cooking.*

**Delmonico Ice Cream or Creme Glacee**

*About 9 servings*

Scald over low heat but do not boil:

1½ cups milk

Stir in until dissolved:

¾ cup sugar

⅛ teaspoon salt

Pour the milk slowly over:

2 or 3 beaten egg yolks

Beat these ingredients until well blended. Stir and cook in a double boiler over – but not in – hot water until thick and smooth. Chill. Add:

1 tablespoon vanilla

1 cup whipping cream

1 cup cream

Fold this mixture into the custard. Churn freeze.

They give three *more* recipes for vanilla ice cream, proving just how various the singular can be.

Again from the past, William Jeanes, chief confectioner at the famed London firm of Gunter's, Confectioners to Her Majesty [the reference is to Victoria and Gunter's no longer exists] gave this recipe in his *Modern Confectioner.*

**Vanilla Ice Cream**

Chop up half an ounce of Vanilla, pound it very fine in a metal mortar. Take five or six ounces of sugar, add it by degrees to the Vanilla, and pound together. When done, put this into a pint of fresh cream, with the yolks of a few eggs; make hot over a fire (but do not boil). Strain through a sieve. When sufficiently cool, put it in the freezing-pot, and work it well.

The contemporary food writer Craig Claiborne gives two recipes for vanilla in his *The New York Times Cook Book.*

**French Vanilla Ice Cream**

*About 1½ quarts*

1½ cups milk

2½ cups light cream

1 vanilla bean

8 egg yolks

¾ cup sugar

¼ teaspoon salt

1. Scald the milk, cream and vanilla bean in the top of a double boiler. Remove vanilla bean.

2. Blend the egg yolks with the sugar and salt. Stir in some of the scalded milk and return to the mixture in the double boiler. Cook, stirring until thick (the mixture will coat a metal spoon.)

3. Remove from the hot water and cool quickly in cold water, stirring occasionally. Chill thoroughly. Freeze in a hand-crank or electric freezer.

**Vanilla Ice Cream**

*About 1½ quarts*

2 cups milk

¾ cup sugar

4 teaspoons flour

¼ teaspoon salt

3 egg yolks or two whole eggs

2 teaspoons vanilla extract

2 cups light cream

1. Scald the milk in a double boiler.

2. Mix the sugar flour and salt. Add the hot milk, stirring, and return to the double boiler. Stir over boiling water until thickened.

3. Beat the egg yolks or whole eggs and add a small portion of the hot mixture. Return to the remaining hot mixture and cook, stirring occasionally, until the mixture coats a metal spoon. Chill thoroughly.

4. Add the vanilla and cream and freeze in a hand-crank or electric freezer.

Maria Parloa, in her 1883 *New Cook Book,* gives the following instructions:

**Vanilla Ice Cream**

The foundation given in this rule is suitable for all kinds of ice cream. One generous pint of milk, one cupful of sugar, half a cupful of flour, scant; two eggs, one quart of cream, one tablespoonful of vanilla extract, and when the cream is added, another tea-cupful of sugar. Let the milk come to a boil. Beat the first cupful of sugar, the flour and eggs together, and stir into the boiling milk. Cook twenty minutes, stirring often. Set away to cool, and when cool add the sugar, seasoning and cream, and freeze.

In *The Ladies own Cookbook,* Mrs. Jane Warren writing in 1891, offers a bit of business acumen about the connection between confectioners and – while they were still called that – Ice Cream Saloons.

Confectioners, generally, add Ice Cream Saloons to their stores. The additional expense is small: the relative profit quite large. Apart from the direct sales, it leads indirectly to the purchase of large quantities of confectionery by Ice Cream customers. Following we give some of the most popular recipes for well liked Ices:

### Ice Cream – No. 1

10 quarts pure cream
3½ pounds choicest refined sugar,
¼ gill extract of vanilla.

Stir the mixture thoroughly, then pour it into a can, much larger than the mixture: the can must be packed hard in ice. Let it freeze – over half an hour.

### Ice Cream – No. 2

6 pints of cream,
6 pints fresh milk,
½ pound sugar
2 eggs

Having given the eggs a good beating, renew the beating in can, and stir: Flavor and freeze.

To either of these recipes add half a pint of any kind of fruit juice to each quart of the mixture. No additional flavor.

The great chef Escoffier begins with an overall recipe to which countless flavorings can be added. An extraordinary number in fact: beginning under the heading, "Vanilla Ice Cream Preparations" and number 2,748 (Almond Ice Cream), he continues through Ices, Coupes, Iced Biscuits, Bombes, Mousses, Puddings, Souffles, and Sherbets, ending at number 2,933 with something called Spooms.

### Ice Cream Preparation (General Recipe)

*Composition pour Glace-Créme*

Work two thirds lb. of sugar and ten eggyolks in a saucepan until the mixture reaches the ribbon-stage. Dilute it, little by little, with one quart of boiling milk, and stir over a moderate fire until the preparation coats the withdrawn spoon. Avoid boiling, as it might separate the custard. Strain the whole into a basin and stir it from time to time until it is quite cold.

N.B. – For the various ice cream preparations, the amount of sugar and number of egg-yolks, as also the procedure, do not change. They are only distinguishable by the particular flavor or infusion which may happen to characterize them.

### Vanilla Ice Cream

*Glace-Créme a la Vanille*

When the milk has boiled, steep in it one large stick of vanilla for twenty minutes.

N.B. – If these various preparations are required to more creamy, the milk may be wholly or partly replaced by fresh cream. Also when the preparation is congealed, it may be combined with one-sixth pint of whipped cream per quart.

– ESCOFFIER

The *only* recipe for ice cream in *The Flavor of France* by Narcissa G. and Narcisse Chamberlain is one given for vanilla which underlines a curious fact about several outstanding writers on food. In Vol. 1 of Julia Child's and Simone Beck's famous *The Art of French Cooking* not a page is devoted to ice cream (a fact corrected in Vol. 2). Nor will a reader find any reference to it in the current five volume collection by the distinguished Californian M. F. K. Fisher. In José Wilson's otherwise splendidly written *American Cooking: The Eastern Heartland* in the Time-Life series, *Foods of the World,* the only discussion of ice cream is a delightful section devoted to the extraordinary molded concoctions created by Mollie and Fred Zendler in Philadelphia. And this in a book covering New York, New Jersey, Pennsylvania, Ohio, Michigan, Indiana and Illinois. *Cooking of the British Isles* in the same Time-Life series, makes no mention of ice cream either. It seems all very odd.

In any event here is the Chamberlain's recipe:

### French Vanilla Ice Cream (Glace Vanille)

Scald 2 cups of milk in a saucepan. Turn off the flame and steep a vanilla bean in the milk for 20 minutes. Beat 6 egg yolks in the top of a double boiler until they are thick and lemon colored. Stir in 1¼ cups of granulated sugar, then slowly add the warm milk. Cook the mixture over barely simmering, never boiling water, stirring constantly for about 7 minutes, or until it just coats the spoon. Remove the top of the double boiler immediately, set it in cold water to cool the custard, and stir in 2 cups of heavy cream.

This ice cream should, of course, be made in a hand freezer. However, if it must be done in the regrigerator, turn the controls to "very cold" and put the custard in a deep ice tray in the freezing compartment until it reaches the mushy stage. Then spoon it into a chilled bowl and beat it hard with an egg beater. Return it to the tray, freeze it some more, beat it again, and then leave it to freeze solid for at least 3 hours, covered with wax paper to keep crystals from forming on top. Makes 3 pints.

Raymond Oliver gives this recipe for vanilla ice cream in *La Cuisine*. It is proceeded by a note from the editors to the effect that the French usually freeze their ice cream in the traditional freezer but that it can be frozen in an ordinary ice tray in the refrigerator. However, they stress that the temperature should then be set at its *lowest* and that the result will be less smooth.

### Parfait Glace a la Vanille/Vanilla Ice Cream

Pour the heavy cream into a bowl, set this bowl in another bowl full of ice, and beat until the cream thickens. Gradually add ½ cup of the sugar and continue beating until it is very stiff. Beat the egg yolks and the remaining sugar until the mixture is white and fluffy.

Fold in the whipped cream and the vanilla. Pour the mixture into two 1 quart shallow metal pans and freeze until the mixture begins to harden at the edges. Remove from the freezer and beat energetically for 1 minute. Return to the freezer for 2 hours, or until firm.

4 cups heavy cream
¾ cup superfine sugar

4 egg yolks
2 teaspoons vanilla extract

Besides vanilla the other two members of ice cream-dom's "blessed trinity" in terms of popularity and prevelance are chocolate and strawberry. Here then, are more recipes along with one or two new sources.*

### Chocolate Ice Cream

Is made in the same way as the vanilla ice cream, adding a flavoring of chocolate and a little vanilla powder. For instance, to make a quart and a half of cream: Make the boiled custard with the yolks of six eggs, half a pound of sugar, one pint of boiled milk, and a teaspoon (not heaping) of vanilla powder. Pound smooth four ounces of chocolate; add a little sugar and one or two tablespoonfuls of hot water. Stir it over the fire until it is perfectly smooth. Add this and a tablespoonful of thin, dissolved gelatine to the hot custard. When about to set in the freezer; add one pint of cream, whipped.

– HENDERSON

* In all cases where reference is made to another or basic recipe, refer to that section, i.e. a vanilla base or freezing process will appear in the section first dealing with it.

*The Saint Louis Cookbook* from which the following recipe is taken, is a delightful collection "chosen from favorites of friends of the St. Louis Symphony; music lovers, orchestra members; guest artists and celebrities from all over the world who came to help St. Louis celebrate her 200th birthday." St. Louis is the place where the first ice cream cone "happened" during another celebration – the Louisiana Purchase Exposition in 1904.

### Chocolate Ice Cream

Two 1 ounce squares
  unsweetened chocolate
2 cups sugar
2 tablespoons hot water

1 tablespoon cocoa
1 quart thin cream
2 cups heavy cream, whipped

Dissolve chocolate, sugar, water and cocoa in double boiler. Stir until very smooth. Add thin cream. Fold in whipped cream. Pour into freezer can and freeze following directions above. Makes about 2 quarts.

ST. LOUIS
(MRS EDWARD J. WALSH JR.)

### Chocolate Ice Cream
#### Glace-Creme au Chocolat

Dissolve eight oz. of grated chocolate in half pint of water, and add one quart of boiled milk, in which a large stick of vanilla has previously been steeped. For this preparation, eight oz. of sugar and seven egg yolks will be found sufficient, if the chocolate used is sweet.

ESCOFFIER

## Chocolate Ice Cream

Take four ounces of good chocolate, dissolve it in a small quantity of water, stir it on a slow fire, and mix it with a pint of cream and eight ounces of sugar. Stir thoroughly, and strain through a sieve; and when the chocolate is cold, put it in the freezing-pot, and work it well.

JEANES

A variation from Robert Carrier's *Great Dishes of the World*.

## Chocolate Ice Cream

4 egg yolks
¼ pound sugar
1 pinch salt
¾ pint single cream

2 ounces melted chocolate
1 teaspoon vanilla
½ pint double cream, whipped

Beat eggs yolks, sugar and salt until lemon colored. Scald single cream and add to egg and sugar mixture, whisking until mixture is well blended.

Pour mixture into top of a double saucepan and cook over water, stirring continuously, until custard coats spoon.

Strain through a fine sieve; stir in melted chocolate and vanilla and set aside to chill.

Mix whipped cream with chocolate custard mixture and freeze for at least 3 hours.

Another world famous French cookbook is *Larousse Gastronomique* by Propea Montagne. Here is one recipe from it:

## Chocolate Ice Cream

*Glace au Chocolat*

Add to a quart (litre) of boiled milk flavored with vanilla, 1⅓ cups (250 grams) of grated chocolate dissolved in 1 cup (2 decilitres) of water.

The chocolate being sweet in itself, only 1 cup (250 grams) of sugar should be used instead of the 1⅓ cups (300 grams) indicated in the instructions for Ice Cream mixture.

LAROUSSE

## Strawberry Ice Cream

Sprinkle sugar over strawberries, mash them well, and rub them through a sieve. To a pint of the juice add half a pint of good cream. Make it very sweet. Freeze it in the usual way and, when beginning to set, stir in lightly one pint of cream (whipped), and, lastly a handful of whole strawberries, sweetened. Put it into a mold, which imbed in ice. Or, when fresh strawberries cannot be obtained, there is no more delicious cream than that made with the French bottled strawberries. Mix the juice in the bottle with the cream, and add the whipped cream and the whole strawberries, when the juice etc., have partly set in the freezer.

Many prefer this cream of a darker red color, which is obtained by using prepared cochineal.

HENDERSON

## Parfait Glace aux Fraises/Strawberry Ice Cream

Proceed as in Vanilla Ice Cream and add ¼ cup strawberry cordial and 1 cup pureed strawberries to the egg yolks before folding in the whipped cream.

OLIVER

This next recipe is from *Summer Cooking* by the marvelous Elizabeth David.

## Strawberry Ice Cream

Add ¼ pint of whipped cream to preparation made exactly as for the water ice below, and freeze for 2½ hours at the maximum freezing temperature.*

This recipe is by Joyce and Christopher W. Dueker from *The Old Fashioned Homemade Ice Cream Cookbook* which is full of helpful precautions and delightful original recipes.

## Strawberry Ice Cream

1 cup fresh strawberries
½ cup sugar
1 pint Half and Half*
2 teaspoons pure vanilla extract
1 teaspoon lemon juice
a few grains salt

Mash the berries and mix with the sugar. Let them stand at room temperature for about one hour, then mix with the remaining ingredients. Chill, crank and freeze.

* For those who own a modern refrigerator with a capacious ice cave or a deep freeze compartment, there is a recently invented French electrical sorbetiere which eliminates the necessity to use ice trays.

* The Duekers have a very intelligent suggestion to make with regard to choosing cream. They note that "heavy whipping cream with about 35 per cent butterfat content makes the richest ice cream; however, it is very expensive, high in calories, and really too rich for most tastes. Light cream, with 20 per cent butterfat, would be a good compromise. We prefer Half and Half, which has 12% butterfat, since it gives a good richness without being overly fattening. When we want richer ice cream, we simply combine Half and Half with heavy whipping cream, using equal amounts of each."

# FURTHER FLAVORS

**Tutti Frutti Parfait**

*About 6 servings*

Cover and soak:

1 cup chopped candied fruit

in a combination of:

Brandy, rum, liqueur and syrup from canned stewed fruit. Drain well. Reserve liquid for flavoring puddings. Soak:

1 teaspoon gelatin

in 2 tablespoons water

Dissolve it over hot water. Boil to the thread stage:

$\frac{1}{2}$ cup water

$\frac{1}{2}$ cup sugar

Beat until stiff but not dry

2 egg whites

Pour the syrup over the egg whites in a fine stream, beating constantly. Add the dissolved gelatin and continue beating until mixture thickens somewhat. Beat in drained fruit. Whip until thickened but not stiff:

1 cup whipping cream

1 teaspoon vanilla

Fold into fruit and egg mixture. Still-freeze in a mold or in foil covered refrigerator trays. Serve topped with whipped cream and candied cherries.

ROMBAUER

**Tutti Frutti**

When a rich vanilla cream is partly frozen, candied cherries, English currants, chopped raisins, chopped citron, or any other candied fruits, chopped rather fine, are added; add about the same quantity of fruit as there is of ice cream. Mold and imbed in ice and salt. It may be served surrounded with whipped cream.

HENDERSON

**Glacé Fruit Ice Cream/Parfait Glace aux Fruits Confits**

Soak 1 cup diced glaceed fruits in 1 cup rum for several hours. Make a Vanilla Ice Cream, and add $\frac{1}{4}$ additional cup of sugar and $\frac{1}{4}$ cup Grand Marnier to the egg yolks before folding in the whipped cream. Omit the vanilla.

OLIVER

**Asparagus Ice Cream**

*Glacé Creme aux Asperges*

Parboil six oz. of asparagus tips for two minutes. Thoroughly drain them; quickly pound them, together with a few tablespoons of milk, and set this asparagus paste to steep in the boiled milk.

ESCOFFIER

**Rhubarb Ice Cream
(Parker House, Boston, Mass.)**

2 cups water

$2\frac{1}{2}$ lbs rhubarb, cut in pieces

$2\frac{1}{4}$ cups sugar

4 cups heavy cream, whipped

Add water to rhubarb and boil 5 to 10 minutes. Add sugar; cool and add cream. Pack in freezer in finely chopped ice and rock salt and freeze. Makes about 2 quarts ice cream.

WOLCOTT

**Parfait Glacé a
L'Ananas/Pineapple Ice Cream**

Proceed as in Vanilla Ice Cream and add $\frac{1}{4}$ cup pineapple cordial and 1 cup drained canned pineapple, finely diced, to the egg yolks before folding in the whipped cream. Omit the vanilla.

OLIVER

**Pineapple Ice Cream II**

We heartily recommend this water-packed "no sugar added" canned pineapple for your ice cream.*

1 pint Half and Half

$\frac{1}{4}$ cup sugar

1 cup canned water-packed crushed pineapple (without added sugar)

A few grains of salt

DUCKER

* The Duckers warn that "fresh pineapple contains the enzyme bromelin, which breaks down proteins ... the enzyme partially digests the cream ... The solution is to heat the pineapple, which inactivates the enzyme ... Canned pineapple doesn't usually taste much like the fresh ... but a new type ... has been developed ... Pineapple Ice Cream II is made with this."

**Concord Grape Ice Cream
(Parker House, Boston, Mass.)**

1 pound Concord grapes
½ pound Malaga grapes
½ pound seedless grapes
½ pound Tokay grapes
2⅓ cups sugar
4 cups heavy cream, whipped

Pick grapes from stems; wash. Heat the grapes but do not boil; press the mixture through a sieve. Combine grape juice, sugar; cool and add cream. Pack in freezer in finely chopped ice and rock salt and freeze. Makes about 2 quarts.

WOLCOTT

The next two recipes are from the evocatively titled *American Food, The Gastronomic Story from Colonial Days to the President* by Evan Jones.

## Avocado Ice Cream

1 cup milk
1 cup light cream
¼ cup sugar
3 egg yolks, well beaten
1 cup avocado pulp
½ cup chopped pistachio nuts

Combine milk, cream and sugar, and heat to boiling point, stirring constantly. Pour over beaten egg yolks and blend well. Add avocado pulp and pistachios, stirring till smooth. Cool and turn into refrigerator trays; freeze. When firm, put in a chilled bowl and beat until smooth. Return to trays and freeze. Repeat beating in chilled bowl. Freeze for 2 hours and serve. Makes about 1½ quarts.

## Greengage Ice Cream

Some time after small, green, delicious plums were first cultivated in England, they acquired the surname of Sir William Gage and colonial plum orchards were started in Virginia before the Revolution. Mrs. Raffold's cookbook provided Old Dominion ladies with a recipe for ice cream that required no mechanical freezer, and her cook book also told them how to make greengage preserves. The two combined became a favorite dessert at the King's Arms in Williamsburg.

1 jar (11½ ozs) greengage preserves
2 small lemons, juiced
1 cup sugar
¼ tsp salt
3 cups heavy cream
3 cups milk

Mix all ingredients and pour into a flat freezer container. Freeze for 2 hours. Remove from freezer and beat; return to freezer. Continue freezing; remove and beat again. Freeze until firm. Makes 2 quarts.

## Orange Pineapple Ice Cream
### (Grace Ross, Northampton, Mass.)

1 cup crushed pineapple
1 cup orange juice

1½ cups sugar
1 cup milk
½ pint cream, whipped

Mix pineapple, orange juice and sugar and let stand overnight. Add milk and cream. Freeze.
Serves 6.

WOLCOTT

## Greengage Plum Ice Cream

*12 servings*

Drain:
   3½ cups canned greengage plums
Put them through a ricer. There should be about 1½ cups pulp.
Soak:
   1½ teaspoons gelatin
in ¼ cup cold water
Heat to boiling point:
   2 cups milk
   ¾ to 1 cup sugar
⅛ teaspoon salt
Dissolve the gelatin in hot milk. Cool, then add the plum pulp and
   2 tablespoons lemon juice
Chill the mixture until slushy. Add when whipped, until thickened but not stiff:
   2 cups whipping cream
Still freeze the ice cream in a mold or in covered trays.

ROMBAUER

271

**Pistachio Ice Cream**

*Glacé Creme aux Pistaches*

Pound two oz. of sweet almonds, and two and a half oz. of freshly peeled pistachios; moistening them with a few drops of milk. Set the paste to steep for twenty minutes in the boiled milk.

ESCOFFIER

**Pistachio Ice Cream**

*About 9 servings*

A pretty Christmas dessert served in a meringue tart garnished with whipped cream and cherries.
Shell: 4 ozs pistachio nuts
Blanch them. Pound them in a mortar with a few drops rose water.
Add to them
    ¼ cup sugar
    ¼ cup cream
    1 teaspoon vanilla
    ½ teaspoon almond extract
    a little green coloring
Stir these ingredients until the sugar is dissolved. Heat but do not boil:
    1 cup cream
Add and stir until dissolved:
    ¾ cup sugar
    ⅛ teaspoon salt
Chill these ingredients. Add the pistachio mixture and
    2 cups whipping cream
    1 cup cream.
Churn freeze.

ROMBAUER

**Pistachio Ice Cream**

*About 1 quart*

½ cup sugar
1 tablespoon cornstarch
1 cup light cream
½ cup milk
2 eggs, slightly beaten
¼ teaspoon salt
1 teaspoon vanilla extract
½ teaspoon almond extract
1 cup heavy cream, whipped
½ cup finely chopped pistachio nuts

1. Set the refrigerator control for fast freezing.
2. Mix the sugar and cornstarch in the top of a double boiler. Add the light cream and milk and bring to a boil over direct heat stirring constantly.
3. Mix the eggs with the salt and add a little of the hot mixture, stirring. Return to the top of the double boiler and cook, stirring, over simmering water until the mixture thickens. Cool.
4. Add the flavorings. Pour the mixture into freezer trays and freeze until firm.
5. Transfer the mixture to a bowl, break up the lumps and beat in an electric mixer or by hand until soft but not mushy.
6. Fold in the whipped cream and nuts. Return to the freezer trays and freeze until firm.

CLAIBORNE

As might be expected *The Alice B. Toklas Cook Book* when it appeared, proved to be utterly idiosyncratic and enthralling. Herewith:

**Mary Oliver,** *London*

**Birthday Ice Cream for Adults**

Toast 2 slices of dark brown bread spread lavishly with butter on both sides. Cut into small cubes. Cover with egg nog made of 2 eggs and 1 cup rum. Add 1 quart cream and freeze.

**Burnt Ice Cream**

Take one pint of Custard Ice (see page 00) and add half a wine glass of burnt sugar. Freeze it.

JEANES

**Praline Ice Cream**

*Glacé au Praline*

Add to a quart (litre) of vanilla custard cream, prepared as described in the recipe for ice cream mixture ¼ lb (125 grams) of praline of burnt almonds, pounded, rubbed through a sieve or put through a grinder. The same method is used for burnt hazlenuts, walnuts, pistachio ground nuts or peanuts.

LAROUSSE

**Singapore Ice Cream**

Stir 1½ cups sugar with 12 yolks of eggs until they are thick and pale yellow. Slowly add 4 cups hot cream in which a vanilla pod cut in half vertically has been steeping. Mix thoroughly, pour into saucepan and stir constantly with a wooden spoon over lowest heat until the spoon is thickly covered. Remove from heat and pour through a fine sieve into bowl. Remove vanilla and wash the two pieces well in cold water. They may be used again. If you do not use vanilla bean, add 1 tablespoon vanilla extract. Stir the mixture from time to time until cold. Before putting to freeze stir in 1 cup diced ginger, as completely drained as possible of its syrup and 1 cup not too finely chopped blanched pistachio nuts. Then mix in two cups whipped cream. Put to freeze. It is not necessary to stir during freezing. When frozen take out of mold and decorate with 1 cup whipped cream flavored with 2 tablespoons ginger syrup.

TOKLAS

**Green Tea Ice Cream**

2 oz. Green Tea, 8 oz. Sugar

Take three parts of a cupful of the best Green Tea, and pour boiling water over it. The water should just cover the Tea; let it stand until the strength is extracted, then pour it through a fine sieve into a pint of cream. Sweeten with eight ounces of sugar, and freeze as Custard Ices.

JEANES

**Tea Ice Cream**
**Glacé au The**

Prepare the cream in the usual way with a mixture of 1 quart (7½ decilitres) milk and 1½ cups (3 decilitres) of very strong, strained tea.

The same method is used for the preparation of ice creams flavored with peppermint, lime-flower or verbena infusions.

LAROUSSE

**Ice Cream without Eggs (American Recipe)**
**Glace sans Oeufs**

Boil together 1 quart (litre) of milk, 1 quart (litre) of cream and 1 cup (250 grams) of sugar.

Bend with 4 tablespoons (45 grams) of corn starch. Rub through a hair sieve. Let it cool, stirring often.

Flavor with vanilla, lemon or orange zest, coffee, chocolate, liquers etc. Freeze in the usual way.

LAROUSSE

**Plombiers Ice Cream**
**Glace Plombiers**

The Mixture. Pound thoroughly in a mortar a scant 2 cups (300 grams) of blanched fresh almonds and 2 tablespoons (20 grams) of blanched bitter almonds. Mix with milk. Add 1½ quarts (litres) of scalded cream.

Strain this mixture, pressing it down in the strainer to extract all the milk.

Stir 10 yolks of eggs thoroughly with 1⅓ cups (300 grams) of sugar in a saucepan. Add the milk to this mixture.

Heat this cream of egg milk and sugar on the stove without bringing it to the boil as for Custard cream. Remove it from the stove and stir it vigorously for 3 minutes. Rub it through a sieve. Freeze this mixture in a freezer, stirring it from time to time with a spatula. When the mixture is partly frozen, add 1 pint (6 decilitres) of whipped cream. Continue the freezing process.

Drain off any water in the bucket and immerse the freezer once more. Cover it completely with ice and salt and leave it for 2 hours. Scoop out the ice cream with a ball scoop and arrange the balls in a pyramid on a dish covered with a folded napkin. Pour apricot jam over the ice cream.

LAROUSSE

**Fruit Buttermilk Ice Cream**

*About 5 servings*

This is a low fat dish and quite acceptable.
Combine: 1 cup sweetened fruit puree: apricot, peach or strawberry
with: 2 tablespoons lemon juice
⅛ teaspoon salt
1½ cups buttermilk
Still-freeze.

ROMBAUER

**Persimmon Ice Cream**

*About 6 servings*

A California creation.
Put through a ricer:
4 ripe Japanese persimmons
Add:
2 tablespoons sugar
6 tablespoons lemon juice
Whip until thickened but not stiff:
2 cups whipping cream
Still-freeze in a mold or in foil covered regrigerator trays.

ROMBAUER

**Nougat Ice Cream**

Heat 3 cups thin cream in saucepan over low heat. Stir 6 yolks of eggs and add the hot cream. Put over lowest heat and stir until spoon is coated. Remove from flame and stirring continuously pour it slowly over 1 cup honey (preferably orange flower). Add 1 tablespoon orange-flower water. Strain, and when cold incorporate 1½ cups whipped cream and fold in 3 whites of eggs beaten stiff, ¾ cup pistachio nuts that have been blanched, skinned and thoroughly dried, and half cup of blanched almonds cut in half lengthways (with the point of a knife they open very easily while still moist). Flavor with 1 tablespoon orange-flower water and freeze.

TOKLAS

273

# Sherbets and Ices

First, words about the preparation of sherbets and ices by the great Ecoffier whose book *A Guide to the Fine Art of Cookery* has become one of the crucial works about preparing food.

## Preparation for Sherbets

Sherbets are made from any liqueur ice preparation at 15°; or they may be prepared as follows:– For one quart of preparation, take the juice of two lemons and one orange, half-a-pint of port wine, of Samos wine, of Sauterne, or other good wine; and add cold syrup at 22° until the saccharometer registers 15°.

For liqueur sherbets, allow about one-fifth pint of liqueur per quart of the preparation; but remember that this is subject to the kind of liqueur used. For the quantity just prescribed, use syrup at 18° or 19°, which the subsequent addition of liqueur reduces to the proper degree. Whatever be the kind of liqueur, the latter should only be added when the Sherbet is completely frozen; that is to say, at the last moment. Fruit sherbets are generally prepared from the juices and syrups of juicy fruits. Fruit purees are scarcely suited to this mode of procedure, and they are only resorted to in exceptional cases.

*The Freezing of Sherbets.* – Pour the preparation into the freezer, which should have been previously packed, and keep the utensil moving. Remove portions of the preparation from the sides of the receptacle as fast as they adhere, and mix them with the whole, until the latter is completely congealed; remembering not to stir at all during the freezing process. When the preparation is firm enough, mix with it, gently, the quarter of its weight of Italian meringue or very stiffly whipped cream; and finish by the addition of the liqueur.

*The Serving of Sherbets.* Take some of the Sherbet preparation in a spoon, and set it in sherbet or sherry glasses, shaping it to a point. When the Sherbet is prepared with wine, sprinkle the preparation when it is in the glasses with a tablespoon of the selected wine. The consistency of a Sherbet, of any kind, should be such as to permit it being drunk.

## Preparation for Fruit Ices

The base of these preparations is a syrup of sugar ... to which a puree of fruit, a flavoring or a liqueur is added, which will give the ice its character. All these preparations require lemon juice, the quantity of which varies according to the acidity of the fruit used, but which, even in the case of the tartest fruits, should not measure less than the amount that may be extracted from a whole lemon per quart of the preparation. Orange juice may also be used, more especially for red fruit ices; while the juices of the orange and the lemons combined throw the flavor of the fruit under treatment into remarkable relief. In the season the juices are extracted from fresh fruit, pressed and rubbed through a fine sieve. When the season is over the preserved juice of fruit is used.

All red fruit ices are improved, once they are set, by an addition of a half pint of raw, fresh cream per quart of the preparation.

In regard to ices made from syrups and fruit, their preparation may measure from 15° to 30° or 32° (saccharometer) respectively. (The use of the saccharometer for gauging the sugar content of syrups is still in use today by the manufacturers and probably by chefs in large establishments. In only a few dessert recipes are directions given for measuring the sugar mixture by degrees. If the reader, when inspired by the combinations and the wonderful flavors the recipes suggest, wishes to make such an instrument he may put the instructions to profitable use by measuring with a Brix Hydrometer, which takes the place of a saccharometer.

The hydrometer is plunged into a hydrometer jar filled with syrup. The syrup must be 68° Fahrenheit, since the instrument is regulated to measure at this temperature. According to the density of the sugar content, the hydrometer will sink into the syrup. The reading on the graduated scale indicates the amount of sugar in the syrup.

(A Brix hydrometer may be purchased in many stores and through the Taylor Instrument Companies of Rochester, New York. They sell for a little more than two dollars.)

## Granites

Granites answer the same purpose as Sherbets, while they may also be introduced into certain culinary preparations.

The bases of these preparations consist of very thin syrups made from fruit juices, and not overreaching 14° (saccharometer). Granites consist only of iced syrups, and are not combined with any Italian or other meringue.

As in the case of the Sherbets, but more particularly in regard to these, the cook should remember not to stir the syrup during the freezing process, lest it separate; and, when it is congealed, it should form a light, granulated mass.

ESCOFFIER

## Fruit Ice

*About 10 servings*

Be careful not to use more than one part sugar for every four parts liquid, as too much sugar prevents freezing. Use:
    1 cup any fruit puree
Add to taste:
    lemon juice
Combine with:
    4 cups water
Churn freeze. If adding Liqueur have the ice almost completely churned before you do so, as the high alcoholic content tends to prevent the freezing.

ROMBAUER

## Currant Ice

Boil one quart of water and a pound of sugar until reduced about a pint – i.e., until a pint of water has boiled away; skim it, take it off the fire, and add a pint of currant juice; when partly frozen, stir in the beaten whites of four eggs. Mold, and freeze again. A good ice for fever patients.

HENDERSON

## Grapefruit Sherbet

*About 4 servings*

Soak:
    2 teaspoons gelatin
in:
    $\frac{1}{2}$ cup cold water
Boil for 10 minutes:
    1 cup sugar
    1 cup water
Dissolve the gelatin in the hot syrup. Chill.
Add to it:
    $\frac{1}{4}$ cup lemon juice
    2 cups fresh grapefruit juice
    $\frac{1}{2}$ cup orange juice
    $\frac{1}{4}$ teaspoon salt
Beat until stiff but not dry and add:
    2 egg whites
Still-freeze. Serve in grapefruit shells.

ROMBAUER

## Cranberry Sherbet

*About 8 servings*

Boil until soft:
    1 quart cranberries
    1$\frac{1}{4}$ cups water
Strain the juice and put berries through a sieve. Add to them and boil for 5 minutes:
    1$\frac{3}{4}$ cups sugar
    1 cup water
Soak:
    2 teaspoons gelatin
in:
    $\frac{1}{4}$ cup cold water
Dissolve the gelatin in the hot juice. Chill. Beat until stiff, but not dry and add:
    2 egg whites
Still-freeze. Serve in orange cups.

ROMBAUER

## Apricot

If the apricots are very ripe, press them through a food mill or puree them in a blender without cooking them. If they are slightly hard, poach them in 2 cups of sugar syrup for 5 minutes. Drain and then puree them.

Dissolve the sugar in the water, boil for 5 minutes, and combine this syrup with the apricot puree. Cool completely and then fold in the egg whites and the lemon juice. Pour the mixture into a 4-cup shallow metal pan and freeze until firm around the edges. Remove from the freezer and beat the mixture energetically for 1 minute. Return to the freezer until firm. Serve the sherbet in a chilled dish.
    $\frac{1}{2}$ pound apricots, pitted
    1$\frac{3}{4}$ cups sugar
    1 cup water
    2 egg whites, stiffly beaten
    Juice of 1 lemon

Note: The temperature of freezing compartments of many home refrigerators is not low enough to completely freeze sherbets. If you are in doubt, add 1 envelope of unflavored gelatine softened in $\frac{1}{4}$ cup of water to the hot syrup and fruit puree before cooling the mixture.

OLIVER

## Pineapple Buttermilk Sherbet

1 quart buttermilk
2 cups sugar
$\frac{1}{2}$ cup lemon juice
2 teaspoons grated lemon rind
2 cups crushed Pineapple
2 egg whites stiffly beaten

Combine buttermilk, sugar, lemon juice, rind and pineapple. Stir until sugar dissolves. Fold in egg whites. Have freezer control set at "coldest". Freeze in ice trays until mushy. Beat in chilled bowl until smooth. Return to trays and freeze until firm, about 30 minutes.
    Makes 6 servings

– St. LOUIS (Mrs. J. Russelll Wilson)

## Sorbet aux Framboises/Raspberry Sherbet

Proceed as in Apricot Sherbet substituting 2 cups raspberry puree for the apricot puree and 2 tablespoons of kirsch for the lemon juice.

OLIVER

## Tea Sherbet

Make the tea very strong, strain it and let it cool. Dissolve the sugar in the water and add the vanilla bean, halved lengthwise, and the greated orange and lemon rinds. Boil for 5 minutes.

Remove the vanilla bean from this syrup, then add the tea, the orange and lemon juices and the rum. Cool completely. Fold in the beaten egg whites and pour the mixture into a 4-cup shallow metal pan. Freeze until the edges are firm, remove from the freezer, and beat energetically for 1 minute. Return to the freezer.
    1 cup very strong tea
    1$\frac{3}{4}$ cups sugar
    1 cup water
    1 piece vanilla bean 6 inches long

    Grated rind of 1 orange and 1 lemon
    Juice of 1 orange and 1 lemon
    $\frac{1}{4}$ cup Rum
    2 egg whites stiffly beaten

OLIVER

**Mint Sherbet or Ice**

*About 9 servings*

A refreshing alternate for the mint jelly which traditionally accompanies lamb.
Prepare:

Any orange or lemon ice or sherbet

After the syrup reaches the boiling point, pour it over:

½ cup fresh chopped mint leaves

Steep briefly, drain out the mint leaves and add dissolved gelatin, if necessary.

ROMBAUER

**Lemon Milk Sherbet**

*About 9 servings*

Dissolve:

1⅓ cups sugar

in:

7 tablespoons lemon juice

Stir these ingredients slowly into:

3½ cups milk or milk and cream

If the milk curdles it will not affect texture after freezing. Churn freeze.

ROMBAUER

**Lemon Sherbet**

Proceed as in Apricot Sherbet substituting the pureed pulp and grated rind of 3 lemons for the apricot puree. If desired the sherbet may be flavored with 2 tablespoons of Curacao before adding the egg whites.

OLIVER

**Lemon Ice**

4 cups hot water

2 cups sugar

1 tablespoon grated lemon rind

¾ cup lemon juice

Stir water and sugar until sugar dissolves. Boil 5 minutes without stirring. Cool. Add lemon rind and juice. Pour into freezer can and freeze following directions above. Makes 1½ quarts.

ST. LOUIS. (Mrs. J. Eugene Baker)

**Orange Ice**

Use only 2 cups water. Use only ¼ cup lemon juice. Add 2 cups orange juice with lemon rind and juice.

– ST. LOUIS. (Mrs. J. Eugene Baker)

Victor Bennett was for many years a distinguished steward on cruise ships, especially in the Pacific. The following recipe is from his collection, *The Polynesian Cookbook.*

**Fruit Ice (6-8)**

¾ cups ripe mango or papaya, pureed juice of 1 lemon or lime

⅓ cup honey

½ teaspoon gelatin

¼ cup cold water

sprigs of fresh mint

orange liqueur

Combine pureed fruit with lemon juice and honey. Soak gelatin in cold water 3 minutes; then melt over hot water. Combine fruit mixture with gelatine, and freeze in ice tray at normal temperature. Ice should be on mushy side. Serve in parfait glasses garnished with mint and drizzled with liqueur.

**Violet Ice**

Put half a lb. of cleaned violet petals into one and one-half pints of boiling syrup. Let them steep for ten minutes; strain the whole through a sieve; let it cool and finish it with the juice of three lemons. The preparation should measure from 20° to 21°fl

ESCOFFIER

Writing in the 30's, Charles H. Baker, Jr., a kind of Noel Coward character – all snobbery and good sense – found steamship travel and foreign shores very special. One envisages a world where men in dinner jackets and slicked down hair escorting women in uneven hem lengths devilishly waving cigarettes about. In fact, one is certain that, during the day at least, those marvelous vanilla colored flannel trousers and white linen suits generally referred to with the adjective "ice cream", were much in evidence. The following is taken from *The Gentleman's Companion.*

**A Sherbet of Violets,** *alla* **Fiesole**

There is no valid reason for dedicating this lovely ice to Fiesole, for it might have happened anywhere a chef drew breath with romance in his heart. But the fact is we were once during a stay in Florence, impelled to call upon an American lady who for reasons of her own had taken up dilatory domicile in a jewel-like 17th Century villa near Fiesole. This sweet, served in a garden-close framed in century-old cedars, out of which popped marble Daphnes and Satyrs and Fauns and what not, and the almond trees foamed with bloom shall always remind us tenderly of Fiesole – and the lady. . . . To duplicate the dish is quite easy.

Put 2 cups of sugar in a saucepan and add just enough water to make a fairly heavy syrup; simmering gently for 10 minutes. Now add ¼ cup Creme de Violette and simmer 5 minutes longer to dissipate some of the alcohol which would otherwise hinder freezing. Draw off fire and cool, meanwhile adding 2 cups of grape juice and the strained juice of 1 small lemon or 2 limes. Now put in the ice cream freezer and when almost frozen add the white of 1 egg and 2 tbsp. confectioner's sugar whipped together. Freeze well. Serve in crystal sherbet glasses with underplate garnished with a green violet leaf and 3 violet flowers mounted on top of the sherbet in glass . . ."

### Liqueur Ice Preparations

These preparations are made by adding to the syrup or the cream which forms the base of the ice a given quantity of the selected liqueur, the latter being generally added when the preparation is cold. The proportion of one-fifth pint of liqueur per quart of syrup may be taken as an average. Subject to the requirements this liqueur flavor may be intensified with strong tea for rum ices; with orange-rind for Curacao-flavored ices, with fresh, crushed cherry stones for Kirsch ices, etc.

ESCOFFIER

### Orange Rum Sherbet

*About 1½ pints*

2 teaspoons unflavored gelatin
¾ cup cold water
¾ cup sugar
1 cup orange juice
1½ tablespoons lime juice
½ cup light rum
1 tablespoon grated orange rind
Few grains salt.

1. Soften the gelatin in one-quarter cup of the water.
2. Combine the remaining water and the sugar and boil one minute. Add the gelatin and stir until dissolved. Add the orange and lime juice, rum, orange rind and salt. Strain and cool.
3. Pour into freezing tray; set refrigerator at point for freezing ice cream and freeze to a mush.
4. Place the mixture in a chilled bowl and beat with a rotary beater until smooth. Return to the tray and freeze, stirring several times, until almost firm. (Too hard a sherbet has an unpleasant texture.)

CLAIBORNE

### Sunset Ice

Select one pound of fine very ripe strawberries, and put them in a silver timbale. Sprinkle them with ten ounces of powdered sugar and one liqueur glass of Grand-Marnier liqueur; cover the timbale and keep it on ice for half an hour.

Then rub the strawberries through a sieve; and with their puree, make a preparation after the directions given under Fruit Ices. Freeze this preparation in the freezer, and, when it is set, combine with it one pint of whipped cream. Now cover the freezer; surround it again with ice if necessary, and keep it thus for thirty-five to forty minutes. This done, put the ice preparation with care in pyramid form in crystal bowls.

N.B. This ice gets its name from its color, which should be that of the western sky during a fine sunset.

ESCOFFIER

### CHAMPAGNE SHERBERT

*About 8 servings*

Stir until dissolved and boil for about 5 minutes until thick:
1¼ cups sugar
1 cup water
Cool. Stir in:
1½ cups champagne
3 tablespoons lemon juice
Churn freeze until almost set. Fold in:
Meringue
When ready to serve, pour over each portion:
2 tablespoons champagne

ROMBAUER

# MUCH MORE THAN JUST DESSERTS

**A miscellany of variations and combinations of ice cream and ices, sauces and fruit – some classics some serendipitous.**

## Coupes

Although the combination of ice creams with various flavors is common in America, the idea is of French origin. In France coupes are almost invariably served in the open-shaped glasses commonly associated with champagne. They may be served in any stemmed glass, however.

Coupes may be garnished with whipped cream, candied fruits, chopped nuts, candied flowers, mint leaves and chopped fresh or canned fruit.

The most famous coupe is perhaps the Coupe Melba, named in honor of Dame Nellie Melba, the Australian operatic soprano [by Escoffier in 1894] invented. Coupe Melba: Top vanilla ice cream with half a peach and spoon over it pureed raspberries sweetened to taste. Garnish with whipped cream and tosted slivered almonds.

Coupe Romanoff: Top vanilla ice cream with fresh, sweetened strawberries marinated in kirsch. Spoon over them sweetened pureed raspberries and garnish with whipped cream.

Coupe Jacques: Arrange vanilla ice cream by spoonfuls vertically in a serving glass. Cover each spoonful with mixed fruits cut in small cubes to fill the space between the ice cream mounds.

CLAIBORNE

## Peach Melba

1 pound can peach halves drained
   (or 8 peach halves)
½ cup water
½ cup sugar
1 teaspoon vanilla
1 quart vanilla ice cream
10 oz package frozen raspberries,
   thawed and pureed

Mix water, sugar and vanilla. Boil gently 10 minutes. Pour into shallow 14 x 10 inch pan. Arrange peaches in single layer in syrup. Bake at 350° for 10 minutes. Put peaches on ice cream in individual serving dishes. Pour raspberry puree over each. Makes 8 servings.

ST. LOUIS (Mrs Carl P. Daniel)

## Kona Coupe Hawaiian

*(Serves 3)*

6 tblsp chocolate syrup
1 pint vanilla ice cream
½ cup heavy cream, whipped
3 tblsp. Kona coffee liqueur
3 tblsp. Cointreau
3 tblsp. chopped toasted macadamia nuts

Spoon 2 tblsp. chocolate syrup into each of 3 small brandy snifters. Place scoop of ice cream in each. Top with whipped cream. Drizzle tblsp. each liqueur over cream in each snifter, and sprinkle with nuts.

BENNETT

## Coupe Crapotte

Fill champagne glasses or ice-cups three quarters full with a smooth layer of peach ice cream. Arrange on top a mixture of equal quantities of alpine strawberries and raspberries, previously steeped in kummel and chilled.

Cover the fruit with a layer of whipped cream piped through a forcing (pastry) bag with a fluted nozzle.

Decorate the top with fresh blanched almonds and crystallized violets. Arrange the glasses on a tray covered with a paper d'oyley.

LAROUSSE

## Coupe Jacques

Fill champagne glasses or ice cups with equal quantities of lemon ice and strawberry ice, with a space between. Put in the middle of the glass a heaped tablespoon of fresh fruit steeped in kirsch. Decorate with crystallized cherries and halved fresh almonds. Sprinkle on top a few drops of kirsch.

LAROUSSE

## Coupe Grimaldi

Fresh pineapple cut in inch squares is macerated in kirsch for 1 hour, drained, placed in a glass and covered with mandarin orange or tangerine sorbet decorated with sweetened but unflavored whipped cream and crystallized violets.

LAROUSSE

## Coupes D'Antigny

Fill the bowls three-quarters with Alpine-strawberry ice, or, failing this, four-seasons strawberry ice, combined with very light and strongly-flavored raw cream. The two most perfect examples of this cream are the "Fleurette Normande", and that which in the South of France is called "Creme Nicoise", and which comes from Alpine pastures. (In the United States we have very fine rich cream from Jersey and Guernsey cows, and all cream is graded according to butter fat content. This recipe calls for a 24-30% cream.)

Upon the ice of each bowl set a half-peach, poached in vanilla flavored syrup; and veil the whole thinly with spun sugar.

ESCOFFIER

## Coupes Reve de Bebe

Fill the bowls half with pineapple ice and half with raspberry ice. Between the two ices set a line of small strawberries, steeped in orange juice. Border the bowls with whipped cream, and sprinkle the latter with crystallized violets.

ESCOFFIER

### German Steamer Baked Ice Cream

This dish was at least a curiosity, served at the table of one of the German steamers. A flat, round sponge cake served as a base. A circular mold of very hard frozen ice cream was placed on this, and then covered with a *meringue,* or whipped white of egg, sweetened and flavored. The surface was quickly colored with a red-hot salamander, which gave the dish the appearance of being baked.

The gentleman who told me about this dish insisted that it was put into the oven and quickly colored, as the egg surrounding the cream was a sufficiently good non-conductor of heat to protect the ice for one or two minutes. However, there is less risk with a salamander.

HENDERSON

### Baked Alaska, Tropical, et l'auteur

Our birthday, which occurs for better or worse on Christmas day, found us in Panama that winter of 1933. Theodore, matchless emperor of the Grill Room on SS. RELIANCE — recently and unhappily burned at her dock — was always a magician with cookery ideas. So this Baked Alaska was whipped up especially for us with enough tropical touches to make it worthy of notation; and here's a secret — we had it repeated in New York for our pre-wedding dinner!

One brick of rich tutti-frutti ice cream serves 4 . . . Now we need a plank or big cookie sheet. Next comes a sponge or angel's food cake layer 1" thick and same size or, better still, at least ¾" larger than the ice cream unit, in order to retain its subsequent jacket of meringue.

. . . Beat 6 tbsp sugar, 4 to 5 egg whites, and 1 tsp of white rum, kirschwasser, or orange Curaçao, until very stiff. Mount sponge cake on plank, ice cream on cake, and spread on meringue in an even layer over everything. Now dust with 1 tbsp finely chopped cashew nuts mixed with the same of grated fresh coconut kernel. Have oven already hot, around 450°; brown meringue, and serve with utmost speed thereafter . . . Please never attempt water ices in Baked Alaska; they simply won't stand the heat, and collapse with disastrous aquatic results!

BAKER

### Frozen Souffle

This is not a recipe but a way of serving ice cream. Line the sides of a 6-cup souffle dish with strong paper so the paper extends an inch or two above the dish. Fill the souffle dish up to the edge of the paper with the ice cream mixture after it has been partially frozen and beaten. Decorate the top with ground toasted almonds, chocolate curls, or minced glaceed fruits; the decorations should match the flavor of the ice cream. Freeze until firm. Remove the paper collar before serving.

In this way you can make souffles with any kind of ice cream, such as orange, vanilla, chocolate, strawberry, Cointreau etc.

OLIVER

### Pumpkin Meringue Ice Cream Pie

1½ cups heavy cream
3 egg yolks
¾ cup brown sugar
1 scant tbs cornstarch
    salt
1¼ cups mashed cooked pumpkin
¾ tsp ground ginger
¾ tsp ground cinnamon
¾ tsp grated nutmeg
¾ tsp grated lemon rind
2 tbs dark rum
1½ cups heavy cream, whipped
¾ cup finely chopped walnuts
1/3 cup finely minced preserved
    gingerroot
1 prebaked 10 inch pie shell

### Meringue:
2 egg whites
cream of tartar
½ cup vanilla sugar (scant)

Scald cream. Beat yolks until lemon-colored, stir in brown sugar and cornstarch, then add hot cream. Cook over boiling water until custard begins to thicken (180°), adding a pinch salt. Remove from heat; mix pumpkin with ginger, cinnamon, nutmeg and lemon rind, then stir into custard; beat mixture over ice while adding rum. When cool, fold in whipped cream, chopped walnuts and minced gingerroot. Freeze in ice cream freezer, or in a metal bowl in a refrigerator freezing compartment. Beat twice during first 2 half-hour periods of freezing. Soften ice cream made in refrigerator by removing to lower shelf; when it reaches a stiff but spreadable consistency fill pie shell and return to freezing compartment.

Just before serving beat 2 egg whites with a pinch of cream of tartar until peaks form; add sugar gradually until mixture has firm meringue consistency. (If vanilla sugar is unavailable add a little vanilla extract to plain sugar.) Spread meringue over ice cream, making sure edges are nearly sealed; put under broiler until lightly browned. Serve immediately.

Makes 6 - 8 servings.

JONES

## Marrons Plombiere

We offer this as one of the finest desserts we have ever known.

... In few cases does a true French chef use what old Susan Rainey called "store-bought" ice cream, but fabricates it himself very easily indeed.

Beat the yolks of 8 eggs with 1 cup of sugar. Stir this into 1 qt of rich milk flavored with vanilla to taste. Heat slowly in a double boiler, stirring with a wooden spoon until it thickens. At this point step up the tempo with $\frac{1}{2}$ cup finely chopped marrons lusciously soaked in a little dark rum, and 1 tbsp kirschwasser. Put into the ice cream freezer, freeze; then pack in individual molds and press on a top layer of more rum-soaked marrons, broken into bits. Keep packed in ice and salt, or better still put into the freeze chamber of the refrigerator. Serve garnished with whipped cream, slightly sweetened, flavored with vanilla and a tbsp more of kirsch. Dust a tiny bit of grated marron on top, and that's it!

BAKER

## Bombe Nero

Take a dome mold and coat it with vanilla ice cream with caramel; fill it with vanilla mousse, combined with small, imitation truffles the size of small nuts, made from chocolate.

Turn out the Bombe on a thin cushion of Punch Biscuit . . . of the same diameter as the Bombe. Cover the whole with a thin layer of Italian meringue . . . and on top, set a small receptacle made of Italian meringue dried in an almost cold oven. Decorate the sides by means of a pastry bag with meringue, and set the whole in the oven to glaze quickly.

On taking the Bombe out of the oven, pour some hot rum into the bowl, and light it when serving.

ESCOFFIER

## Bombe L'Algerienne

Line the bombe mold with tangerine ice. Fill with pineapple ice, to which pieces of crystallized pineapple steeped in kirsch have been added.

LAROUSSE

## Bombe Alhambra

Line the mold with vanilla ice cream. Fill with strawberry flavored mousse (bombe) mixture. After turning out surround the bombe with large strawberries steeped in kirsch.

LAROUSSE

## Bombe Americaine

Line the mold with strawberry ice cream. Fill with mousse (bombe) mixture flavored with tangerine. Decorate the bombe with pistachio ice cream put through a forcing (pastry) bag. See Tangerine ice for preparing the syrup for the mixture.

LAROUSSE

## Bombe Dauphinoise

Line the mold with pineapple ice. Fill with whipped cream flavored with green chartreuse.

LAROUSSE

## Bombe Monselet

Line the mold with tangerine ice. Fill with mousse (bombe) mixture flavored with port and mixed with candied orange peel cut into little pieces and steeped in champagne brandy.

LAROUSSE

## Iced Appled a la Normande

Scoop out some large, sound cooking apples without damaging the skins. Immense the hollowed out apples for a few minutes in boiling syrup, so that they are slightly cooked.

From the pulp make either a plain ice cream or a mousse (bombe) mixture. Flavor this with calvados.

If the apples are filled with mousse mixture, chill them in plenty of ice and salt for about 2 hours.

If they are filled with plain ice cream, freeze the mixture first and fill the skins just before serving.

LAROUSSE

## Iced Pineapple

Choose a large pineapple, regular in shape, with the plume of its tufted top left on. Remove the tufted top by a clean cut about $\frac{3}{4}$ inch below the crown. Keep it to use as a lid.

Carefully remove all the flesh leaving on the walls and on the bottom of the unbroken rind a thickness of pulp of about $\frac{1}{2}$ inch. Dust the pineapple shell inside with two tablespoons of sugar. Sprinkle with 2 tablespoons of kirsch and leave to saturate in a cold place for about 2 hours.

Just before serving fill the unbroken pineapple rind with pineapple ice cream prepared from the pulp removed earlier, with shredded pineapple steeped in kirsch added to it.

Put the pineapple on a napkin or a block of ice, slightly hollowed out in the middle, and replace the tufted crown on top.

LAROUSSE

### Iced Melon (filled)

Slice off the top of a large cantaloupe melon, near the stem. Remove all liquid and seeds.

Using a large spoon scoop out all the pulp, being careful not to damage the rind. Using this pulp make a water ice or ice cream flavored with kirsch.

Just before serving fill the melon with this ice. Serve the melon on a napkin or in a large glass dish, surrounded with crushed ice.

LAROUSSE

### Princess Papulie's Hawaiian Delight

*(Serves four)*

1 cup grated coconut, toasted dark brown
1 cup grated coconut, toasted light brown
1 cup raw coconut
4 pineapple rings, browned on both sides on hot grill
4 Queen Anne cherries
4 vanilla ice-cream balls
1 tblsp. sweet butter
1 heaping tblsp. brown sugar
2 jiggers Cointreau
3 jiggers dark rum
4 silver-dollar-size slices pound cake

Arrange dark brown coconut in center of large platter, with raw coconut around it and light brown coconut around that. Place grilled pineapple around outer coconut ring. Place cherry in center of each pineapple ring. Place ice cream balls on coconut. Present platter to guests; heat butter in crepe pan over direct heat or in frying pan on stove; add sugar, and blend. Sauté pineapple rings on one side; and Cointreau and rum, and flame. While fruit is flaming, quickly roll ice cream balls in coconut, and place on pound cake in glass desert dishes. Place pineapple ring on top of each ice cream-coconut ball, and ladle flaming syrup over each.

BENNET

### Honey Mousse
### which is a delicate and haunting memory – among others not pertinent to mention – of time-mellowed restaurant laperouse

Laperouse has, easily for half a century, been considered one of Paris' fine restaurants . . . Mousse au Miel was our sweet, that day; and the amateur will find it easily created in his own kitchen . . . Beat the yolks of 6 eggs so fresh they really should have been scheduled for laying tomorrow – for vintage eggs popping up in a honey mousse are just as bad as a vintage sweetheart popping up on a honeymoon! – together with 1½ cups of strained honey – the darker the more flavorful . . . Put in a double boiler and stir diligently until it thickens. Chill well and fold in the whites of 3 eggs beaten stiff; then work in a pint of very heavy cream, also whipped. Now pack in mold or molds, and store in the freezing chamber of the refrigerator exactly the same as Plombiere aux Marrons, and do not agitate while freezing. Garnish with a dusting of finely chopped pistachio nuts, or better still do not garnish at all. There is something about the simplicity of this dessert so delicately perfumed and flavored with the lovely gift of honey, that needs no additions whatsoever.

BAKER

### Vanilla Ice Cream, Paula, Being another fine origination of Theodore on the reliance especially for our (then) one year bride

We had just run into a dustry February no'theaster out of La Guayra, but it flattened out off the rocky coast of Dutch Curaçao and to celebrate everyone's returned good humor there was a dinner given, with this fragrant dessert as a fitting period to it all . . . Arrange 1 brick of vanilla or tutti-frutti ice cream in a suitable dish, slightly over-capacity, and garnish the edges with glace fruits. Brown 4 tbsp of finely chopped Brazillnuts in hot butter, and have these all drained and ready. Heap them on the ice cream in the form of a miniature volcano cone. First moisten this nut mountain with 1 tbsp orange Curaçao, then with one tbsp heated brandy; serve flaming.

BAKER

### Plum Pudding Ice Cream

Frances Parkinson Keyes, a transplanted Virginian who lived in New England and later spent much time in Louisiana, was a novelist with a probing interest in American food; she wrote once of finding in an old newspaper a recipe for a Christmas dinner ice cream invented by Yankee cooks. This is the way Plum Pudding Ice Cream was made for a recent twentieth-century holiday.

1 cup seedless raisins
½ cup chopped candied orange peel or dried currants
applejack or other brandy
1 cup sugar
4 oz unsweetened chocolate
1 qt buttermilk
¾ tsp ground cloves
¾ tsp ground cinnamon
1 tsp vanilla extract
4 egg whites

Day before making, put fruits in a bowl and barely cover with applejack, set aside to macerate at

### Ice Cream Cake

John Kenyon gives a recipe for an ice cream cake using gin in his book Mangoes and Monsoons which deals with tropical cookery from Ceylon to Siam and Uganda to Panama.

2 eggs
1 pint cream
4 tablespoons icing sugar
1 dessertspoon gin
1 sponge cake
1 bar dark chocolate

Whip the egg whites until stiff. Whip ¾ pint cream; add the sugar and, if you prefer it – vanilla, although 1 dessertspoon gin gives a sharper flavor. Beat in the egg whites, pour into trays and freezer. When frozen take out and cut into slices and put between the layers of sponge cake. Whip the rest of the cream, pour over top and cover with shaved chocolate. Serves 4 to 6.

### Homage a "Coco"

This way of serving ice cream was thought up one day by the author and San Francisco restauranteur Fred Kuh while discussing the genius of the French designer Gabrielle Chanel. The idea was to see if we could match her talent for achieving the maximum effectiveness through the minimum of visible means.

Over a serving of French vanilla ice cream pour a generous splash of crème de menthe. Dust the top with the finest after-dinner kind of coffee available.

### Snow Ice Cream

This is the ancestor of all frozen delights and a favorite winter scoop for small fry. Arrange attractively in a chilled bowl, trying not to compact it:
    Fresh clean snow
Pour over it:
    Sweetened fruit juice
or a mixture of:
    Cream
    Sugar
    Vanilla

least overnight; most of liquid should be absorbed. Put sugar, chocolate, and about 3 tablespoons of the buttermilk in a saucepan or top part of a double boiler over hot water and heat just enough to melt chocolate and meld it with sugar; stir in cloves, cinnamon, and vanilla. Beat egg whites until peaks form. Combine sugar-chocolate mixture with buttermilk, then fold in egg whites. Pour into freezer containers and freeze for about 3 hours, then stir well. Repeat at 3 hour intervals twice.

Makes 12 or more servings.

                                    JONES

### Custard Ices

Beat up the yolks of seven or eight new-laid eggs, pour them into a copper pan; add a pint of good cream, and mix together gently. Take the extreme outside rind of a lemon, as thin as you can pare it and one slice of the lemon; add them to the cream. Place the pan on the fire, and stir constantly with a wooden whisk. You must not let the cream boil, as it would then curdle and be spoilt. When it gets thick, and refuses to obey the motion of stirring, remove it from the fire, for it is done. It now requires to be sweetened; add half a pound of pounded sugar (or what suits your taste) and pass through a sieve. Sometimes half milk and half cream are used, when two or three extra eggs must be mixed in. You boil the milk and cream, and add the eggs and lemon. All new cream and less eggs, however, make the best custard. Flavor as you think necessary.

## Three Sauces for the Fun of Them
### (all from *The Saint Louis Cookbook*)

Berry Sauce
1 cup sugar
¼ cup soft butter
1 egg white

1 cup mashed berries
    (strawberries, raspberries, blueberries)

Beat sugar and butter to a cream; add egg white beaten to a froth. Stir in mashed berries. Makes 2 cups sauce.

### Maple Sauce for Vanilla Ice Cream

Boil maple syrup to 227°F or until it spins a fine short thread when dropped from spoon. Cool slightly and poor over ice cream.

### Grandmother's Vanilla Sauce

Many recipes were sent to us like this one ... as passed on from grandmothers, great-grandmothers or word-of-mouth! Old time cooks left much to taste and this sauce is one that will work to suit anyone's taste.

Mix a scant tea cup of sugar and a good tablespoon flour. Add a lump of butter and a beaten egg. Use about 1 cup boiling water and a little vanilla. Pour a small amount of the boiling water into egg mixture. Mix well. Then put this mixture into rest of boiling water and boil until it thickens. Then add vanilla. Add more water, if necessary.

(Mrs Herschel J. Drabelle) (St. LOUIS)

## Homemade Ice Cream cones

$\frac{1}{2}$ cup cake flour
$\frac{1}{4}$ cup sugar
2 tablespoons cornstarch
Dash salt
$\frac{1}{4}$ cup cooking oil
2 egg whites
2 tablespoons water
$\frac{1}{2}$ teaspoon vanilla

In mixing bowl, sift together flour, sugar, cornstarch, and salt. Add oil and egg whites; stir till smooth. Add water and vanilla; mix well. Make one cone at a time: pour about $1\frac{1}{2}$ tablespoons batter onto lightly greased skillet or griddle, spreading batter to a 4-inch circle. Cook over low heat for 4 minutes or till lightly browned. With wide spatula, lift and turn; cook 1 minute more. Working quickly, roll batter into a cone shape; secure with wooden pick. Cool on a baking sheet. Remove picks when cones are cool. Makes 8 to 10 cones.

from Better Homes and Gardens, June 1973.

**Please note that there are differences between metric and non-metric measurements and between British and American measurements.**

**The standard American measuring cup holds 8 ounces, and there are 4 cups to the quart. The English quart contains 5 American cups.**

| | | |
|---|---|---|
| The American pint | = | 16 ounces |
| $\frac{1}{2}$ pint | = | 8 ounces |
| 1 quart | = | 32 ounces |
| The English Imperial pint | = | 20 ounces |
| $\frac{1}{2}$ pint | = | 10 ounces |
| 1 quart | = | 40 ounces |

### LIQUID MEASUREMENTS

| English | | American |
|---|---|---|
| 1 gallon = 4 quarts = 8 pints | = | 10 pints = $1\frac{1}{4}$ gallons |
| 1 quart = 2 pints = 40 oz | = | $2\frac{1}{2}$ pints = 5 cups |
| 1 pint = 20 oz | = | $1\frac{1}{4}$ pints = $2\frac{1}{2}$ cups |
| $\frac{1}{2}$ pint = 10 oz | | |
| 2 oz = 4 tablespoons | = | $1\frac{1}{4}$ cups = $\frac{1}{4}$ cup |
| 1 tablespoon = $\frac{1}{2}$ oz | = | $\frac{1}{2}$ oz |
| 1 teaspoon = $\frac{1}{4}$ tablespoon | = | 1 teaspoon = $\frac{1}{3}$ tablespoon |

| | | | | | | |
|---|---|---|---|---|---|---|
| 1 litre | = | 1000 gr | = | approx. 35 fl oz | = | $1\frac{3}{4}$ pints |
| $\frac{1}{2}$ litre | = | 500 gr | = | approx. $17\frac{1}{2}$ fl oz | = | $\frac{3}{4}$ pints plus 5 tablespoons |
| $\frac{1}{4}$ litre | = | 250 gr | = | approx. $8\frac{3}{4}$ fl oz | = | $\frac{1}{2}$ pint less $2\frac{1}{2}$ tablespoons |

### SOLID MEASUREMENTS

| Metric | | English |
|---|---|---|
| 1000 gr (1 kg) | = | approx. 2 lbs 3 oz |
| 500 gr | = | approx. 1 lb $1\frac{1}{2}$ oz |
| 250 gr | = | approx. 9 oz |
| 125 gr | = | approx. $4\frac{1}{4}$ oz |
| 100 gr | = | approx. $3\frac{1}{2}$ oz |

# RALPH POMEROY

The gifts of poets often turn out to be ideal for projects involving discoveries, descriptions and disclosures. And the eyes of a painter can enlarge those gifts that much more. Ralph Pomeroy is both poet and painter and from those twin trunks has found himself branching out in any number of directions. He has been Travel and Entertainment Editor for *House & Garden;* has worked in a number of art galleries, directing one or two; been a university professor; exhibited as a painter; read his poems and lectured on art. As an art critic he has been on the editorial staff of *Art News* in America and *Art & Artists* in England and contributed to many other art publications. In the United States he has given poetry readings cross-country in colleges and universities. He is represented in more than a dozen anthologies, including *The New Yorker Book of Poets* and the Anchor *A Controversy of Poets*. His poems have been widely published in magazines both in the United States and Great Britain and three books of his verse have been published. Through his work as a museum curator he has created and helped create a number of important exhibitions and contributed to exhibition catalogues. He has worked as a soda jerk (during his college days) and as a bartender in San Francisco.

Mr. Pomeroy was educated at the Art Institute of Chicago, the University of Illinois and the University of Chicago. He has also been a member of the faculty of the San Francisco State University, lecturing in Comparative Literature – a field particularly suited to his multi-talents. One of his most popular classes dealt with the interplay between writing and art and was called "Pablo and Gertrude and Marcel and Claude" – respectively, Picasso, Stein, Proust and Monet.

At present Mr. Pomeroy is working on a new book of poems, a novel and a study of Navajo abstraction.

His published books include:
*Stills & Movies* (poems) 1961
*The Canaries as They Are* (poems) 1965
*In the Financial District* (poems) 1968
*Soft Art* 1969
*Stamos* (full-scale monograph) 1974

Among anthologies including his work are:
*The New Yorker Book of Poems*
*A Controversy of Poets*
*A Garland for Dylan Thomas*
*Poems from the Hungarian Revolution*
*The Male Muse*
*Under Eight Lines*

# ANOTHER HELPING:
## MORE BOOKS THAT TALK ABOUT ICE CREAM

The Alice B. Toklas Cook Book – *Alice B. Toklas*
American Food, The Gastronomique Story From
Colonial Days to the Present – *Evan Jones*
The American Soda Book – *James W. Tufts*
The Art of French Cooking, Vol. 2 – *Simone Beck
and Julia Child*
La Cuisine – *Raymond Oliver*
The Escoffier Cook Book – *A. Escoffier*
The Flavor of France – *N. G. and N. Chamberlain*
The Food of Italy – *Waverly Root*
The Gentleman's Companion
– *Charles H. Baker, Jr.*
The Great American Ice Cream Book
– *Paul Dickson*
Great Dishes of the World – *Robert Carrier*
Gunter's Modern Confectioner – *William Jeanes*
Ice Cream – *W. S. Arbuckle*
Ice Cream Making and Selling – *Edited by
Godfrey Staines*
Ices and Soda Fountain Drinks – *P. Michael*
Joy of Cooking – *I. S. Becker and M. R. Becker*
Larousse Gastronomique – *Prosper Montagne*
The Ladies Own Cook Book – *Mrs. Jane Warren*
Let's Sell Ice Cream – *George W. Hennerich*
Mangoes and Monsoons – *John Kenyon*
My Father Alberto – *Romilda Peri Gould.*
The New England Yankee Cook Book
– *Imogene Wolcott*
The New York Times Cook Book
– *Craig Claiborne*
The Old Fashioned Home-made Ice Cream Book
– *J. and C. Dueker*
Miss Parloa's New Cook Book – *Maria Parloa*
The Polynesian Cook Book – *Victor Bennett*
Practical Cooking and Dinner Giving
– *Mrs. Mary F. Henderson*
The Saint Louis Cook Book – *Group of authors*
The Standard Manual of Sodas and Other
Beverages – *A. Emil Hiss*
Summer Cooking – *Elizabeth David*

*The New Yorker* November 4, 1974